At Home with Pornography

Women, Sex, and Everyday Life

Jane Juffer

NEW YORK UNIVERSITY PRESS

New York and London

NEW YORK UNIVERSITY PRESS
New York and London

Copyright © 1998 by New York University
All rights reserved

Library of Congress Cataloging-in-Publication Data
Juffer, Jane, 1962–
At home with pornography : women, sex, and everyday life / Jane Juffer.
p. cm.
Includes bibliographical references (p.) and index.
ISBN 0-8147-4236-X (cloth : acid-free paper). —ISBN 0-8147-4237-8
(pbk. : acid-free paper)
1. Pornography—Social aspects. 2. Women and erotica. 3. Women—
Sexual behavior. 4. Women consumers. I. Title.
HQ471.J83   1998
363.4'7—dc21   97-45413
                           CIP

New York University Press books are printed on acid-free paper,
and their binding materials are chosen for strength and durability.

Manufactured in the United States of America

10 9 8 7 6 5 4 3 2 1

2/08

Contents

Acknowledgments

This project would not have been possible without the daily inspiration and encouragement provided me by Carol Inskeep. Her insightful comments on all aspects of everyday life often kept me going.

James Hay gave endless consideration to the arguments presented here. His patience, ideas, and cooking all provided critical nourishment.

Thanks to Siobhan Senier for her careful readings of much of this project. I am grateful as well to Michael Bérubé, Larry Grossberg, Amanda Anderson, and Cary Nelson for their suggestions and encouragement. Thanks also to Elizabeth Coleman and Vivian Wagner for their comments on individual chapters.

I want to thank Eric Zinner at New York University Press for bearing with me throughout the completion of this project and for his support along the way. This book was made possible through fellowships granted to me by the Graduate College and the Department of English at the University of Illinois at Urbana-Champaign.

My parents, Peg and Ron Juffer, gave me all kinds of non-judgmental support. And thanks most of all to Alex, who so sweetly kept asking me, "Is your book done yet, Mama?"

A shorter version of chapter four was published in *Social Text* 48 (Fall 1996): 27–48. Reprinted with permission.

Introduction

From the Profane to the Mundane

Pornography is not often a subject linked to the mundane.

Take, for example, the controversy surrounding the 1996 release of Milos Forman's film *The People vs. Larry Flynt*. The main players in the porn debates resurfaced, using the platform created by the film to make the same arguments they have always made about pornography and women. Larry King brings together *Hustler* publisher Larry Flynt and televangelist Jerry Falwell; Falwell likens Flynt to a Nazi and says that "pornography is a scourge on society, demeaning to women and children." Flynt responds that he has tremendous respect for women and that there is no element of coercion in the production of his magazine: "The models pose willingly . . . for every one who posed, there's another ten thousand in line." Gloria Steinem is interviewed in the news coverage, represented as the spokesperson for all feminists; on CNN she proclaims that you are not a feminist unless you are against pornography. In an Arts and Entertainment channel biography of Flynt, Steinem objects to the film's portrayal of the publisher as a hero of First Amendment battles: "Larry Flynt's portrayal of women, pornographically, is a contributing factor to the terrific danger in which women find themselves walking around the street. It legitimizes it."

These positions demonstrate how different players in the porn debates often extract it from the conditions in which it is produced and consumed in order to represent a political position that has very little to do with the mundane uses to which pornography is actually put. In their uneasy alliance, both the religious Right and antiporn feminists have argued that pornographic texts like *Hustler* turn all men into victimizers/rapists/child molesters and all women into victims, of either physical violence or objectification. Flynt's easy denial of the victim charge—thousands of women are actually waiting to pose for *Hustler*—asserts a freestanding agency, as do First Amendment arguments that champion the rights of individuals and admonish opponents of porn to simply "not buy it if you don't like it." The most insightful voice in the Larry Flynt coverage was Laura Kipnis, a Northwestern University professor and author of a book on pornography, *Bound and Gagged*, who despite being positioned by the Arts and Entertainment show as a supporter of Flynt, presents in her book a multidimensional examination of *Hustler*, focusing on the complex imbrications of class, gender, and sexuality. Kipnis refuses to stake her argument on clear antiporn or proporn arguments, and in this respect, *Bound and Gagged* is a long overdue contribution to a politics of pornography that exceeds this tired binary. However, Kipnis does remain invested in positing pornography as an indicator of politics rather than as an everyday practice. "Certainly everyone's entitled to better orgasms— wherever and whenever they can be had," she says, but this is not the point of her book: "once you've accomplished that [better orgasms], there's still the issue of what pornography means as a form of culture, and why it's so meaningful to our culture, especially now" (x). Pornography is so meaningful, argues Kipnis, because of its transgressiveness, its propensity to reveal the insecurities of our collective national psyche. In this formulation, all of pornography's consumers become transgressors of certain cultural codes.

In the two decades of debates around pornography since second-wave feminism raised it as a primary concern, we remain mired in a fruitless back and forth about the status of women in relation to the genre: hapless victims or transgressive agents? The question is no longer a useful one, if indeed it ever was. The effects of pornography—indeed, of even one pornographic magazine—have been given an overdetermining power to shape the lives of women, children, and men. This inflational rhetoric has kept us from considering a much more important, albeit less dramatic, set of questions: What are the material and discursive conditions in which *different kinds* of pornography are produced, distributed, obtained, and consumed? How do the particular sites at which pornography is produced, obtained, and consumed shape its meanings and uses? In their emphasis on the overwhelming power of the texts, the various players in the pornography debates have actually inhibited an understanding of many important questions surrounding sexuality, not the least of which is most definitely what is necessary for women to have better orgasms.

The pornography debates testify to the power of the repression/liberation dichotomy, which Foucault so thoroughly critiqued; the various speakers seemingly step outside the repression of pornography, or the repression of those who want to censor pornography, in order to explain how, one day, sex will be better. Of course, I participate in this desire to speak the "truth" about sex, to the degree that this project aims to offer a new position on pornography. However, this "new" position is not one of liberation or transgression but rather one of domestication. I aim not to prove my own transgressiveness by speaking about forbidden texts, but rather to examine critically how the genre of sexually explicit materials aimed at women intersects with their everyday lives in ways that sometimes challenge and sometimes reinforce dominant conceptions of home and domesticity. The subjects of this book—women's literary erotica, masturbation discourse, adult cable programming, couples' video porn, cybersex, sex toys for women, lingerie catalogs, and sexual self-help books—all represent various ways sex is domesticated, brought in from the wild, so to speak, and controlled by women for their pleasures within a particular, constantly redefined space called the "home." Ranging across a number of sites at which these texts and artifacts are produced, this book examines the texts' attempts to reconcile the erotic with the everyday, to infuse sexual representations and products with elements of the mundane, yet to retain enough distance between the mundane and the profane so as to preserve a potential realm of fantasy, to avoid drowning in the details that need to be acknowledged and yet threaten to overwhelm the excesses of sex.

This emphasis on the reconciliation of the everyday with the erotic is a characteristic that distinguishes erotica from much pornography; as Steven Marcus wrote in *The Other Victorians*, pornography often represents a placeless "pornotopia," a land of endless fantasies. However, this convention of pornography is not consistent across the genre, particularly as it increasingly addresses women as potential consumers; erotica and pornography often overlap in their conventions. My emphasis, however, is on the importance of the various distinctions that get made between different kinds of sexually explicit materials: erotica, "adult" cable programming, instructional sex videos for couples, pornography. Although these distinctions are fairly easy to deconstruct, I am not interested in deconstruction as an academic exercise. Rather, I analyze how these various distinctions shape the distribution and circulation of sexually explicit materials, making some texts more accessible than others. We must not dismiss the erotica/porn distinction—as many critics have—but rather analyze how it works to determine women's access to sexually explicit materials; erotica is a kind of pornography, neither removed from the genre nor able to be homogenized within this group of diverse texts. How, for example, does something that is marketed as erotica circulate differently than something marketed as pornography, even when the content sometimes seems quite similar?

Access has been an issue largely ignored in the pornography debates. Antiporn feminists don't consider access a problem because, they argue, pornography is everywhere. Some antiporn activists, such as Andrea Dworkin, even argue that women's erotica can't exist in a society overdetermined by patriarchal values; indeed, the very question of whether there is such a thing as women's erotica elicits this response: "I think that the question itself is part of the male agenda around pornography . . . because the male question always is, is there gonna be something left for me?" ("Dworkin on Dworkin," 210–11). Conversely, prosexuality feminists too often have celebrated women's ability to appropriate any kind of pornographic texts for their pleasures, in a manner agreeing with Dworkin's assumption that all texts are formed in a patriarchal, pornographic world but that women can operate as subversive agents within this world. Perhaps because of this shared assumption that the erotica/ pornography distinction is not a particularly fruitful one to make in terms of advancing a political position, the debate around whether there is indeed something distinct about erotica seems to have faded into the background even as the genre has grown; perhaps erotica's very mainstream nature has indicated its seeming failure to stand for any kind of political position. Discussions of more brazen, public performances and representations of sex, such as those by Robert Mapplethorpe, Karen Finley, Marlon Riggs, Madonna, and Annie Sprinkle, have dominated academic discussions, participating in the larger interest in cultural studies and other fields in the politics of the public sphere and performance art.

Certainly feminists have good reason to valorize public performances of sex: so much of the history of women and sexuality has been one of containment to a private sphere of procreation. Furthermore, that history is still with us; the continued attempts to regulate pornography are just one example of how women get connected to a private sphere that needs to be protected from explicit sexual representations, where we are positioned as victims or moral regulators. Without dismissing the importance of work on sex and the public sphere, we must not cede the territory of the home to conservatives nor dismiss texts that try to fit within conceptions of domesticity just because they do not correspond to academic assumptions about what constitutes a radical or transgressive text. The home, in all its different manifestations, is, after all, where most women consume sexually explicit materials; my emphasis on domestication is meant to capture the importance of the home while retaining its constant connection to other sites—not just to one undifferentiated public sphere. As Roger Silverstone writes in reference to television, domestication entails "the capacity of a social group to appropriate technological artifacts and delivery systems into a culture—its own spaces and times, its own aesthetic and its own functioning—to control them, and to render them more or less 'invisible' within the daily routines of daily life" (98).

Women's domestication of pornography has historically involved the taming of a traditionally male genre—including erotica, with its foundation in canonical male writings—and rewriting/reworking it within everyday routines. The goal may be, however, not to render pornography invisible within daily routines but rather to carve out spaces for its consumption and for fantasy within these daily routines. In the oscillation between public and private spheres, in this struggle for control, we must analyze the conditions of access, which are determined not only by textual content but also through the publication, distribution, circulation, and reception of texts.

This book begins with a concentrated focus on print materials—masturbation discourse and literary erotica—then maps connections to other technologies, including the computer, cable, video, and sexually related products such as lingerie as it is marketed in the Victoria's Secret catalogs. I give print erotica more attention because women have had a longer, more productive history writing and reading erotica than they have in producing or watching visual porn; indeed, the number of erotic books published between 1991 and 1996 increased 324 percent while the overall number of books published increased by only 83 percent, according to the *Subject Guide to Books in Print,* and the majority of those books are women-authored. Women don't have a greater biological attraction to print than visual materials—as the popular stereotype goes—but rather a greater access to the means of production and consumption. Women as producers and consumers are increasingly entering and slowly redefining the traditionally male domain of visual pornography,[1] but that change is happening quite slowly even as the pornography industry continues to expand in fairly conventional ways. *Newsweek* reported in a special issue on the pornography industry in February 1997 that in 1996, "Americans spent more than $8 billion on hard-core videos, peep shows, live sex acts, adult cable programming, sexual devices, computer porn, and sex magazines—an amount much larger than Hollywood's box office receipts" and that by far the largest consumers in this industry are men (Schlosser, 44, 46).[2] Certainly women are watching pornography, but they are not fully being addressed as pornography's consumers, either through textual content or through methods of distribution and sales. Although technologies like the Internet offer women considerable potential in terms of accessing pornography, it is also just as likely that the intensifying interactivity of different technologies of pornography works to consolidate the genre's already existing tendencies to focus on male consumers. Furthermore, access to erotica or porn depends on conditions of women's lives that have nothing to do with erotica or porn—child care, housework, leisure time, knowledge about new technologies—all of which contribute to porn's continued male address and greater access; simply put, men generally have more time and mobility to access and consume porn than do women.

Although sexually explicit materials aimed specifically at women likely generate only a portion of the money garnered by the porn industry, the growth of the two categories should be seen as interrelated, part of an overall expansion of the commodification of sex. In fact, much of the sexually explicit material discussed in this book stands to profit from the continued association of pornograpy with men, carving out its marketing niche as a clear alternative to pornography. In the nearly twenty-five years since the publication of Nancy Friday's *My Secret Garden* in 1973, erotica written specifically by women for women has increasingly been recognized by publishers, distributors, and consumers as a genre distinct from porn, functioning within a broader genre of what we might call "identity erotica." In March 1993, for example, *Nation* reviewer Lennard Davis called the genre "socially acceptable erotica" and reviewed seven collections, targeting women, gays, lesbians, married couples, and African Americans. Even the more brazen erotica, such as the collections edited by outspoken lesbian sex radical Susie Bright, are now published and marketed by mainstream houses under respectable covers and sold in B. Dalton and Barnes and Noble stores across the country, sometimes in the "literary anthology" section, sometimes in a specifically marked "erotica" section, as in the Borders bookstore chain. The diverse genre I am calling domesticated porn also includes sexual self-help books and videos on couples' sex, such as John Gray's mini-industry of texts derived from his huge best-seller, *Men Are from Mars, Women Are from Venus*, and the Playboy line of videos for couples, such as *The Secrets of Making Love to the Same Person . . . Forever*. Adult cable programming often focuses on the question of women's fantasies and desires and therefore must also be included in the proliferation of texts that have been domesticated for home consumption.

Women's access to the production and consumption of erotic materials also occurs as part of a larger political context in which visual pornography is regularly demonized as a threat to the home, regulated quite heavily, and contrasted to the legally and aesthetically legitimated genre of erotica. In varying ways, all the texts discussed in this book try to distance themselves from pornography even as they draw on many of the same conventions. The literary erotica, for example, relies on a specific aesthetic privileging that extends its purposes beyond immediate sexual gratification into the realm of finding the truth of one's identity through the texts of women writers who reveal the falsity of pornography's claims about women and sex. In this respect, the erotica seems co-opted, potentially essentialist, consolidating some of the very norms about gender and sexuality that dominant discourse seeks to ensure, such as the more consensual, less aggressive nature of female sexuality. Yet some erotica has used the safe space of the literary to greatly expand notions of female desire, including selections that in other contexts would be labeled pornographic. Sex education videos for couples also illustrate the complicated position that domesticated porn occupies: they sometimes use excerpts from hard-core porn in order to emphasize the importance of female orgasm through clitoral stimulation, yet they usually legitimate the images through their emphasis on a better partnership, often referring to marriage and monogamy.

What then unites this diverse set of texts I am calling domesticated porn? Textually, the most recurrent feature is the emphasis on female orgasm; the clitoris reigns supreme, and it does so within the routines of everyday life. Indeed, establishing the connections between sex and everyday life is another common convention of these texts. But the diversity of the genre must be retained in the interest of understanding the different kinds of everyday lives addressed: John Gray's *Mars and Venus in the Bedroom* posits a much different kind of everyday life than does *Pleasure in the Word: Erotic Writing by Latin American Women*. Still, these texts are united by their attempt to distinguish themselves from pornography, thus circulating in different, more legitimate venues and making themselves more available for many women as aids to sexual pleasure.

To understand access, we must have a theory of agency, with agency defined as the relationship between the individual subject and the different forces that enable and constrict her movement between sites where sexually explicit materials are available and back to the home, where it is consumed. Feminists, both antipornography and anticensorship, have failed to produce a theory of agency in relation to pornography precisely because the discussions have been dislocated, occurring at a highly generalized level far removed from the conditions of everyday life. This level of abstraction has positioned women as victims or freestanding agents rather than considering the particularities of texts and how they are positioned differently given the circumstances that surround their consumption. My aim, as an alternative, is to conceptualize domesticated porn as a genre formed across sites and social relations, and thus to begin to understand the power relations that determine both its production and its consumption, and to formulate a politics of pornography that considers specific ways women's choices in relation to erotica/porn are both constricted and enabled. Such a focus shifts the emphasis away from pornography as a discourse of either universal power or individual appropriation (both of which transcend specific places); rather, it emphasizes pornography as a discourse of everyday significance, shaped by its relations to particular sites.

Pornography, Power, and Place

If domestication involves an oscillation between public and private spheres, then understanding agency means situating women as consumers in a constant movement between public and private places, retaining the materiality of the home without isolating it from other sites. For it is only in this manner that we begin to understand the question of agency: not as an issue of individual interpretation of singular texts but rather as a question of, to use Lawrence Grossberg's definition, "relations of participation and access, the possibilities of moving into particular sites of activity and power, and of belonging to them in such a way as to be able to actually enact their powers" (99). I want to first identify and briefly elaborate three premises regarding women's location in relation to pornography;

each premise characterizes a position in the pornography debates that inhibits analysis of agency within women's everyday lives because of its lack of attention to places as relationally defined.

Premise 1: Victim status is guaranteed if the victim's identity can be fixed in one place, and that place is defined as a site of stasis.

Because chapter 1 discusses this premise in detail, I will only say here, briefly, that much governmental discourse in the past twenty years around pornography has been concerned with establishing pornography as a threat to the home in order to guarantee women's status as victims within the domestic sphere. This regulatory impetus to define and protect a private sphere follows in the tradition of many of the legal decisions of the twentieth century that attempted to protect a class of private sphere victims—women and children—from pornographic texts that circulated in public but always threaten(ed) to spill over into the sanctity of the home.

In order to prove pornography's threat, much governmental discourse, such as the 1986 Meese Commission, *purports* to establish porn's multiple locations; however, the commission's examination of the multiple sites of pornography worked not to define any of these sites relationally but rather to prove that pornography was such a pervasive and violent presence as to be threatening the very boundedness of the home. They were searching, to use geographer Doreen Massey's descriptions of reactionary definitions of place, for a reason to be able to reassert the home as a site of "fixity and security of identity in the middle of all the movement and change . . . [to give it] an unproblematical identity . . . constructed out of an introverted, inward-looking history based on delving into the past for internalized origins" (151–52). If agency, as I describe above, is a question of movement into positions of access, governmental discourse on pornography seeks to ensure women's victim status in order to limit their mobility outside the home and thus their access to porn; it also defines their tasks *within* the home so as not to acknowledge the intersections of (nonprocreative) sexuality and other gendered, domestic roles.

Premise 2: Victim status is guaranteed if the victim's identity is not tied to any one place but rather doomed to placelessness.

In many respects the antipornography feminists have produced a similar victim discourse, sometimes in collusion with conservative politicians, as in the 1986 Meese Commission hearings. As critics have noted, Catharine MacKinnon, Andrea Dworkin, and other antipornography feminists are firmly committed to an ahistorical politics of victimizer and victimized, in which men and women are ceaselessly confined to play out the roles to which pornography, seemingly, has the sole power to confine them. I don't want to rehearse this criticism of the antiporn position— which has been eloquently stated elsewhere[3]—rather, I want to emphasize the extreme placelessness of the antiporn position. Pornography exists everywhere, and everywhere manifests itself in the same manner; from cyberspace to Bosnia, women and children are destined to everywhere be its victims, without ever achieving access to positions that might help them reconfigure pornography's meanings and uses. Indeed, pornography's meanings and uses cannot be reconfigured outside the oppressive male paradigm, according to most antiporn feminists, because pornography is literally what it is—an objectification and debasement of women. There is no acknowledgment of the subtleties and complexities of representation, of individual users' abilities to manipulate texts differently, of the entire realm of fantasy to which pornography speaks. In Robin Morgan's oft-quoted phrase, "Pornography is the theory, rape the practice."

The Meese Commission used the porn-is-pervasive argument in order to justify the need to draw boundaries around a threatened home; the antiporn feminists claim that porn is pervasive in order to justify their claims that porn knows no boundaries and thus neither should the attempts to declare a huge category of texts to be violations of women's civil rights. Questions of agency defined in terms of access, mobility, and the capacity to move into positions of power so as to be able to produce, distribute, or gain access to pornography of choice are rendered moot because pornography is already everywhere, always available and accessible. This argument actually limits access; not surprisingly, a repercussion of their legal efforts has been the confiscation of gay and lesbian erotica, including one of Andrea Dworkin's own novels in Toronto (Canada passed antipornography legislation modeled on the Dworkin-MacKinnon ordinance that the U.S. Supreme Court declared unconstitutional). By blanketing all porn under one condemning definition, the antiporn feminists provide the basis for censorship efforts that are more likely to limit access of sexually explicit material to women and gay men than to halt the sale of mainstream heterosexual porn.[4] As noted earlier, this homogenization of porn is sometimes extended to include women's erotica; although Gloria Steinem has argued for a distinction between erotica and porn, Dworkin dismisses not only that distinction but even the need for women-friendly erotica, if it could, in a more ideal world, exist: "I have a question as to why people would need it [erotica], if they were making love with each other and happy" ("Dworkin on Dworkin," 211).

The problems with this decontextualized and ahistoricized position are manifested in MacKinnon's recent article in the *Georgetown Law Journal*, where she responds to the 1995 release by Carnegie Mellon University of a huge study on users of pornography on the Internet. MacKinnon gives a very grudging nod to the study, which emphasized the prolific use, by men, of obscene, often violent sexual imagery. All the study did, says MacKinnon, was recognize what was already there: "Like pornography everywhere else, before and after it becomes Carnegie Mellon's 'images' in cyberspace, it is women's lives" (1,960). Despite the obvious differences cyberporn represents in production, distribution, and access, MacKinnon consistently denies them in order to assert that "the harms pornography does are no different online than anywhere else" and "in whatever form pornography exists, its harms remain harms to the equality of women" (1,966).

MacKinnon ridiculously simplifies the complex world of cyberporn. As many commentators on cybersex have noted, the computer offers multiple opportunities for identity bending, as users are free to adopt the gender, age, sexuality, race, physical appearance, and other characteristics they so choose. And on the Net, the line between producers and consumers of pornography breaks down as users download pornographic images and texts from adult bulletin boards and post them to newsgroups, themselves becoming disseminators if not exactly the "original" producers of images. MacKinnon tries to retain her argument that the actual material production victimizes women performers; in a convoluted footnote, she claims that even though interactive porn allows users to customize on the screen their desired stimuli without "the acts first being performed on a live woman," this freedom could actually "escalate the harms done through consumption." It seems more plausible, as Carlin Meyer argues in the same issue of the *Georgetown Law Journal*, that technology will actually *decrease* the demand for live performances, due to "Easy pirating, posting and sharing" and "sophisticated graphic techniques. . . . Bodies can be created and manipulated out of old images; faces can be reused with slight alterations to create new pornography" (2,001).

Perhaps the most damaging aspect of MacKinnon's argument on porn in terms of women's agency is her refusal to consider the question of access: as long as pornography always performs the same function no matter what place it manifests itself, women have no incentive to learn how to access it in a manner (on the Internet, for example) that might facilitate an exploration of sexual desires in the "privacy" of one's home.

Premise 3: Agent status is guaranteed if the agent's identity is defined in terms of his or her ability to evade confinement to any place, able to freely transgress boundaries of public and private.

Having stated this premise so baldly, I want to take some time to trace the historical context and sympathetically explain why so many prosexuality feminists have been eager (although often too eager) to posit women as agents of pornography. I say "sympathetically" because largely I agree with many of the arguments made by prosexuality feminists, often posited in the interest of countering the positions presented by conservatives and antipornography feminists. However, it is precisely because prosexuality feminists have remained in a generally reactive position that we have failed to define an effective politics of pornography that is situated in more than just the pornography debates.

For example, the influential anthology *Caught Looking: Feminism, Pornography, and Censorship,* composed by members of the Feminist Anti-Censorship Taskforce (FACT) and published in 1986, devotes most of its essays to countering the various arguments of the antipornography movement. Thus, even though one of *Caught Looking*'s main points is that antiporn feminists wrongly emphasize pornography as the cause of women's oppression, the anthology offers only limited suggestions on what might constitute an effective alternative politics. The essays begin to articulate such a politics, but it is largely a politics of negation: prosexuality feminism is not anti-pleasure, not rigidly gendered, not victim-assigning, and so forth. Indeed, it is precisely the antipornography position's rigidity that prompts these feminists to refuse to define their politics too definitively. As Ann Snitow writes, "Since one of the faults of antipornography theory is its misplaced concreteness, I can't be correspondingly specific about how I would go about working to alter the often limited, rapacious or dreary sexual culture in which women—and also men—now live" (17). Snitow follows this statement with a series of important questions about pornography, sex, and gender, questions that it is perhaps unfair to say that the anthology should answer. Admittedly, countering the antiporn position does move in the direction of an alternative politics, even as it remains invested in the terms of the antiporn argument. For example, an article by Lisa Duggan, Nan D. Hunter, and Carole S. Vance details the dangerous assumptions in antipornography legislation, including the Dworkin-MacKinnon antipornography ordinance that was adopted by the city of Indianapolis and later ruled unconstitutional by the U.S. Supreme Court. Other essays in *Caught Looking* rightly take on other misguided assumptions of the antipornography movement: the conflation of fantasy and reality, for example, and the demonization of all heterosexual sex as rape. Juxtaposed provocatively amidst the essays are a wide variety of pornographic images, ranging from the "artistic" to hard-core pornography, straight, gay, bondage—almost everything one could imagine being construed as pornographic. The authors make no attempt to contextualize or read the images, which is in keeping with their insistence in the essays that women be allowed to pursue sexual pleasure in nonjudgmental contexts, rather than be consigned to be the victims of false consciousness if they are aroused by images that seem to demean or objectify women.

Caught Looking represents, in some ways, what I am trying to define as an effective politics of pornography. It attempts to address some of the conditions of consumption, such as feminist politics and legal decisions, that determine when, where, and how women can buy and consume pornography. Within these conditions, it places pornographic images and tells viewers, "Do with them what you will. We make no judgments about desire." Yet because the anthology remains at a fairly general, reactive level, it also represents the beginnings of what I perceive to be the increasingly placeless discourse of prosexuality feminism. Aside from Paula Webster's brief personal recounting of a tour of New York's Forty-Second Street, none of the essays address questions of production and distribution; in fact, the decontextualization of the images suggests a certain ahistoricity, as Linda Williams notes in analyzing the anthology (*Hard Core*, 28). The anthology valorizes the individual viewer/reader's ability to interpret, to transgress codes and conditions in order to arrive at a state of pleasure. Although I certainly don't want to deny this realm of individual pleasure, I also want to argue that asserting it alone does not do much toward transforming the conditions of access that define most women's consumption of pornography. In other words, it counters the victim status posited by antipornography feminists and conservatives by asserting a kind of agency that is based on the powers of the individual; furthermore, the agency is usually connected to a kind of transgression—either the transgressive text or the act of transgressing mainstream texts. We are now certainly at the point where we can move beyond reacting to antipornography feminists and articulate a politics of pornography that does a more comprehensive job of addressing issues of production, access, and consumption, one that includes but is not limited to the questions of the subversive powers of individual consumers.

Certainly some people have made these kinds of broader arguments; Linda Williams's book *Hard Core* addresses the historical conditions of the development of the genre of hard-core pornography, refusing to take simplistic positions in terms of women's objectifications or pleasures. More often, however, the prosexuality collections that have emerged in the last decade valorize the public proliferation of transgressive texts that violate boundaries of public and private, straight and gay, and so forth, and locate in the interpretation of these subversive texts a degree of agency. Although this tendency is not *necessarily* wrong, it has not emphasized the importance of studying pornography in relation to the specific places it is produced, distributed, and consumed, and it has, furthermore, focused attention on the seemingly implicit liberation of an undifferentiated public sphere. For example, in three volumes of prosexuality essays on the pornography debates published in the early 1990s, only a handful of the forty-three total essays even mention the proliferation of erotic texts, both print and video, aimed at women produced in the last twenty years; no essay analyzes in any detail the growth in women's literary erotica.[5] The majority of the essays take up pornography as a political issue, staking a claim to a certain feminist politics by arguing against the antiporn feminists and governmental attempts at censorship and regulation. Given this urge to regulate, it is understandable that the essays that do take up in detail the discussion of specific texts rather than the general politics of pornography focus on transgressive representations that directly challenge the homogenizing, antisex tendencies of antiporn politics. In the *Sex Exposed* volume, for example, Kobena Mercer describes how readings of Robert Mapplethorpe's photos of black men represent a "perverse aesthetic of promiscuous intertextuality" (106) that makes the sexual black male visible through a transgression of sexual and artistic boundaries; in *Dirty Looks: Women, Power, and Pornography*, two essays celebrate postmodern porn performer Annie Sprinkle's border crossings. I am not dismissing the importance of work by Mapplethorpe or Sprinkle, or of critical essays on their work; rather, I am pointing to the limitations of a progressive politics that relies on an analysis of transgressive texts to the exclusion of other kinds of pornography.

Let me break down my argument about agency and placelessness into two main parts. First, prosexuality feminist responses are increasingly characterized by an assumption that places and spaces don't really matter, mainly because sexual representations have so thoroughly pervaded our society as to render moot the question of public/private sphere politics. Note the similar disregard of place here and in the Dworkin-MacKinnon position. In *Dirty Looks*, Linda Williams argues that it is increasingly difficult to declare that "sex is a private matter, since sex has, in effect, become so very public a matter, even to those who would argue to keep it private" ("Second Thoughts," 48). Although I agree with Williams's emphasis on the impossibility of defining a clearly marked private sphere, her argument erases the distinctions between different kinds of places, emphasizing instead that sex has become so public a matter as to be everywhere available (48).

Unfettered by the public/private divide, performance artists like Annie Sprinkle become relentless agents of sexual experimentation, willfully violating various boundaries that have contained female sexuality. Here is Chris Straayer on Sprinkle: "Breathing orgasms into non-genital sex, and spirituality into orgasms, Sprinkle seduces deconstruction. Exercising a 'queer' ideology arising from contemporary gay and lesbian subculture, she confounds pornography's boundaries, transgresses ours, and wraps us in her own. Pornography's naturalist philosophy spreads outward, merging private and public realms, simultaneously intensifying and diffusing the pornographic sensibility" (156). Similarly, Williams applauds Sprinkle's transgression of the art-pornography dichotomy, arguing that her refusal to recognize the boundary between these two categories maps onto the difficulty of "drawing clear lines between what is dirty and what is clean, what is properly brought on scene and what should be kept off (ob)scene." This latter issue, adds Williams, "no longer seems the crux of a feminist sexual politics" ("Agent," 177). Sprinkle, she says, "has a way of defusing and going beyond, rather than directly confronting, familiar oppositions," such as mother/daughter, artist/whore.

Thus the second manner in which these responses stop short of theorizing agency: the obliteration of spaces is tied to a belief in the transformative power of representation and interpretation as fairly isolated practices. Granted, both Williams and Straayer retain the importance of place insofar as they argue that Sprinkle's performance art is an example

of the transgressiveness that has enhanced women's mobility; to this degree, they move beyond issues of textual interpretation. However,
Williams and Straayer both suggest that it is through the reading/viewing
of individual texts, such as Sprinkle's performances, that women may, like
Sprinkle, liberate themselves into a world of polymorphous, orgasmic sexuality freed of material boundaries. As such, Sprinkle facilitates a "merging [of] private and public realms, simultaneously intensifying and
diffusing the pornographic sensibility" (Straayer), and she "defuses" and
"goes beyond" traditional dichotomies (Williams). What does it mean to
somewhat uncritically celebrate a "merging" of public and private realms?
Although Sprinkle's work is certainly important in challenging the clear
containment of women to a private sphere, one performance artist's transgressive abilities begin to substitute for the conditions that determine the
sexual practices of most women. When Williams and Straayer celebrate a
politics of transgression of public/private spaces, they valorize the politically radical space of the public without locating it in relation to other
sites. In so doing, they elide the very real materiality of the home for many
women, producing a placeless model of agency that does not challenge
conservative attempts to inhibit access through claiming a particular definition of home. Despite Sprinkle's emphasis on the merging of public/pri-
vate spheres, her work is still conditioned by the places in which she
performs; this in turn leads to broader, material questions: Who attends
her performances? How do reviews of her work circulate? What are the
implications for her work on governmental policy on pornography?

With the renewed fervor around the sanctity of the home, it is crucial
for feminists not to cede the home as the territory of right-wing conservatives; it is precisely because of this articulation to a conservative agenda
that feminists must seek ways to redefine the home in more progressive
ways. This does not mean reasserting clear-cut boundaries around the
home, but rather asking how representations of female sexuality may act
as one of a set of social relations to redefine female sexuality and sexual
relations within the home in ways that diminish the distance between the
public and the private, between the pornographic and the everyday, *without erasing the distinction*. To do this, we must consider the whole array
of available sexual representations, not merely the "baddest" or most
transgressive, but also those that seem quite limited in their challenge to
gender and sex roles. More important, we must ask how those representations shape individual consciousness only insofar as they exist within
sets of social relations that shape the material transformation of the sites

at which women purchase and consume pornography. Doing so requires an examination of the different social relations that variously determine the relationship between sexuality and women; for example, *Pleasure in the Word* testifies to the particular cultural conditions that make it difficult for many Latina and Latin American women to gain access to both the production and consumption of sexually explicit materials.

Laura Kipnis's *Bound and Gagged* also celebrates pornography's transgressive capacity; however, her texts are not postmodern works like Sprinkle's but rather popular pornography, from the rather mainstream *Hustler* to more marginal forms, including transvestite porn and fat porn. Kipnis argues that pornography is so stringently regulated precisely because it probes too revealingly our cultural and individual psyches:

> Pornography provides a realm of transgression that is, in effect, a counter-aesthetics to dominant norms for bodies, sexualities, and desire itself.... What shapes these genres [of pornography]—their content, their raw materials—are precisely the items blackballed from the rest of culture. This watchfully dialectical relation pornography maintains to the mainstream culture makes it nothing less than a form of cultural critique. It refuses to let us so easily off the hook for our hypocrisies. Or our unconsciouses. (166)

Kipnis sounds quite like a populist version of Susan Sontag, who argued in her famous 1967 essay "The Pornographic Imagination" that pornographic literature explores the demonic forces of the sexual imagination, representing "one of the extreme forms of human consciousness." The pornographic artist is a "broker in madness," whose "principal means of fascinating is to advance one step further in the dialectic of outrage. He seeks to make his work repulsive, obscure, inaccessible; in short, to give what is, or seems to be *not* wanted" (45). Both Kipnis and Sontag sublimate the immediate sexual purposes and gratifications of porn—while not dismissing them completely—preferring rather to point to the ways it acts as a form of cultural critique. Kipnis is much more attentive to the material and regulatory conditions shaping pornography and much less eager than Sontag to defend a realm of high art dependent on the singular artist (for Sontag, this meant expanding the notion of a realist aesthetic to include the avant-garde erotic literature such as Pauline Réage's *Story of O* and Bataille's novel *The Eye*). However, their arguments are similarly prescriptive in that both find *inherent* in the content of pornography something transgressive, which transcends in importance the specificities of individual texts and their uses.

I want to agree in one important way with both Sontag and Kipnis: the realm of sexual desire should not be policed, and individual preferences should not be judged. As Kipnis says, "Why a specific individual has this or that sexual preference hasn't been my concern here. . . . What the cultural critic wants to account for is the 'why' behind forms of fandom, and behind the existence of particular genres of popular culture, and to distill from them the knowledge they impart about the social" (166). In this respect, pornography does act as a kind of resistant force to regulatory attempts that try to deny the excesses of fantasy in the interest of restricting various kinds of freedoms, including women's rights to sexually explicit materials. However, the knowledge that Kipnis distills from pornography continually returns to its status as a transgressive genre, albeit transgressive in different ways: fat porn, for example, transgresses social mores about proper bodies, while geriatric porn transgresses the assumption that older people do not have sexual desires. However, transgression should not be used as the sole standard of examination; for one, not all pornography tries to be transgressive, and not all pornography circulates in conditions that stress its transgressive qualities. Indeed, focusing exclusively on pornography's transgressiveness may actually impede an analysis of who has access to it under what conditions, for in Kipnis's analysis, all pornography circulates under the rubric of transgression. Kipnis is continually caught up in the contradictions of wanting to see pornography as valuable because of its transgressive status and yet positing it as just another cultural form that should be analyzed with the same tools and perspective as other kinds of texts. For example, she argues in her chapter "How to Look at Pornography" that "pornography obeys certain rules, and its primary rule is transgression. Like your boorish cousin, its greatest pleasure is to locate each and every one of society's taboos, prohibitions, and proprieties and systematically transgress them, one by one" (164). On the other hand, Kipnis also argues against the tendency to isolate pornography from other cultural forms: "What disastrous thing would happen," she asks rhetorically, "if we were to—just experimentally, provisionally—approach pornography as we would any other cultural form, applying to it the same modes of respectful analysis" (64). The problem is that Kipnis does not approach pornography as she would any other cultural form but rather as the ultimate indicator of societal hypocrisies and standards: there is only one way to look at pornography, and that is by locating its taboos. Thus, Kipnis replicates the very strategy of antiporn feminists of which she is so critical: "the endless attention pornography commands, whether from its consumers or its protesters ... has less to do with its obvious content (sex) than with what might be called its political philosophy" (162). This is precisely what *Bound and Gagged* does: sacrifice an examination of the possibilities of different ways of consuming porn, which obviously relies on its content, for the political statement that porn makes, a position that makes it fairly easy to conflate consumers and protesters.

These proponents of transgression, in other words, are all making a form of the argument Hans Robert Jauss made in *Toward an Aesthetic of Reception*. Jauss proposed that the power of a work of art—indeed, the claim to aesthetic status—lies in the text's ability to violate the reader's "horizon of expectations," a transgression that in turn prompts a new moral recognition. Says Jauss, "Thus a literary work with an unfamiliar aesthetic form can break through the expectations of its readers and at the same time confront them with a question, the solution to which remains lacking for them in the religiously or officially sanctioned morals" (44).

The problem with this emphasis on the violation of norms, or transgression, is not with transgression itself; rather it is that transgression seemingly exists in the aesthetic form itself and awaits the critic, who will make the transgressive meaning available for (appropriately trained) readers. Although for Jauss the "new" is not only an aesthetic but also a historical category reliant on audience, his notion of history and reception is fairly limited. He relies on a universalized and implied literary reader, one with the cultural capital necessary to recognize a text's power to violate certain horizons. Similarly, much of the prosexuality work I have discussed assumes a certain kind of reader, one who is abstracted from specific conditions of access and consumption.

The claim for transgression, in other words, is in no small part a result of the academic critic's own environment and desire to generate new interpretations, new ways of reading texts in the interest of producing new ways of seeing—what Evan Watkins calls the fascination with "ideologies of the new." Says Watkins, "Such ideologies construct a series of value claims that depend on trying to dislocate work, free it from the 'institutionalized' structures where it occurs" (16). Rather than valorizing the production of new interpretations of texts without regard to their limited circulation, Watkins says, academics in English—and we can usefully expand his argument here to include other academic critics—would do well to inquire into the material conditions under which most people consume texts. We should emphasize the dependable and predictable rather than the new:

> My focus on popular cultures . . . points to the exploitation of the "realistic" and familiar, on the premise that if you're working where you can't afford a slowdown in the same way, the material of the labor process in English isn't going to help you much unless you can do something else with it. The undependability that comes from making strange is only an advantage if you've got the time and control over work processes to dictate the subsequent direction of work. If you don't, then what you want from a Stevens poem is not always a making strange, an invitation to work, an occasion for an extended labor process of reading, but rather . . . a dependable set of details you can take and use in some other way where you are. (273)

The persistent academic emphasis on making the pornographic "strange"—violating gender roles, pointing out hypocrisies, and so on—thus may not work in the contexts in which readers use the texts, for the stimulation of sexual pleasure and fantasy. Indeed, I want to argue that the critic should not concern herself with what works as a sexual fantasy for any particular reader; celebrating pornography's transgressiveness may lead to a certain dictation of appropriate desires. For example, Kipnis's emphasis on transgression leaves little room for the possibility that women don't want to read texts that continually represent taboos but rather texts that help them reconcile the world of fantasy with their everyday lives. In other words, valorizing the act of reading certain (transgressive) texts potentially hierarchizes desire in a manner that might actually inhibit its expression and could play into a conservative politics of correct and incorrect sexual expression. How should one look at pornography? As a text that, consumed correctly, will liberate your sexual psyche from an oppressive society that tries to deny desire.

In his chapter on pornography in *No Respect*, Andrew Ross critiques the intellectual impetus to use pornography as an educative body of texts; in a thesis that generally coincides with my own, Ross says that the academic interest in texts, manifested in the relationship between representation and reality, has resulted in the "neglect [of] the actual conditions under which the great bulk of pornography has been produced and consumed as an object of popular taste" (175). Ross does not attempt any such analysis himself; he devotes this chapter largely to substantiating his critique of intellectuals, arguing that any intellectual attempt to use pornography to educate the citizenry mistakenly assumes that the unconscious can be taught (200). Ross celebrates pornography as a genre whose "popularity lies in its *refusal* to be educated" (201), which suggests that critics should make no judgments at all about pornographic texts. However, Ross contradicts this position by arguing that Candida Royalle's Femme Productions videos are themselves examples of an attempt to educate desire and thus do not qualify as erotic texts. He says about *The Pick-Up*, a 1987 Femme Productions video that eroticizes the use of a condom, "*The Pick-Up* is clearly presenting iself as an attempt to educate desire, but it is just as likely to achieve overkill, and demonstrates how and why education of this sort can often be a turn-off" (199). Who is the intellectual now? Ross clearly positions himself as the judge of erotic tastes in relation to Femme videos despite simultaneously arguing that intellectuals should not attempt to use pornography to make claims about desire. My answer is not to disregard texts in favor of examining solely the conditions of their production and consumption; rather, I propose that we nonjudgmentally consider pornographic texts themselves as participants in the production of conditions that determine pornography's consumption. In this view, the critic analyzes the integration of condoms into an erotic video not in terms of whether or not it is erotic (for whom, after all?) but rather in terms of how it intersects with other conditions of women's access, such as the need to practice safer sex.

What to Do with Texts

I have thus arrived at an important point of intersection in my project: the valorization of the new, manifested in the interpretation of texts, that occurs in both prosexuality feminist work on pornography and much literary analysis and some cultural studies. Although there are many other, different factors that shape these two fields, their coincidence is particularly important for my work, situated as it is within an English department and attempting to make an intervention in the politics of pornography. The intersecting question, simply put, is this: What do we as critics do with texts, both literary texts and the other kinds of texts, from different media, that constitute a genre? What does it mean—if we accept Watkins's claim about the continued valorization of the new—to emphasize the predictable and mundane?

To begin to answer this question, I want to draw on Tony Bennett's

Outside Literature, where he argues that literary criticism (his focus is Marxist criticism) has been characterized by an aesthetic discourse that positions the critic as the interpreter of deep meanings, the one who inculcates the reader into a process of self-formation based on the meaning the critic has found in the text. Although I have some reservations with Bennett's argument, I find his theories useful for developing a theory of texts and genre that preserves their specificity without valorizing the interpretation of texts as a process guaranteeing political change. In that sense, Watkins and Bennett share a concern for constructing an approach to the study of texts that positions the critic not as judge or, in Bennett's words, moral exemplar, but rather as a describer, so to speak, of the conditions that shape the interpretation of texts.

Bennett argues that texts should not be privileged as a site from which to read *through* to their underlying social conditions. Instead, says Bennett, "Literature is itself a field of social relationships in its own right and one which interacts with other fields in which social relationships are organised and constituted *in the same way as they interact with it and on the same level*" (108). Following Bennett, then, I have in this book traced the connections between literary erotica and the other kinds of texts that constitute the genre of domesticated porn, constantly demonstrating the ways these different technologies of pornography interact within a particular set of conditions surrounding the home and domesticity. I argue that we must treat pornographic literature as a field—not as a set of texts representing the desires we deem appropriate for women to feel upon reading or viewing the text. We must ask, What are the multiple sites and sets of social relations that determine the relationship between pornography and home for women consumers? How is the genre of domesticated pornography located within this field of relations? (By "located," I mean to indicate a position that is shaped by sites such as governmental discourse, yet reshapes them as well.) Constituting a genre is an impure enterprise, as John Frow and Meaghan Morris indicate: "The mixing of discourses and genres in much work in cultural studies has to do with its methodological impurity, perhaps with a certain fruitful insecurity about its legitimacy as a discipline, but perhaps too with the way in which it conceives its objects as being relational (a network of connections) rather than substantial" (xix).

To say that domesticated porn is composed of various kinds of texts, each of which is produced at different sites that then must be connected in order to constitute the genre, is to begin to understand the manner in which agency is *a matter not of subjectivity by itself* but rather of the material conditions that facilitate the subject's structured mobility. We must examine the various material and discursive sites that define mobility and locate the individual texts as one position among these sites. Thus, my project is not only an effort to situate these texts within a much broader field of social relations in the interest of defining an effective politics of pornography, it is also an effort to demonstrate a kind of cultural studies that preserves the specificities of different technologies yet shows how their meanings are determined only in relation to each other. I thus distance myself considerably from methodologies that define a genre solely in terms of a single body of texts—literary, film, television, and so on—as most genre studies still do. A cultural studies critic engaged in pursuit of the mundane implications of consumption, then, acknowledges that the text's meaning is determined as much by factors outside the text as by factors within it.

We as critics can never step outside textual interpretation; indeed, much of this project is a series of interpretations of different texts within particular contexts. But we can avoid the search for deep, intrinsic meanings that produces the judgmental claims of value that both Watkins and Bennett object to, and that surfaces even in Ross's desire to distance himself from intellectual "reformist zeal." In some ways, we are no better off with transgression as a normative value than we were with the nuclear family or the missionary position. Avoiding prescriptive claims means that we must not read erotic texts as a gauge of the author's or presumed reader's ability to violate gendered and sexualized norms. Using transgression as the standard of interpretation, one could easily dismiss much of the erotica I analyze as co-opted, reinforcing gendered norms and essentialist notions of female sexuality. Rather, I address the texts as themselves sites where notions of home and sexuality are produced; the texts, in relation to other sites, thus become places where issues of access are partially determined.

It may seem that my emphasis on texts as participants in determining conditions of access flattens the question of fantasy, which is clearly a central component of the textual "work" that erotica does. In fact, this is what the antipornography feminists do—conflate reality and fantasy, take pornography literally, ignore the complexities and uncertainties of interpretation. In contrast, however, I want to make as much room for fantasy as possible by examining the conditions under which it occurs. The question, then, is not what kinds of fantasies women will have after reading a certain erotic story or viewing an erotic cable show, but rather how the representation of fantasies within the contexts of everyday life legitimates the spaces for fantasies that may or may not reproduce the one represented. Also, how are the conditions for fantasy limited and facilitated by governmental discourse that demonizes some kinds of porn and implicitly valorizes erotica and some soft-core porn? How does the commodification of lingerie through a hugely successful company like Victoria's Secret affect the erotic possibilities of fiction that references lacy bras and underwear? I can make no direct connections between these conditions and the fantasies that result—indeed, that is precisely what I am trying to avoid, a kind of prescriptive connection between social conditions and fantasies. However, in focusing on the social conditions surrounding pornography and erotica, I am emphasizing that, indeed, social conditions structure fantasy, in ways that we can't exactly determine but that nevertheless can be changed. The masturbation texts of the 1970s that emphasized the importance of clitoral orgasm, for example, clearly helped produce conditions in which women were more likely to read erotica as a masturbatory aid—although the fantasies that accompanied masturbation are beyond the critic's determination. Emphasizing how texts themselves are participants in setting the rules for access leads to a politics of pornography in which questions of access predominate: How do we arrive at the political, social, and economic conditions in which women are "free" to consume whatever pornography they desire? That would constitute transgression in the material sense of the word.

Domestication and Commodification

The concept of domestication may conjure up images of the white middle-class housewife, suggesting a coherent category of women. However, as this book shows, domestication encompasses many different identity groups with different conceptions of everyday life (including the suburban housewife). For example, women's literary erotica has increasingly been characterized by an appeal to multiple identities as they are articulated to race, class, sexual preference, and age; in recent years, volumes of erotica for Asian Americans, African Americans, Latin American women, and Chicanos/as have been published. Although some of the women's erotica devoted to the historical recovery of women's erotic writings often does presume a category of white women, other volumes of erotica, such as the *Herotica* series, foreground questions of difference within each volume. Lesbian, straight, and bisexual stories constitute the mix of many volumes, with the exception of the more conservative texts dedicated to saving marriages through better sex. Because domestication is a matter not just of textual content but also of publication and circulation, all the texts that circulate broadly under the rubric of better sex for women help produce and are produced by the politics of greater access within a capitalist economy.

Indeed, commodification is a necessary component of domestication; the process of domesticating a volume of erotica, a vibrator, a garter belt, or an adult video depends on the item's availability as a commodity. Its meaning, however, is not inevitably contaminated by its status as a commodity; a commodity is defined not by a set of internal properties but rather by the nature of the exchange process. As the commodity enters the home, thus, its meaning is redefined—a vibrator bought in the Sears department store as a back massager may also (or instead) be used to stimulate the clitoris. Although some erotica tries to define itself as a purer, less commodified form than the big industry of pornography, its success as a genre that is now marketed widely in mainstream bookstores depends, clearly, on its commodification, a process that promises to multiply women's uses of sexually explicit materials. Much lesbian erotica, for example, foregrounds its role in the development of a politicized lesbian community, something that couldn't be accomplished if the erotica did not circulate widely. In the introduction to *Best Lesbian Erotica, 1997,* Jewelle Gomez has this to say about the importance of open access: "For me as a black lesbian, to pick stories and poems embodying lesbian desire, knowing that they will be published in a book sold in bookstores around the country, not under the counter but on the shelves—this remains a most political act. It is akin to reaching out that first time to touch my best friend's body" (Taormino, 15). Radical politics is thus linked to commodification.

It's important to note, as well, that all forms of sexual representation are commodified to varying degrees, from hard-core porn to Annie Sprinkle's performances. If we don't acknowledge this omnipresent albeit uneven process, we run the risk of invoking, once again, the high art/low art distinction, in which the "good" form of sexually explicit material is available only to an elite few, while the masses wallow in their low-brow porn. A more instructive approach is to inquire into the relationships between making a product palatable for relatively widespread marketing, the content necessary for that commodification to occur, and the possible uses that result. Such an approach reveals that some products do well precisely because they are easily assimilated into a mainstream politics that valorizes sexually explicit products as long as they reinforce certain dominant conceptions of love and marriage (such as the John Gray texts) or of the pursuit of feminine beauty (such as the Victoria's Secret catalogs). However, other products share shelf space with John Gray even as they valorize more marginal sexual practices and challenge conceptions of romantic, heterosexual love.

If domestication is a negotiation between public and private spheres, then we can establish a sort of continuum: the texts that try to deny this relationship, as if existing in an isolated private sphere, participate more fully in the family values discourse valorizing the traditional nuclear, heterosexual family. When texts lend themselves to domestication as a process of making more open the fluidity of the public/private boundaries while retaining their material importance, then the kind of control women gain over sexually explicit materials is more likely to challenge the family values agenda. Thus, although I want to distance this project from any judgmental claims about the appropriate desires women should feel upon reading certain texts, I do not ignore the ways texts become part of and help reproduce various kinds of distinctions, distinctions that will themselves become part of the conditions of access. As John Frow writes, drawing on Bourdieu,

> ... the primary business of culture is distinction, the stratification of tastes in such a way as to construct and reinforce differentiations of social status which correspond, *in historically variable and often highly mediated ways*, to achieved or aspired-to class position. Cultural discrimination involves a constant negotiation of position with the aim of naturalizing one's own set of values, distinguishing them from the values of others, and attempting more or less forcefully to impose one's values on others. It is thus not just a matter of self-definition but also of struggle for social legitimation. (85)

The struggle manifested in many of these texts is that of distinguishing themselves from pornography, a distinction that has relevance to stratifications of class, gender, and sexuality, as I describe more in chapter 3, and that is shaped by the historical and contemporary regulation of pornography and legitimation of erotica, as I describe in chapter 1. To say, then, that certain texts participate more fully in a family values agenda than others is to point to the ways the texts try to blend into a national discourse that will, presumably, make the process of marketing texts that deal with the problematic area of sex more palatable to a public wary of pornography. The content of texts is only one of many variables that constitute the struggle for legitimation; content partially determines but also sometimes contradicts the possibilities of marketing, circulation, and consumption. For example, the identity erotica anthologies often make a strong claim about the ability of the text to clearly define women's sexual desires—a distinction that legitimates a difference from pornography and facilitates circulation—yet then include a set of stories that show how variable, and sometimes "pornographic," women's desires are. Furthermore, readers are very capable of disarticulating certain aspects of texts from others. Couples may find John Gray's instructions on clitoral orgasm very useful for their sexual practices without necessarily endorsing his overall emphasis on heterosexual monogamy and marriage.

At one level, then, this book endorses all the texts discussed as participants in the production of conditions of women's access to sexually explicit materials; the proliferation of texts directed at women and couples that focus on the clitoral orgasm and women's fantasies and pleasures is so important that it requires nonjudgmental description, as well as the recognition that the practices endorsed in texts will be employed in different manners. At another level, I do not claim that all texts are equally accessible to all women; each chapter examines what Frow calls the "struggle for social legitimation" amidst these various texts as they are produced in relation to other discourses, from governmental regulation of pornography to dominant conceptions of what constitutes a "couple." Examining the struggle for legitimation leads to an understanding of the variability of access. For example, adult cable programming already must struggle for legitimacy within a governmental discourse that holds visual pornography to stiffer regulatory standards than those for print; one way of showing its distance from pornography (as well as its appeal to a broader audience) is to foreground its use by couples as an aid to better sex within marriage—something Playboy has done in some of its programming. Still, this strategy doesn't always guarantee greater legitimation; a 1997 Supreme Court ruling upheld a requirement that cable companies either completely block the audio and visual signals of adult programming channels to nonsubscribers or limit the hours of programming to 10 P.M. to 6 A.M. Because blocking audio signals is a very costly endeavor, many local cable franchisers are choosing to limit the hours of programming. This ruling most certainly affects women's access to the

Playboy and Spice channels, and it might also affect women's perceptions of what constitutes legitimate material for their consumption. The court ruling and the programming content do not ultimately determine how women might use the content of certain shows to build a particular fantasy; I am more concerned with analyzing the regulation of texts and the texts produced in this environment than with the actual uses to which women ultimately put them—for it is impossible to study the "actual" life of fantasy without devolving into the judgments of desire I have criticized.

This brief example, elaborated in chapter 1, indicates the importance of examining the genre of domesticated porn across a number of dispersed sites rather than as a coherent category of texts defined by their similar textual characteristics or even as a contract between reader and text. Defining the genre is a process of connecting the various discourses shaping the genre, of constantly going out from the text to other discourses and from the home to other sites. Following Foucault, then, I am trying to challenge the unity of certain categories in order to reconstitute them as a kind of "regulated dispersion"—the term Ernesto Laclau and Chantal Mouffe use to describe Foucault's notion of discourse. The objects that together constitute the genre of domesticated porn exist not as a coherent unity but in a field of regulated dispersion. The objects are regulated at a series of dispersed sites of production of rules about sexuality and subject formation—governmental discourse, popular women's magazines, the gay and lesbian rights movement, and so forth. By connecting these sites, I am practicing what Laclau and Mouffe describe as articulation: "any practice establishing a relation among elements such that their identity is modified as a result of the articulatory practice" (105).

Chapter 1 charts the history of pornography regulation in this country, showing the always present but recently reinvigorated attempts to use porn to regulate sexual relations within the home. I describe these regulatory attempts across a variety of technologies—the Internet, cable television, and pornographic videos—leading up to the current historical conjuncture of these various technologies within the "private" sphere. Governmental discourse and actual regulation (arrests, for example, of Internet porn disseminators) shape local consumption in a highly mediated but nevertheless material way, dependent on a series of other facilitating and restrictive factors that occur at the local level; I demonstrate these local variables through a brief case study of my own community, Champaign-Urbana, Illinois.

Chapter 2 focuses on the 1970s as a decade in which the discourses of second-wave feminism, sex therapy, and consumerism legitimated the practice of masturbation through clitoral stimulation. Much of this discourse emphasized the idea that women's desires should not be subsumed to everyday demands even as the right to masturbation and orgasm was posited in a normalizing manner. Nancy Friday's *My Secret Garden* and numerous studies on the female orgasm, including Masters and Johnson's work, stressed the possibility that sexual pleasure and fantasy could mesh with the realities of everyday life. In legitimating masturbation and emphasizing the clitoris, these texts also laid the foundation for the claim by contemporary erotica to a specific women's language based on the body. The concept of the female body was a contested one, however. As I show in my discussion of the vibrator's reception as a masturbatory aid in the 1970s, many women were initially reluctant to endorse its use because it represented the "technologization" of sex, the coming together of the natural and the mechanical. Despite these anxieties, vibrators have increasingly gained legitimacy as domestic pleasure tools; furthermore, I argue that the vibrator debates serve as a useful historical transition into the current debates about virtual sex and the potential for women to domesticate the computer in the interest of sexual pleasure.

Chapter 3 takes up the specifically aesthetic distinction made by identity erotica in its attempt to distinguish itself from pornography. I critique the tendency in cultural studies to dismiss aesthetic claims as inherently elitist and placeless and the move by poststructuralist feminists to dismiss identity-based politics as engaged in an essentialist project of whole subjectivity. Both positions hamper an engagement with the popular spheres in which an invocation of aesthetics is strategically important. Indeed, it is precisely the erotica's claims to aesthetic status in relation to subjectivity that legitimates it in a manner that guarantees accessibility in a very material way. Women's erotica has become an increasingly mainstream category for large publishing houses, distributors, and chain bookstores because of the genre's insistence on its literary nature and its appeal to women as a class of readers within the home. I focus on Down There Press's *Herotica* series and the British series Black Lace, which is widely distributed in the United States, in order to illustrate how—and where—erotica's aesthetic claims circulate.

Perhaps as a nostalgic response to the development of new technologies that hold the potential for a kind of "disembodied sex" transcending boundaries of public and private, the 1990s have seen a resurgence in the popularity of Victorian erotica; several publishing houses have reprinted

excerpts from Victorian underground pornography, such as *The Pearl,*
and published "Victorian" erotica written by contemporary authors. In
chapter 4 I analyze the Victorian fetish, including in this phenomenon the
hugely profitable Victoria's Secret lingerie catalog, which also capitalizes
on a kind of highly mediated Victorian nostalgia. The desire for a time
when boundaries between private and public were more clearly fixed—a
domestication that tries to deny the oscillating relationship between
sites—also participates in and helps produce a kind of erotica that is
friendly to the family values proponents. The emphasis on sex as a private, heterosexual affair of the bedroom characterizes many of the better-
sex-for-couples texts I look at in chapter 5. For example, John Gray's
depictions of female anatomy and his valorization of the specificity of female pleasure seem to draw on feminist texts; however, the manner in
which pleasure gets linked to heterosexual, procreative marriages coincides with a definition of family and sexual practices that explicitly ex-
cludes gay, lesbian, and other alternative families. Candida Royalle's
Femme Productions video company illustrates the more progressive edge
of this emphasis on couples, still relying on some of the tenets of heterosexual privilege but expanding conceptions of women's pleasure within
relationships outside the more cloying aspects of romance.

The texts analyzed in chapters 4 and 5 can't be dismissed as purely nostalgic or fully complicit in the conservative backlash against feminism and
gay rights. The Victoria's Secret catalogs and the sale of lingerie more generally suggest that there are many gaps between the production and the
consumption of these products; furthermore, Victoria's Secret's textual
and visual address to the independent working woman refutes any easy
categorization of its pleasures as fully subsumed under a male gaze. Lingerie as a commodity assumes a different life when it enters the pages of
women's erotica, where characters use and discard it in order to enhance
a wide variety of sexual practices. Similarly, chapter 5 does not concede
that any and all referencing of couples and sex falls into the family values
agenda; the doors of the bedroom are not irrevocably closed to change.

In chapter 6, I examine the growth of cable as a technology accessible
to many women within the space of the home. Erotic series and features
on the premium cable channels have helped redefine women's televisual
narratives, foregrounding the woman protagonist in pursuit of her sexual
pleasures, often to the near exclusion of male characters. I trace some
connections between the different kinds of programs, analyzing the
agency represented in terms of movement between public and private

sites of different figures, such as the suburban housewife, the femme fatale, and the career woman. Although the kinds of everyday life represented are mainly white, heterosexual, and upwardly mobile, the premium channels do a better job of addressing women as viewers than does the Playboy channel, which has also tried to attract women viewers to its cable programming.

Pornography has been seen by its various commentators as a production and a representation of great power, able to claim victims or liberate agents, seemingly transcending the more mundane details that define the situations in which most people consume the texts. A more effective politics of pornography would seek to place it *within* the routines of everyday life; I say this not in order to equate pleasure and desire with dishes and diapers, but rather to work toward the conditions in which the latter does not overwhelm the former, in which agency is a question of access to the times and places in which pleasure and desire, including the consumption of pornography, can be freely practiced.

1

Home Sweet Pornographic Home?

Governmental Discourse and Women's Paths to Pornography

On August 22, 1996, President Clinton signed a "welfare reform" bill that effectively eliminates the federal guarantee of cash assistance for the country's poorest children, saving the U.S. government $55 billion over six years. The bill abolished Aid to Families with Dependent Children, which, according to the *New York Times*, provides monthly cash benefits to 12.8 million people, including 8 million children (Pear, A10). It established a lifetime limit of five years on welfare payments to any family and required most adults to work within two years of receiving aid. In a little reported but telling provision, the bill mandated that mothers who refuse to divulge the identity of their children's fathers will immediately have their aid withdrawn.

Critics were quick to condemn the bill for punishing children for the sins of their mothers. No one, however, at least in the mainstream debates, took objection to the demonization of single motherhood and the implication, sometimes overtly stated, that "illegitimacy" has caused a whole series of social problems. As William Bennett proclaimed, "Illegitimacy is America's most serious social problem" (16). This polemic was central to the political discourse on welfare reform, from conservative guru Charles Murray's December 1994 broadside in *Commentary* to Clinton's decision to sign the bill. In urging passage of the bill, Senator Phil Gramm of Texas lamented the fact that "When we started the current welfare program, two-parent families were the norm in poor families in America. Today two-parent families are the exception. When we started the current welfare program, the illegitimacy rate was roughly one quarter of what it is today." For Gramm, fathers are the victims of the welfare system, mothers the manipulative benefactors: "Our current welfare program has failed. It has driven fathers out of the household" (Pear, A10).

Similarly, in Charles Murray's analysis of welfare mothers in the United States, their sexuality, expressed outside marriage, indicates a degree of agency that must be dissipated by containment within a traditionally gendered marital relationship. How to achieve this containment? Cut off their financial resources and force them to find a husband. Better yet, start earlier, with fathers who run a properly patriarchal household. Let's not make this complex, says Murray; the answer to the rise of babies born "out of wedlock" is not "sex education, counseling, and the like"; change will occur only when "young people have had it drummed into their heads from their earliest memories that having a baby without a husband entails awful consequences." He adds, "Subtle moral reasoning is not the response that works. 'My father would kill me' is the kind of response that works" (31). In this manner, the single mother is hypothetically recontained within a nuclear family, a sexuality deemed too mobile is reined in, and a simple answer to a complex social issue is proposed: marriage in the family values tradition.

The welfare repeal law was one of a series of governmental acts in the election year 1996 that showed just how narrow the attempt to define "family values" has become, at least in Washington. Republican presidential candidate Bob Dole took swipes at Hollywood for its violence and lack of sexual standards,[1] echoing then vice president Dan Quayle's 1992 attack on the television show *Murphy Brown*, when Candice Bergen's character decided to become a single mother, flouting, said Quayle, the importance of fatherhood.[2] In the summer of 1996 the U.S. Congress passed the Defense of Marriage Act, which defined marriage as the union between one man and one woman; Clinton signed it into law in September. Again, "aberrant" sexuality was blamed for the "demise of civilization." The bill's author, Representative Bob Barr, a Republican from Georgia, said the act was needed because "the flames of hedonism, the flames of narcissism, the flames of self-centered morality are licking at the very foundation of our society, the family unit" (qtd. in Jerry Gray, A8). With Clinton staying just one degree to the left of Dole, election year 1996 had become an exercise in scapegoating sexuality and gender in lieu of taking on a series of complex social issues. Rather than addressing issues like poverty, inner-city joblessness, racism, violence, and education inequities, Congress and the president saw fit to blame single mothers and

same-sex marriages and reassert the importance of a traditionally config-
ured, heterosexual family.

Governmental attempts to regulate pornography must be situated
within the political context of the policing of sexuality for the sake of a
mythical set of family values. The same legislators who vote to eliminate
welfare proclaim their concern for women and children in hyperbolic
debate about pornography on the Internet. By juxtaposing the welfare debate with the pornography debate, we can understand some of the
hypocrisy of governmental policy: women are dangerous sexual agents
when they take money from the state yet, according to reports like those
issued by the Meese Commission, helpless sexual victims in a society sat-
urated by pornography. These governmental positions legitimate the
withdrawal of necessary and humane funding and substitute a much less
costly rhetoric about the evils of pornography. Both, in different ways,
work to limit women's sexual freedom. An effective politics of pornography, as I argue in my introduction, must not answer the governmental
strategy by inflating the importance of pornography as a transgressive
text, the common retort of prosexuality feminists; rather, access to and
consumption of erotica and pornography must be situated in relation to
women's everyday lives, as only one of the many elements that potentially
constitute part of their everyday routines.

Much governmental discourse on pornography in the last twenty years
has sought to use the "problem" of pornography to reinstate certain
norms about what constitutes a healthy sexuality and a proper family.
The fact that pornography consumption has increasingly become concentrated in the home, moving from the more public and regulatable
spheres of adult theaters and bookstores to computers, cable television,
and home video recorders has made it easier, in certain respects, for government to claim that pornography threatens the sanctity of the home
and the innocence of its (young/female) inhabitants. In the first part of
this chapter, I trace the gradual shifting of governmental prosecution of
porn from its presence in relatively public spaces to its circulation via
technologies within the home. Governmental reports like the one issued
by the Meese Commission, congressional regulation of cable, and attempted policing of the Internet combine to set up a model of domesticity that demonizes pornography in several ways. According to this model,
pornography is consumed by men who are likely to mimic its purportedly
violent and objectifying representations of women; the porn industry literally oppresses women; and women who consume pornography either

are forced to do so or, if they claim to like it, are victims of false consciousness who need to be educated about their proper sexuality. We must understand this governmental discourse in order to effectively formulate a politics of pornography that reclaims the home as a site where women can consume pornography—if they so choose—rather than abdicating it as a site of conservative regulation. The study of pornography in relation to domesticity is thus important at two levels: as a strategic way of analyzing the methods through which patriarchal institutions attempt to use pornography in order to recontain female sexuality and as a practical inquiry into the material realities of pornography consumption for women.

Reclaiming the home means making it a site where women can consume pornography that they like without feeling guilty about its relationship to their other roles within the home. This involves asking questions about women's movements, both within and outside the home: Where can women find pornography or erotica? Why might they consider it inimical to the home? Do they feel comfortable and safe buying it in locations outside their homes, or through technologies inside their homes? How do women's other activities—work, household chores, child care, leisure activities—affect their abilities to consume pornography? And how are the home and relations within the home redefined through these movements? Does the governmental demonization and regulation of pornography make it easier for women to access erotica? The effects of this regulation, except in the case of direct prosecutions of obscenity, are often hard to gauge, in part because the consumption of pornography via cable, video, and computer technology in the home is a much more difficult and complicated act to regulate than the public display of sex that characterizes adult theaters and strip bars. Governmental discourse shapes local consumption in a highly mediated but nevertheless material way, dependent on a series of other facilitating and restrictive factors that occur at the local level. In the conclusion to this chapter, I consider how the different governmental attempts to regulate porn converge with local efforts to police public displays of sex in my community of Champaign-Urbana, Illinois.

Pornography and the Struggle for Access

Throughout the twentieth century in the United States, attempts to regulate pornography across a number of spheres—legal, medical, governmental, antipornography feminist—have often been undertaken in the name of protecting a class of victims most threatened by pornography's presence. Regulation intends to protect these victims from access to pornography by preventing its circulation in the places where those victims are assumed to reside. Usually there is a strict dichotomy between the public sphere perpetrators—producers, disseminators, and users of porn—and their private sphere victims—women and children who are connected to the sanctity of the home. With the exception of some historical periods of relative deregulation of pornography, we can say that from the Comstock laws of the early twentieth century through the latest debates on Internet pornography, regulators have tried to pinpoint pornography's victims and define them as virtually powerless against a growing tide of increasingly violent and harmful pornography. The state, in various manifestations, thus becomes the agent, authorized to protect pornography's victims by preventing them from exposure to the harmful texts as well as to limit pornography's use by potential "victimizers" who supposedly imitate the texts.

These private/public debates point to—without often developing—the importance of access: that is, we must consider the history of pornography in this country as not only a battle over representation but also a battle for access to the specific spaces where those representations occur. The feminist struggle for access to public sphere representation is so critical because for much of this century, court rulings, other governmental proceedings, and the pornography industries have worked, in different but often overlapping ways, to limit access to pornography to men. Yet, as I argued in the introduction, too often the feminist arguments on pornography operate at a similarly general level, leaving intact reductive notions of public and private spaces and thus failing to analyze the material conditions that constrict and enable women's access to pornography.

Great Britain established the legal precedent for protection of the private sphere with the passage of its first anti-obscenity legislation in 1857, the Obscene Publications Act; it sought to protect young middle-class women whose pornography consisted of the romantic novel. In 1868 the famous *Regina v. Hicklin* case, which was to become the basis of much early U.S. obscenity law, arose from similar concerns.[3] In it, Lord Chief Justice Cockburn remarked, "This work, I am told, is sold at the corners of the streets, and in all directions, and of course, it falls into the hands of the persons of all classes, young and old, and the minds of the hitherto pure are exposed to the danger of contamination and pollution from the impurity it contains" (qtd. in Kendrick, 122). As Walter Kendrick notes, Cockburn's concern was that the text in question circulated not among gentlemen in private but in the streets. Much pornography in late nineteenth-century Britain was circulated only among upper-class bibliophiles who amassed private collections that never drew the attention of the courts or the public because of their limited circulation and high price (Kendrick, 77).

In the United States, circulation of sex-related materials through the mail in the late nineteenth century provided the grist for the zealous mill of Anthony Comstock, the Post Office special agent who for forty-three years enforced an 1873 law—which quickly became known as the Comstock law—prohibiting distribution of any "obscene, lewd, lascivious book, pamphlet, picture, paper, print or other publication of an indecent character, or any article or thing designed or intended for the prevention of conception or procuring of abortion" (qtd. in Kendrick, 134). As Lauren Berlant describes it, Comstock "installed this regime of anxiety and textual terror by invoking the image of youth, and in particular, the stipulated standard of the little girl whose morals, mind, acts, body, and identity would certainly be corrupted by contact with adult immorality" (388). This standard figured heavily in court decisions on obscenity for much of the twentieth century and continues to haunt governmental commissions like the 1986 Attorney General's Commission on Pornography and the 1995 Communications Decency Act.

The pornography that did circulate during and after the Comstock days was the stag film, the predecessor to the modern hard-core narrative. These illegally made, silent, one-reel films were often enjoyed privately by groups of men, providing what Linda Williams describes in *Hard Core* as a kind of male bonding experience that was narratively structured so as to create the need for the fulfillment of sexual desire in other venues, such as prostitution. Stag films were often shown in brothels in Europe and in exclusive male clubs in the United States, to which prostitutes were often invited. The circulation of the stag films thus limited women's access to pornography at several levels—their illicit production, their private showings, and their association with prostitution.

Court cases in the first half of this century—even those that are hailed for their recognition that certain (literary) works should be freed from regulation—implicitly denied women the right to consume sexually explicit material. For example, legal scholar Edward de Grazia hails the 1933 decision freeing James Joyce's *Ulysses* as the first step toward loosening the courts' dependence on the standard of the little girl. De Grazia says that Judge John M. Woolsey fashioned a new legal rule to replace *Hicklin*: "*Ulysses* should not be judged by a tendency that novel might have to corrupt the morals of young girls, but rather by the effect on the judge himself—and two friends, whom he privately consulted" (de Grazia, xxi). When Joyce's novel failed to arouse these three gentlemen, Woolsey ruled in favor of the novel; de Grazia writes that "the capacity to arouse lust in the 'average person' now became the prevailing American legal test of whether literature ought to be suppressed for being 'obscene'" (xxi). De Grazia fails to note, however, the gendered nature of the ruling; women, presumably, did not figure as "average" people who consumed potentially pornographic texts but rather, still, as their potential victims.

Making Pornography a "Household Word"

In the first half of this century pornography circulated in mainly private, male-defined venues and was associated with illicit sex. Several events in the 1950s indicated a gradual acceptance of certain kinds of pornography and also of more sexually explicit films that were not called pornography. The 1953 Kinsey report focused attention on the sexual needs of American women; mainstream cinema, according to Richard Dyer, became increasingly explicit in its treatment of sex (26). Marilyn Monroe appeared as the first nude centerfold in the first issue of *Playboy*, also in 1953. *Playboy*'s philosophy, one Monroe helped to foster, was to present female sexuality as healthy and natural, in the form of the "girl next door," as I discuss more in chapter 6. The emphasis on sexuality as a "healthy" part of life would dominate much of the discourse that legitimated it throughout the 1960s; it was a characterization broad enough to encompass even the most hard-core pornography. By 1972, argues Linda Williams, "hardcore pornography had become a household word" (*Hard Core* 99).

Beginning with the 1957 Supreme Court case *United States v. Roth* and continuing into the 1960s, U.S. courts gradually freed all but the most "hard-core" of pornographic materials. Although the court upheld the conviction of Samuel Roth for mailing a magazine containing nude pictures and erotic stories, Supreme Court Justice William Brennan ruled that only material "utterly without redeeming social importance" could be declared obscene. De Grazia argues that Brennan's ruling "produced a significant crack in the country's century-old obscenity law"; during the next decade it became very difficult for prosecutors to prove that a literary, artistic, or social text was "utterly without redeeming social importance." In fact, de Grazia notes, during the decade following the Roth decision, all kinds of sexually explicit texts were freed, from previously banned novels like *Lady Chatterley's Lover* to "blatantly pornographic pulp literature" (323–24). In 1964 the Supreme Court furthered the defense of literary and artistic expression in decisions, authored by Brennan, concerning Henry Miller's *Tropic of Cancer* and Louis Malle's film *The Lovers*. Lower federal and state courts "obediently put the Brennan doctrine to work in reversing obscenity findings in book, film, and magazine censorship cases throughout the country" (de Grazia, 431).

This period of relative deregulation was not without its own set of norms; most obviously, the courts continued to preserve a category—the obscene—that, bereft of social value, does potentially cause harm to its victims, usually posited as victims of men who consume pornography. Also, the process of proving that a work "as a whole" does have "redeeming social value" and that it does not appeal to "prurient interests"—all defining characteristics of obscenity that emerge from this period—continued to uphold aesthetic distinctions between the erotic and the pornographic, or between hard-core and soft-core. As Hunter et al. note, and as I elaborate in the next two chapters, this aesthetic distinction sets in motion a process of self-disciplining, emphasizing "individuals' ability to mediate and order their own sexual interests and to balance the excitations of erotica with an aesthetic appreciation of the work as a whole" (211). The courts thus established a balance "between self-management and legal policing" (Hunter et al., 211). Although the figure of the little girl is not as predominant as it is in either earlier or later juridico-governmental decisions, the need to protect a class of victims from hard-core pornography's users and the need to prove one's own maturity, standing outside the class of users, remain.

However, there was increasing recognition in the 1960s and 1970s that women could join the class of consumers of erotica and even pornography. This is particularly clear in the 1970 Report of the Commission on Obscenity and Pornography, known also as the Lockhart report, which emphasized the rights of adults to purchase and consume whatever sexually explicit material they desire: "In general outline, the Commission recommends that federal, state, and local legislation should not seek to interfere with the rights of adults who wish to do so to read, obtain or view explicit sexual materials" (U.S. Commission on Obscenity, 57). As Hunter et al. note, the arguments in the report are based on a problematic, liberal belief in the rational powers of an individual who is abstracted from particular conditions of ongoing regulation and disciplinization of desire. Nevertheless, the report's insistence that government not interfere with adults' rights to consume pornography represented a critical move away from the juridical characterization of (male) pornography consumers as infantile. In fact, said the report, the regulation of pornography actually creates impediments to a society that perceives sex in a healthy manner because it becomes the "scapegoat for Americans' confusion and ambivalence about sexuality" (311). The report recommended that rather than attempting to regulate pornography—"an inferior source of information about sexual behavior" (312)—the country should devote itself to a massive sex education program, aiming to achieve "an acceptance of sex as a normal and natural part of life and of oneself as a sexual being" (54). In contrast to the Meese Commission and the Internet debates that would occur in the following two decades, the Lockhart report helped to legitimate pornography consumption by explicitly denying its harmfulness and by refuting the idea that pornography is defined in relation to a class of victims who should be denied access to a genre of dangerous texts. Furthermore, the report posited a model of domesticity that made both men and women responsible for fostering open attitudes about sex.

As the pornography industry grew, so did its desire to appeal to women as potential consumers. Linda Williams notes that "for the first time, cinematic works containing hard-core action were reviewed by the entertainment media and viewed by a wide spectrum of the population, including, most significantly, women" (*Hard Core* 99). *Deep Throat* opened in the relatively accessible New Mature World Theater in Times Square and grossed over a million dollars. The legalization and mainstreaming of pornography made it not only more available but also more accountable to the growing feminist movement and its criticisms of pornography. This is not to say, as Williams is careful to note, that the pornography industry fully incorporated feminism into its notions of female pleasure; however, the more pornography tries to appeal to women and couples, the more likely it is to try to represent female pleasure as something distinct from male desire. Williams notes the difference in representations between the largely private stag films of the early twentieth century—which were relatively unconcerned with female pleasure—and much contemporary heterosexual porn, which tries to capture the "truth" of the female orgasm.

But this relative mainstreaming of porn was also accompanied by increased regulation. The owner of the New Mature World Theater was prosecuted twice for obscenity, and the theater was ordered closed in 1973. The same year that *Deep Throat* opened, the U.S. Supreme Court upheld a Detroit city zoning ordinance regulating adult entertainment. The controversial decision was the first of three over the following two decades by the Supreme Court and the first of dozens by lower courts supporting zoning of adult entertainment; the effect of these decisions in more conservative communities has been to erect barriers to the open operation of adult entertainment, sometimes virtually eliminating the spaces in which adult theaters, strip bars, and adult bookstores may operate. Thus, even in the midst of the "freeing" of much pornography from legal regulation, a governmental report that largely dismisses pornography's harms, the generally liberal attitudes about sexuality, and the growing feminist movement, we see the simultaneous attempt, which would increasingly gain impetus throughout the 1980s and 1990s, to contain pornography's public presences.[4] The historical narrative I next construct thus focuses on the reasons pornography has largely become a matter of private sphere regulation and consumption. Although the private sphere is always inextricably intertwined with the kind of public sphere acts of transgression that prosexuality feminists valorize (see introduction), I aim here to preserve the material force of the confines of the home, even as I locate it in relation to other sites.

Zoning Out Pornography's Public Presences

In general, U.S. cities have deployed two strategies to distance adult entertainment from those places connected to the city's "legitimate" values—mainly homes, schools, parks, and churches—because pornography represents a threat to the "quality of urban life." Cities using the "dispersion technique" prohibit adult entertainment establishments from locating in close proximity to each other or to any of the "family values" sites. Cities that deploy the "war zone" technique allow adult entertainment in only one concentrated area, also removed from family sites. Zoning regulation has attempted to preserve the boundedness of a sphere defined in relation to its family values in order to keep it materially removed from pornography; ironically, over roughly the same period of time that adult theaters have largely disappeared from the U.S. landscape, adult videos have been integrated into many mainstream video stores (with the notable exception of the huge chain Blockbuster), thus making them more accessible to a larger portion of the population, in more varied parts of the country, than adult theaters were for many people. What this means, again, is that pornography consumption has become an increasingly privatized activity, raising both the potential and the problems of cutting off sex from more public sites. Zoning out porn's public presences even as it is integrated into mainstream video stores suggests both a legitimation of porn and an embarrassment in its consumption, a reluctance to acknowledge one's shared tastes in a popular culture form through the somewhat public act of viewing. Although women never enjoyed equal access to adult theaters, they did begin to frequent theaters in the 1970s for the showings of such "mainstream" porn films as *Deep Throat.*

Zoning regulations in many communities effectively restricted access for women by locating adult entertainment in areas that were not safe or legitimate spaces for women to frequent. Many local ordinances have relied for validation on a 1972 Supreme Court case, *Young v. American Mini Theatres Inc.,* in which the court upheld the city of Detroit's use of the dispersion technique to scatter adult theaters and severely restrict their available land use. The court ruled five to four in favor of a Detroit ordinance prohibiting a place of "regulated use"—in other words, adult motion picture theaters and some adult bookstores—from locating within a thousand feet of any two other such establishments, or within five hundred feet of a residential area. In rejecting the claim by the theater operators that the ordinance was an unconstitutional content-based regulation, the Court suggested that "low-value speech" warranted less protection than other types of expression (Rohan, 11–47). The Court also found that the adult theaters posed a threat to the city's interest in preserving the quality of urban life, a threat that overrode any claim by the theaters about First Amendment rights. The Court's validation of the dispersion technique had a nationwide impact on the accessibility of pornography, as many cities and towns enacted similar ordinances (Rohan vol. 2, 11–49).[5]

Even the legendary Times Square has fallen victim to zoning laws. In October 1995 the New York City Council approved a package of zoning restrictions on X-rated video stores, peep shows, and topless bars that would, according to the *New York Times*, "essentially eliminate . . . the red-light district of Times Square." Businesses there "will have to shift from adult entertainment, close, or move to a new site that conforms to the zoning requirements. Most of those locations are in industrial areas" (Bastone, 13). The regulations, coming after a long history of attempts by City Hall and the New York state government to clean up the area, cleared the way for Disney's redevelopment of the area; in 1996 Disney and other entertainment companies began transforming the area into a family fun zone.

By the end of the 1980s there were only 350 X-rated theaters operating in the United States, half as many as a decade earlier (Williams, *Hard Core*, 231). This decline continued into the 1990s; *Newsweek* reported that Los Angeles, which once had thirty adult theaters, had only about six in 1997. The reasons for this decline are complex; they include not only zoning ordinances and obscenity prosecutions but also the AIDS epidemic, which has significantly hurt the business of live sex shows in places like Times Square (Landis, 31–32). Furthermore, the boom of the home video market, beginning in the early 1980s, greatly reduced the demand for live sex theaters. *Adult Video News* estimates that the number of hard-core video rentals rose from 75 million in 1985 to 490 million in 1992, then to 665 million in 1996 (Schlosser, 43–44). However, in no small part because they have successfully articulated a connection to the video market, strip clubs have also grown in number, doubling between 1987 and 1992, and reaching 2,500 in 1996 (Schlosser, 48). Strip clubs regularly promote dancers through their association with the porn industry; porn stars often earn more money by stripping than by performing in hard-core videos (Schlosser, 48). Strip clubs are doubly articulated to the porn industry—both through the overlap in performers and the conventions of their routines and through zoning regulations that set them apart as a clearly male form of entertainment. If pornography consumption has become largely concentrated in the home for both men and women through the growth of the home video market and adult cable programming, then men's consumption is a more mobile privatization;[6] men move more freely between sites of accessibility than do women.

In the face of this incorporation of pornography into the private sphere, governmental regulators and the religious Right found themselves in an awkward position. How could they claim that pornography was a growing public menace when it was so clearly becoming increasingly

concentrated in the home, the very space that conservatives were supposed to respect as a site of privacy, a retreat from the pressures of a hectic world? I want next to examine the ways governmental regulation
across three technologies—video, cable, and computer—has tried to ne-
gotiate this contradiction. In the instances of video and cable, governmental discourse has tried to retain the public sphere threat by focusing
on the components of porn's production and distribution; however, Internet sex has thwarted even those attempts to rhetorically preserve
clearly demarcated public and private spheres.

Retaining the Public Sphere Threat: Pornography as Production

The final report of the 1986 Attorney General's Commission on Pornography proposed to regulate what it characterized as public representations of sex in order to provide a rationale for increasing governmental
regulation that would restore sex to its rightful, private status. In order to
justify their recommendations for stepped-up prosecution of obscene materials, the commissioners needed to prove pornography's increasing influence and interference in the public sphere;[7] there was no disagreement
here between the sometimes strange bedfellows of antiporn feminists and
sexist conservatives represented on the commission. Pornography is pervasive, both agreed, thus porn degrades everybody—most importantly
women and children, but men as well (in categorizing men as victims of
porn, conservatives diverged from feminists). Porn is so pervasive a problem that its effects are uncontrollable, further legitimating the commission's recommendations for increased regulation and prosecution. This
regulation of public representations occurs, as Lauren Berlant argues in
"Live Sex Acts," in the name of the protection of privacy—of restoring
sex to its appropriate place in the sanctity of the home, which is challenged by porn's insidious public influences.

One way for the Meese Commission to prove pornography's public
presences—as opposed to focusing on its private consumption—was to
emphasize pornography as a "public" industry that exploited its workers,
particularly the young women actors. The commission's purported concern about the working conditions of porn performers mirrors the argument by antiporn feminists that the material exploitation of women in the
industry equals the material exploitation of all women in this country and
that both should negate any pleasure one might find in watching pornog-

raphy. But in actuality, the commission was most concerned to use its admittedly random and anecdotal evidence not to study the production side of pornography but rather to conflate production and consumption as one massive victimization of young women.

First, the commission stressed the performers' youth—"perhaps the single most common feature of models is their relative, and in the vast majority of cases, absolute youth" (229)—and used this as the starting point for the stereotypical construction of the misguided porn worker.[8] This naïveté was traced to their family lives, which were purportedly characterized by "broken marriages, early parental death, and intense family conflict," as well as child abuse (230). Furthermore, porn performers, due to their work, cannot maintain healthy adult relationships: "Romances as well as family ties are often strained or broken. . . . Many female models live with highly abusive husbands or boyfriends, whose relationship to them is that of pimp to prostitute" (241).

The stories of a handful of pornography performers thus became the means by which the commission scapegoated the industry for a set of social problems that are far more complex and indeed, may have little to do with either the production or consumption of pornography. Furthermore, by continually linking pornography to domestic sphere problems, the commission suggested that anyone who enjoys watching pornography should consider the exploitation of the performers, lest he or she become complicit, or even fall prey to the same troubled private lives. In fact, the commission conflated porn actors with all women in this ominous warning:

> The evidence before us suggests that a substantial minority of women will at some time in their lives be asked to pose for or perform in sexually explicit materials. It appears too that the proportion of women receiving such requests has increased steadily over the past several decades. If our society's appetite for sexually explicit materials continues to grow, or even if it remains at current levels, the decision whether to have sex in front of a camera will confront thousands of Americans. (839–40)

The commission negated the possibility of consent, by either performers or consumers, ignoring countering evidence by sex workers and porn performers—some of whom testified—that they choose to work in the industry, make a lot of money in it (more than male performers), and actually enjoy pornography. Argued the commission, "We submit that few performers are fully able to appreciate the meaning and the magnitude of their decision to engage in sexual performances—and throw away control of the resulting material for the rest of their lives" (245). Then the commission conflated performers with consumers: "Just as it is appropriate to provide consumers with extensive government protections against the consequences of their ignorance, so every adult needs special safeguards against making a decision which even the pornography industry's strongest booster admits 'will haunt her for the rest of her life'" (245). Thus, the Meese Commission's model of domesticity emphasized women's status as victims, in need of state protection and unable to experience sexual pleasure through the consumption of pornography, a body of texts that essentially victimizes them.

The Meese Commission report prompted President Reagan to launch an investigation into porn; although statistics on numbers of porn operators who were convicted are hard to come by, *Newsweek* claims that "Hundreds of producers, distributors, and retailers in the sex industry were indicted and convicted. Many were driven from the business and imprisoned" (Schlosser, 43). The report also helped spawn a series of legislative acts increasing regulation of child pornography; however, these acts are often indiscriminating in their regulation and impede adult access to many forms of pornography. For example, the 1994 Violent Crime Control and Law Enforcement Act includes a provision requiring all production companies of X-rated films to keep a videotaped record of each performer holding an ID card that proves her or his age to be over eighteen. The requirement does not present a moral dilemma for most production companies; indeed, according to the industry journal *Adult Video News,* few in the porn industry have ever wanted to use underage performers. However, the requirement makes it very difficult for production companies to make what's known in the industry as compilation videos— the best of Savanna, the best of Hypatia Lee, and so forth—especially if the videos were made before 1995, since many production companies did not keep proof of age on record. Child pornography laws are often written and then enacted in a manner that restores the figure of the little girl as the standard by which all citizens access—or do not access—pornography.

Retaining the Public Sphere Threat: Pornography's Distribution

The Meese Commission also tried to regulate porn by focusing on methods of distribution, and in this area, cable television presented a particularly thorny problem. During the time the commission was holding its hearings, cable was steadily increasing its presence in U.S. homes; the number of cable subscribers increased from 13 percent of all U.S. households in 1975 to 60.3 percent in 1991.[9] In four separate recommendations calling for stricter regulation of cable television, the commission acknowledged that a man's home is indeed his castle, giving him the right to watch what he desires in the privacy of his abode, and yet condemned the infiltration of porn into the home, via the "trickery" of producers and distributors who evade the public theater rating system and the Federal Communications Commission control over broadcasting media. For example, the commission lamented the fact that "(w)hile a minor under the age of seventeen cannot be admitted into a theatre to view an 'R' rated film without an accompanying parent or guardian, the same films are available to a viewer of any age over cable. . . . These films are sometimes the same films shown in pornography movie theatres and include films which federal and state courts have found to be obscene" (121). The commission tried to establish a mandate for regulating private consumption of porn by linking it to public venues; the commission was clearly struggling, at a time when adult movie theaters were on the wane, to prove a clear public sphere link that would legitimate their private sphere interventions.

This link was established through an emphasis on distribution as a public sphere act that occurs prior to the protected practice of watching cable. Consider, for example, this quote from the Meese Commission's final report:

> An individual may possess and view obscene materials in the privacy of his own home. Despite popular arguments to the contrary, it is well established in decisions by the United States Supreme Court that there is no correlative right to *receive, import, or distribute* the obscene materials. An argument that in the cable area the obscene materials are exhibited to consenting adults only is not a defense to an obscenity prosecution. (104)

The position allows that while individuals are unlikely to be prosecuted for watching a pornographic program on television, cable companies as the disseminators of the material may be motivated to erect various impediments, both material and psychological, to sexually explicit programming for fear of being prosecuted for distributing obscenity. This motivation increases in areas where community sentiment bolsters governmental regulatory discourse; several cable companies have been sued by local groups for their decisions to carry sexually explicit materials. For example, in the mid-1980s, Cincinnati's vice squad successfully pursued obscenity charges against Warner Amex Cable Communications for two films shown on the Playboy Channel. Warner Amex settled out of court and agreed not to distribute "adult oriented sexually explicit materials . . . which are unrated and if rated would receive an X-rating" (Trauth and Huffman, 2).[10]

Furthermore, the Meese Commission—in a proposal that characterizes much regulatory discourse about sex and technology—tried to hold on to a public/private sphere dichotomy by claiming that it is in the public interest to regulate private sphere activity when the potential consumers—or potential victims of consumers—are children; the state is thus sanctioned to act as children's public benefactor. In order to establish a precedent for governmental regulation of cable, the Meese Commission argued that cable functions in the same manner as television and radio, which historically have come under fairly strict FCC supervision precisely because of their accessibility to children. The commission called on Congress to amend the U.S. code to specifically proscribe obscene cable and satellite television programming in the same manner as the code proscribes the use of "any obscene, indecent or profane language by means of radio communication" (92).[11] The commission here seemingly referred to the landmark case of *FCC vs. Pacifica Foundation*; in this decision, which was sparked by a radio broadcast of George Carlin's famous "seven dirty words" routine, the Supreme Court referenced the unique accessibility of the broadcast media to children as a reason for providing less First Amendment protection to broadcasting than to print media (Trauth and Huffman, 23).

By claiming that cable television functions in the same manner as broadcast television and radio, the commission ignored a whole set of conditions that make cable differently accessible to different populations; we see, thus, how the commission's concern for children was in no small part a pretense for regulating pornographic consumption for adults as well. The differences between cable and broadcast television have been established in some legal cases in which cable has been granted more freedom to show sexually explicit material precisely because it can be more easily controlled within the home. In the 1985 case *Cruz vs. Ferre,* for example, a U.S. court of appeals ruled in favor of a group who challenged a city of Miami ordinance that prohibited the distribution of obscene and indecent material through cable television. The city of Miami drew on the

Pacifica decision to argue that cable television operated like broadcast television and thus should be as highly regulated. However, the court of appeals found *Pacifica* to be inapplicable to cable television, drawing on the wording of the *Pacifica* decision itself, which emphasized the "narrowness" of the holding. The appeals court stressed the *differences* between cable and broadcast television: "a cable subscriber must make the affirmative decision to bring Cablevision [the Miami cable operator] into his home. By using the monthly program guide, the Cablevision subscriber may avoid the unpleasant surprises that sometimes occur in broadcast programming" (Carter et al., 498). Additionally, the district court noted, "the ability to protect children is provided through the use of a free 'lockbox' or 'parental key' available from Cablevision" (Carter et al., 498).

Indeed, one would think that if the real concern was protecting children, most conservative parties would be content with effective parental lockboxes, devices that simultaneously preserve the adult's First Amendment rights to consume materials in the privacy of his/her own home and provide a significant measure of protection against children viewing any of the same material. But legislators have succeeded in passing more restrictions on cable in the 1990s. In a significant blow to adult cable channels like Playboy and Spice, the Supreme Court in March 1997 upheld Section 505 of the 1996 Telecommunications Act, which requires that cable operators scramble both audio and video signals for adult programming. If that's impossible—as about 60 percent of all cable operators say it is—then they must limit programming to the so-called safe harbor hours of 10 P.M. to 6 A.M. (Colman, "It's Scramble Time," 44). Although cable companies had previously been required to scramble the video signals of any program at a customer's request, Section 505 requires that cable companies carrying sexually explicit programming install either traps or converter boxes in the homes of all its subscribers, thereby scrambling both audio and video signals, whether the consumers request the scrambling devices or not. According to an estimate in *Broadcasting and Cable*, cable operators could lose from $25 million to $50 million in revenue from adult programming, which amounts to about $131 million a year (Colman, "It's Scramble Time," 44).[12] Obviously, most consumers will have their hours of access curtailed severely.

It is not only these pay-per-view channels that have prompted regulatory action. Of perhaps more concern to conservatives are the public access channels that, under the Cable Communications Policy Act of 1984, must be open at no charge to all local residents who want to broadcast noncommercial matter. The act also requires cable operators to reserve a number of leased access channels for commercial use. The 1984 act, whose impetus was generally deregulatory, prohibited operators from exercising any editorial control over the access channels; in some areas, local groups took advantage of these channels to air programs about sex, from talk shows to performance art. The leased channels have sometimes been used by companies advertising adult films and adult phone lines. Some of the shows, particularly in New York City, produced citizen complaints; in 1992 Senator Jesse Helms succeeded in pushing through an amendment to the 1992 Cable Act that could significantly hamper access to these channels. The Helms amendment gave cable operators discretion to ban indecent programming from the public access channels, rolling back the part of the 1984 act that had prohibited cable operators' editorial control. Furthermore, the 1992 act also requires that any indecent programming a cable operator chooses to allow on leased access channels be placed on a separate channel that is "blocked" until a subscriber makes a written request for unblocking (Lloyd, 6). In upholding this ruling, a U.S. court of appeals claimed that the cumbersome procedure of blocking channels was warranted because "neither lockout devices nor a 'safe harbor' rule limiting indecency to late-night hours would achieve the government's aim of protecting children from exposure to such programming" (Lloyd, 6).

Although restrictions on cable have in some cases been loosened when advocates have proved its distinctiveness from broadcast television, it appears likely that cable could become more highly regulated—in terms of sexual content—the more it interacts with other technologies, especially the Internet. The generally deregulatory 1996 Telecommunications Act greatly expands the possibilities for technology companies to operate on each other's turfs; it is a wide-ranging bill ostensibly designed to increase competition, allowing phone companies and cable television operators to go after the same customers and generally loosening governmental restrictions on what the law calls the National Information Infrastructure, or the information superhighway. However, until the Supreme Court struck down the Communications Decency Act (CDA), which was included in the Telecommunications Act, it appeared that regulation of sexual representations on these different technologies would significantly *increase*, in contrast to the general spirit of the act. And even as the CDA (which made it a crime to use a computer to transmit indecent material to someone under 18)[13] was ruled unconstitutional, antiporn forces in Congress were preparing new bills to regulate the Internet. Senator Pat Murray of Washington announced that she would introduce a bill "that would make it a felony to exploit chat rooms designed for children" (Broder). Cable industry journals were particularly worried about the push into computers when the CDA passed in Congress; writing for *Cablevision*, Chris Nolan sketched one possible scenario: "If a cable programmer runs a World Wide Web site, and at that site one subscriber posts a message that contains a picture of a woman without her shirt on ... that programmer can be found to have violated the law ... [if] the programmer or operator might have made something that could be called 'indecent' available to someone under the age of 18" (46). As technologies become increasingly concentrated and interdependent within the space of the home, government's job in regulating them becomes *somewhat* easier—pass laws regulating one technology, and you've implicated the others. Actually enforcing these laws may be another issue, especially on the Internet.

Cyberporn: Abandoning the Public Sphere Pretense

Pornography on the Internet represents a particularly sticky problem to would-be regulators and policers of sex because even they must acknowledge that cyberspace is impossible to define using traditional concepts of public/private spaces. On the one hand, computer consumption of porn is intensely private, occurring not only in the privacy of one's home (or cubicle/office at work) but also in the isolated, ephemeral interaction of user and screen. On the other hand, the consumption is intensely public, in that information proliferates and spreads to numerous sites, transgressing the physical boundaries that make other kinds of porn outlets, such as bookstores and theaters, much more easily identifiable and regulatable. This slipperiness fuels the regulatory rush: if pornography cannot be literally seized, it can more insidiously enter and affect relations in the home in a manner that cannot be easily regulated, confronting legislators with a whole set of contradictions about the boundaries and privacy of the home.

Of course, as many critics have noted, the fact that cyberporn is not as materially visible as the adult bookstore variety does not *necessarily* make it harder to track down users. In fact, increasingly sophisticated technologies make it relatively easy for different information-gathering powers, from the government to corporations, to gather seemingly private information, ranging from credit ratings to pharmaceutical purchases to visits to sex chat rooms. As Laura Kipnis demonstrates in her analysis of the case of Daniel DePew (see chapter 1), FBI officials are particularly eager to use the Internet to catch/entrap users of pornography that is in anyway connected to children. This ability to survey computer use only exacerbates the question of privacy, especially within the material space of the home, raising a complex set of issues about whose uses should be regulated, and in whose interests.

Given the *potentially* easy accessibility of cyberporn, it should come as no surprise that legislators and conservative religious groups have targeted the medium as a particularly ominous threat to the home and the children who, by their accounts, run the risk of exposure to porn merely by logging on. The cover image on the July 3, 1995, *Newsweek* captured the hysteria: a terrified child, eyes wide, mouth agape, with the headline "Cyberporn: A New Study Shows How Pervasive and Wild It Really Is. Can We Protect Our Kids—and Free Speech?" (see article by Levy). An outpouring of concern about the sanctity of the home and the exposure of children to cyberporn followed the release in the spring of 1995 of an extensive study by Carnegie-Mellon that examined online porn, concluding that its use was ubiquitous and its mainly male users' tastes tended toward the kinky and "perverse."[14]

Senator James Exon spearheaded the passage in Congress of the Communications Decency Act; the rhetoric throughout Senate debates in the summer of 1995 centered sanctimoniously around the issue of family values, with hardly a dissenting voice. Here's Exon:

> The Internet has invaded that protected place [the home] and destroys [children's] innocence. It takes the worst excesses of sexual depravity and places it directly into the child's bedroom, on the computer that their [*sic*] parents purchased in the thought it would help them do their homework or develop their intellect. When sexual violence and gross indecency are available to anyone at the touch of a button, both an individual or a culture becomes desensitized. . . . The images and messages act like a novocaine on our national conscience. (June 14, 1995, S8333)

In the elision between the child exposed to depravity and the belief that "anyone" can gain access to cyberporn, Exon reveals that concern for children is a pretense for regulating all relations in the home in a manner that coincides with conservative definitions of what constitutes a "proper" home.

In this home, parents—but particularly mothers—must act as proper moral guardians of their children's innocence and youth. Thus, the Internet debates added another level of constriction to the model of domesticity posited by the Meese Commission: while women are still posited occasionally as victims of pornography, the debates and media coverage are much more likely to posit women as asexual regulators. Anecdotes during the congressional debate assigned mothers the job of policing their children's sexuality and access to sexual information. In the policing process, the mother demonstrates her own sexual purity and fitness to be a mother—unlike all those single mothers challenging patriarchal authority by raising children without fathers, setting bad examples, and expecting at the same time to receive welfare benefits.

Consider this example, cited by Senator Exon in a June 9, 1995, Senate debate on cyberporn. He relates a story told to him by a female journalist. The woman was, by Exon's account, skeptical of Exon's claims about cyberporn until she logged on to the Internet, with her young daughter by her side. The reporter was "astonished" when she started "doing preliminary searches of what we were getting into. Finally, I recognized it was not something I wanted my daughter to see, *let alone me sharing it with her*" (S8088, emphasis added). In Exon's account, the exposure to cyberporn becomes even more dangerous to the sanctity of the mother-daughter relationship when they share the viewing experience, suggesting that it is as much the mother's morals worrying Exon as the daughter's vulnerability, or perhaps the possibility of a conversation about sex. Conservatives are threatened by the computer's potential to teach children about sex in a medium that invites parental participation rather than governmental censorship.

Mothers are positioned as gatekeepers in several newspaper articles that senators asked to be entered into the Senate record. A *Time* magazine article entered by Iowa senator Charles Grassley quotes several mothers of young boys, all of whom are appalled by the *potential* that their sons could access porn. Says Mary Veed, a mother of three, "Once they get to be a certain age, boys don't always tell Mom what they do." But while mothers become asexual regulators in the debate, fathers, like the young sons who emulate them, retain their sexuality. A letter entered into the record from the National Law Center for Children and Families, endorsing the Exon amendment, concedes that carriers of Internet porn could not be prosecuted if children gained access to the system through the use of "their dad's porn pin number" (June 14, 1995, S8338).

The concern about cyberporn in Washington has contributed to a regulatory atmosphere legitimating obscenity prosecutions of cyberporn users. There have been numerous reports of FBI investigations of cyberporn, especially dealing with children; in July 1996, for example, a federal grand jury indicted sixteen people for joining in a pornography ring that was "effectively an on-line pedophilia club" (Golden, A10). Although this protection of children is in many ways very important, the urge to regulate becomes problematic when it involves prosecution of fantasies that are never enacted. Laura Kipnis documents the prosecution and incarceration of Daniel DePew, who received a thirty-three-year sentence for trading kinky *fantasies* involving children with an FBI agent who was part of an undercover team looking for pedophiles on the Net. The FBI agent, notes Kipnis, is still roaming the streets (see chapter 1 of *Bound and Gagged*).

In the cumulative governmental model of domesticity produced over the past two decades, pornography consumption is antithetical to legitimate activities within the home; indeed, porn on the Internet could threaten the very lives of your children. Furthermore, the virtual elimination of adult theaters and the material isolation of adult bookstores in many towns in the United States (due to the zoning ordinances that make their presence antithetical to family values) impede the possibilities for women to easily access pornography outside the home, either to consume it in other locations or to purchase/rent it in order to consume it in the home. The intended regulatory effect is an isolation of the home from purportedly illicit public sexual activity, a goal that becomes particularly urgent to conservative regulators when it is also clear that through technology, pornography can so easily evade them.

From the National to the Local

Conservative fears about technology's ability to enter the home may be seen in the more general context of postmodern angst, sometimes reflected in a nostalgia for a seemingly more settled time, when public and private spaces could be more easily delineated. The attempts to fix the meaning of home along some traditional notion of family suggests a conservative defensiveness and insecurity, what Doreen Massey calls "a de-

sire for fixity and security of identity in the middle of all the movement
and change" (151)—a desire that is fulfilled by "delving into the past" in
a search for "internalized origins" (152). By freezing the identity of home
in some moment that never actually existed—except perhaps in 1950s
television shows like *Leave It to Beaver*—conservatives believe they can
claim a "moment and a form where they had a power which they can
thereby justify themselves in retaking" (169).

But how effective is this governmental model of domesticity in impeding women's access to all sexually explicit materials? The rest of this book
demonstrates how ineffective governmental discourse is—or at least the
many gaps between governmental policy and local consumption habits.
But I also argue that much of what is accessible to women in somewhat
mainstream venues has been shaped by this regulatory climate that demonizes porn, especially the more hard-core varieties; we have thus seen
over the past two decades a heightened production of domesticated porn,
texts that retain varying levels of sexual explicitness but also employ
strategies of distancing themselves from porn in order to avoid the il-
licit/illegal associations. Before taking up the different kinds of domesticated porn and their places of access more specifically, I want first to
consider an example of the relationship between national and local discourses on porn, showing how, at least in Champaign-Urbana, Illinois,
these discourses have interacted fairly effectively to constrict women's access to many kinds of porn. In beginning to construct an alternative way
of conceptualizing home, then, I am not abdicating the site of the home
because it is inevitably tainted by conservative discourses. Rather, any
home must be situated in relation to both national and local forces; as
Massey argues,

> Instead, then, of thinking of places as areas with boundaries around, they
> can be imagined as articulated moments in networks of social relations and
> understandings, but where a large proportion of those relations, experi-
> ences and understandings are constructed on a far larger scale than what
> we happen to define for that moment as the place itself, whether that be a
> street, or a region, or even a continent. And this in turn allows a sense
> of place which is extroverted, which includes a consciousness of its links
> with the wider world, which integrates in a positive way the global and the
> local. (155)

Determining women's access to sexually explicit material involves determining their potential for mobility between different sites. Access, then,

is shaped by a number of conditions, including governmental regulation; education about technology, such as the Internet; financial resources to buy the technology, from subscribing to cable television to buying a computer; and the time and space in which to consume pornography amidst everyday routines such as work and child care. Furthermore, access is in part a question of content: to the degree that much pornography is still largely produced within the conventions of an industry that has for years catered mainly to male pleasures, access for women on their—albeit diverse—terms is still somewhat limited. This is not to say that women do not find pleasure in a large variety of texts, regardless of to whom they are addressed; however, texts that specifically target women will more likely function to increase access because they often circulate in a manner that legitimates women's sexual pleasures, in turn helping to create the times and spaces in which to exercise those pleasures.

Paths to Pornography: Champaign-Urbana, Illinois

Madonna may have been all the rage in academia in the early 1990s, but some citizens in Champaign-Urbana made clear their disdain for the sexually outrageous pop star. In the winter of 1992–93 in Champaign, Illinois, 327 people filed formal objections to the Champaign public library's decision to buy a copy of *Sex*, Madonna's recently published book of sexually explicit, artistically packaged, expensively priced ($49.95) photographs and writings. More than three hundred people turned out for a library board public hearing, most of them to protest the decision, calling the book obscene and pornographic. Numerous letters to the editor in the local newspaper, the *News-Gazette*, lamented library director George Scheetz's inability to distinguish between art and pornography. Wrote A. G. Baker of adjacent Urbana, "This expensive trash book the library bought is just old-hat porn. Same tired, worthless smut available at the sex shops." Citing the public's right to read a best-selling book, Scheetz stuck to his decision to buy the book, but made it available only to people eighteen and older and kept it at the circulation desk.

In May 1997 a group of parents calling themselves "To Inform People About Schools" protested Urbana High School's use of certain books, including *Native Son, Beloved, Sula, The Color Purple,* and *One Flew over the Cuckoo's Nest.* Their statement claimed that these books contain the kind of subject matter one would expect to find in porno shops. Chester

Fontenot, a professor of English and specialist in African American literature at the University of Illinois, defended the books' status as literature, noting as well that a majority of the books targeted were written by African Americans.

These antiporn crusaders may not be representative of the entire population, but they are a frequently heard voice in the community. They illustrate the manner in which the art/porn distinction is very much alive and kicking here, indicating that the women's erotica I discuss in chapter 3 does legitimate itself in relation to porn the more it can prove its status as art. It is easier for women to travel between their homes and the Barnes and Noble, Borders, or Pages for All Ages bookstores in Champaign than it is to travel between their homes and the Illini Video Arcade.

Pie and Pornography

Champaign's Pie-full Delight restaurant is a local favorite for homemade pies and pastries, quiche and sandwiches, all served in a decidedly Christian ambience. Ornate plaques with Bible verses and catchy phrases about the joys of family life adorn the walls; a Bible sits open next to the cash register. My five-year-old son, Alex, and I stop to get a piece of pie one night, and as we're leaving, he looks across the street and comments, "Look, Mom, 'XXX'—just like the last letter in my name."

Just what the owners of Pie-full feared three years ago when the Illini Video Arcade opened up directly across Springfield Avenue. The Pie-full owners went before the Champaign City Council and asked them to consider zoning regulations that would prohibit the adult video store from operating across the street, but the council turned them down. As one of the arcade's managers points out, this is hardly prime real estate; it's a fairly industrial area, with a scrap metal yard and railroad tracks about a block down the street. And the Illini Video Arcade is probably one of the town's oldest and most steadily profitable establishments; before moving into its current location, it operated for thirty-four years in downtown Champaign. Until 1979 it was an adult theater, but, says owner Frank Lipousky, demand for the theater died down as the home video market boomed. Business has taken off since the operation moved in 1993; regular rental customers have risen to 5,500, from 1,250 three years ago. The arcade has 2,200 titles and claims to be "downstate Illinois's largest" adult video store.

Most of the customers are men—and nearly half of those gay men, judging by their selections, according to Lipousky. Indeed, the porn video arcade is one of the few commercial spaces in this country that are not produced as heterosexual, argues John Champagne in his analysis of the porn arcade: "It is, rather, polymorphously perverse and rendered increasingly so by capital's voracious commodification of everything, including 'aberrant' sexual desires" (84). Champagne concedes that this inclusiveness does not extend to women, noting that in his observations of arcades in four midwestern cities, women rarely frequented the stores. Lipousky agrees that "there's still a stigma attached to women watching porn"; he notes that while women come in groups to buy sex toys for parties, they rarely rent videos. Although industry trade publications estimate that roughly 40 percent of all adult videos are rented by women or couples, over the course of two years of visiting the video arcade at different times of the day and evening, I see only a handful of women renting porn. The same situation holds true for the cordoned-off hard-core sections of the six local general video stores.[15] If indeed more women are watching porn, then this must be the one area where men do the shopping.

The Illini Video Arcade hasn't done much to attract women customers, judging by the video selection and the layout of the store. Five of Candida Royalle's Femme Productions videos are tucked away in the "Classics" section; the store owner says he knows of no other woman porn producer. There are no videos by the handful of lesbian producers, such as Debi Sundahl's Fatale Video Production. Most of the stuff seems predictably sexist and racist; genres include "Big Tits," "Sodomania," "Gang Bang," "Inter-racial" (as if that in itself were pornographic), "Raunch-o-Rama." There's a lesbian section and a "bi-sexual" section, but one wonders how these videos got pulled out—they seem to be variations on the regular porn that features these numbers. There might be plenty of stuff here to turn on women, gay and straight, but it's not organized or represented on the covers so as to make women feel we're just as much a target audience as men.

There's no clearly marked "couples' section," where I might expect to find videos with plot and/or videos that valorize female pleasure, two elements that purportedly characterize couples' porn. But you can sort of tell from the descriptions on the video boxes what audience the producers might be targeting. There are a few dozen that seem to be appealing to a slightly upscale audience, viewers who want some complexity with their cum shots. One day I rent a 1995 production by Wave Video called

Smoke Screen; the video box emphasizes its complicated plot—"Nothing is quite what it seems." The video functions as a simultaneous legitimation and sanitization of pornography, seemingly responding to the antiporn claims that representation is reality by stressing that fantasy is purely fantasy. In the video, two women cousins are reunited after some time apart. Elizabeth, a Valley girl, overhears a conversation her cousin has about a "body" and hears the name "Zelda." From this, Elizabeth, imagination running wild, begins to believe that her cousin is a stripper and has become embroiled in shady affairs, including a murder. Elizabeth and her boyfriend, Andy, use their imagined story about the cousin to construct a series of explicit fantasies with a variety of numbers—anal sex, girl-girl, lots of male cum shots, cunnilingus—all of which occur in the imagined strip bar. At the end of the video, however, we learn that Zelda was just a dog and that Elizabeth's cousin is really just a bartender in a club. The narrative structure allows the viewer to enjoy pornographic fantasies within the "reality" of the monogamous relationship of Elizabeth and Andy; furthermore, Elizabeth's cousin turns out not to be a stripper, which would, ironically enough, tarnish her character. At a meta-level, thus, *Smoke Screen* suggests that pornography is purely fantasy, a facilitator for couple sex.

In fact, it's surprising how frequently the porn videos make a self-referential effort to legitimate the industry by emphasizing its ability to improve sex in relationships, a move that itself might increase access for women fearful of the government characterization of porn's effects. Paradise Visual's 1995 video *Make Me Watch* parodies the myth that women are forced by men to watch pornography; rather, the protagonist, "Sally Layd," watches porn videos because her husband is such a boring lover that she can climax only by watching porn. Sally watches one video while her husband, Donald, has sex with her in the missionary position, as she fruitlessly exhorts him to try some different positions. He climaxes, then says in disgust, "Where do you get these ideas of yours?" Looking at the porn video playing on the TV screen, he says, "Oh, I know—these tapes that are always running. This shit is not fucking normal, you know? It's disgusting." Sally complains about her passionless marriage in a phone call to her friend Laura, who offers to help by showing Donald exactly how to pleasure a woman. When Donald stops by Laura's house (she has just finished watching a porn video), purportedly to pick up Sally's sunglasses, she solicits his help in "figuring out why she gets so wet." She introduces a seemingly befuddled Donald to the art of cunnilingus, even squirting a stream of ejaculate into his mouth. "Oh my God," exclaims Donald. "That's not bad. That's not bad at all! Can you do that again?" And a contrite and educated husband returns home, apologizes to Sally, and tells her he's willing to experiment. "I just want to make you happy," he says. Pornography plays a mediating role in saving their sex life; Sally uses it until her husband learns how to give her pleasure, and Laura has presumably learned from it and uses those lessons to teach Donald how to better service his wife.

Pornography as fantasy material for consenting adults is the message implicit in many porn flicks. In *Venom*, a popular selection produced by Vidco Home Video, ten porn stars perform a vast number of sex acts in what is billed as an expression of their authentic and outrageous sexualities. Says producer Henri Pachard before the MTV-style video begins, "You're going to see something different—exhibitionists given the freedom to expose nasty sexual urges that will amaze a viewer. This extremely personal approach causes the performers to become very vulnerable. . . . They're not fucking for you. They're not fucking for me. They're fucking for themselves." We're thus positioned before the video begins to view pornography as something performers do for their own pleasures; they are at heart exhibitionists, not victims, as governmental discourse would have it. Furthermore, you, the viewer, are the invader on what is essentially a private act; says Pachard, "If you begin to feel that you're invading their privacy, you are." Pachard appeals to the illicit thrill of voyeurism and yet legitimates pornography as a private, fully consensual act.

In fact, it's hard to find anything that doesn't look consensual in porn, even—or perhaps particularly—in the fetish section, where the sado-masochistic and bondage and discipline videos are. Take, for example, Gotham Gold's *Enter into Slavery*. Slave master Hans, with a German accent, seems particularly intent on asking his willing "victims," "Are you doing OK?" as he methodically ties and unties them; they always answer "yes." As is the case with all bondage videos, there is no intercourse. The video seems more like an instruction guide in how to safely practice bondage and discipline than an attempt to show a "real" world of sexual slavery.

The Illini Video Arcade sometimes strikes me as one of the more politically aware public spaces in town; quite often the owner and manager talk with customers about the latest attempts in the state legislature in Springfield to crack down on porn. In April, for example, magazines purchased at the arcade by an undercover agent working for the state's attorney's office became the focus of discussions in the State Judiciary Committee, where conservative legislators were trying to push through a bill that would allow counties to establish their own obscenity standards rather than relying on the statewide standards. (The bill was approved by the committee but eventually defeated.) News coverage of the bill perpetuated the idea that pornography oppresses women and children; Janet LaRue, a lawyer for the National Law Center for Children and Families, was quoted in the local paper saying that hard-core porn is a "tool and a fuel of serial child rapists and sexual predators" (Rooney, A8).

The state's attorney's office also carried its crusade against sex in "public" into one of the two local strip clubs, the Malibu Bay Lounge. On March 31, 1997, thirty SWAT team personnel and at least ten local officers burst into the club, arrested seven dancers—forcing them into the paddy wagon without first letting them get dressed—and taking all the money from the cash registers, bartenders, and dancers. They also arrested the club's owner, Ike Mapson, a prominent African American businessman in the community since 1963, and charged him with keeping a house of prostitution and six counts of pandering. The seven dancers were charged with prostitution. The charges were based on the covert video-recording done by an undercover agent who had paid for private dances and later claimed that the women had made physical contact with him while naked, an apparent violation of the county ordinance and—arguably, if contact did occur—an act of prostitution under Illinois state law. The dancers all denied they had made contact, and the videos are apparently somewhat ambiguous; the nature of the private dance makes it hard to say when slight contact might have been made. Since such ambiguities are common to night club dancing, what does seem clear is that the local Republican authorities are trying to put the club out of business for political reasons, and that racism as well as antiporn zeal is involved. These politics were nicely documented in a piece by Shelley Masar in the local alternative newspaper, the *Octopus*.

Local regulation of porn coincides with national governmental attempts to police video arcades and strip bars, producing a climate in which any kind of pornography is positioned as antithetical to family values. In this context, it hardly seems to matter that more porn companies are modifying the content of their videos to attract women consumers (although the video box covers remain stuck in the old conventions—very few show male bodies, except for gay male porn). In the University of Illinois's newspaper, the *Daily Illini*, a student columnist, Natasha

Rosenstock, describes her visit to the video arcade in a manner that speaks to these limiting conditions. Although Rosenstock doesn't rent any videos—the clerk tells her she's not old enough—she reaches all the same damning conclusions about porn as do the most vociferous antiporn feminists. Describing her discomfort at both the representations and titles on the video boxes and the stares she and her female friend receive from male consumers, Rosenstock concludes that pornography is a primary component in a commercial culture that objectifies and victimizes women, inhibiting communication between men and women. "Women are continually subjugated by these videos, and they aren't even aware of it," she says. The arcade's environment—and a sociology class Rosenstock quotes that is clearly taught by an antiporn professor—is enough to keep Rosenstock from qualifying any of her statements based on the rather mitigating factor that she has never seen a porn video.

Even in more legitimate venues, such as general video stores, women consumers could easily get the impression that antiporn feminists try to foster: all pornography is the same. The small back room of the Old Towne Video store in Champaign—marked with an overhead sign that says "ADULTS ONLY"—is a miniature version of the Illini Video Arcade, except that there are no clearly marked sections and only a handful of gay porn videos. There is an open section in the store marked "Risque," next to Westerns, and it is here that discerning women can find soft-core porn for couples. However, even this section is overwhelmed by a large selection of soft-core videos aimed at straight men, such as Playboy's lingerie videos and Penthouse fantasies.

Cable as a Matter of Life and Death

This is a town that takes its cable television seriously.

When the local cable operator, Time Warner, announced in 1994 its plans to implement a new system through which customers would have to rent a converter box at $3.99 a month per television in order to receive anything above the basic fourteen-channel tier of service, citizens exploded in protest. Time Warner's local general manager, Jim Cochran, even received a death threat. "This is cable television, for Pete's sake," he told the local newspaper, the *News-Gazette*. "If you don't like it, don't buy it" (Zimmer, A2).

But the real problem in Champaign-Urbana, as in most towns and cities—not to mention rural areas—is that there has been only one choice for cable service. Cable systems are operated by private companies that must compete for franchises granted by municipalities, but as of 1991 there were only fifty cities in the country that had competing cable companies. In 1992 Time Warner was the second largest cable operator in the country, serving 7.1 million subscribers (Wasko, 82). However, the fact that cable operators must indeed compete for a community's franchise did seem to make a difference, at least a small one, in terms of Time Warner's accountability to customers—especially when members of the City Council threatened to seek alternative bids. Bowing to petitions signed by hundreds of citizens, Time Warner scaled back its plans to install converter boxes in every home and instead required the boxes only for homes subscribing to the pay-per-view channels.

Although Time Warner says the converter boxes were intended to give customers more flexibility in terms of their package choices—a claim consumers said was a ruse for a packaging scheme that would increase profits—the box also works very well as a form of parental control. The converter box allows parents to block certain channels temporarily by programming a "lock" on them; also, users must enter a four-digit access code before they can gain access to the pay-per-view channels. Furthermore, the converter box blocks both audio and visual signals; otherwise, visual signals are easily blocked but audio signals are very difficult to block.

Choices for adult programming are subject to local regulation in another manner as well—the decisions of franchises about what channels to offer. In Champaign-Urbana, for example, you can get the Playboy channel but not the Spice channel, the other major adult cable channel in the country. Time Warner's division president Sam Napone told me in an interview in July 1996—in an office filled with photos of his large family—that he has never given any thought to offering Spice because "I'm not particularly interested in carrying those kinds of channels. The Playboy channel was on when I got here, so I left it on. As an individual manager, not as a company position, I don't have any interest in putting Spice on." When in the spring of 1997 the Supreme Court upheld the ruling forcing cable operators to scramble adult channels completely or operate only at certain hours (see above), the Champaign franchise restricted the Playboy hours to 10 P.M. to 6 A.M. Furthermore, as Playboy warned, costs have been passed on to consumers; in Champaign-Urbana, for example, the cost of ordering the Playboy channel rose from $4.95 for twelve hours to $4.95 for four hours after the scrambling provision went into place.

There are other somewhat small but still significant ways local cable franchises can impede access to adult channels. Because you must rent a converter box in order to receive the Playboy channel, you cannot make the addition through a simple and somewhat anonymous phone call. You must go into the office, ask for a converter box, receive a somewhat hurried set of instructions on how to hook it up to your VCR and television, then return home and try your luck at following the instructions. The local cable company also limits access to program information about Playboy: while monthly program guides to premium channels like HBO and Cinemax are set out on a table, you have to wait in line and ask the attendant for a Playboy guide.

Cruising the Net

It would seem, on the surface, that cyberporn represents the perfect path out of fairly conservative communities like Champaign-Urbana. No access to an Annie Sprinkle performance? Simply punch up her Web site. No place to buy a vibrator other than the Illini Video Arcade? Simply turn to the Good Vibrations page and order one. And, as I describe in the next chapter, the computer does indeed have considerable potential for expanding women's sexual mobility. But beware: travels into cyberporn may just land you in an even more conservative jurisdiction. The regulation of cyberporn has prompted a revision in what constitutes "community standards"; the 1973 *Miller* decision rejected the notion of a national obscenity standard in favor of community standards designed to permit local communities to decide on their definitions of obscenity. However, because cyberspace is a global community, the question arises as to whose standards apply. Court rulings have to date held that the "government can choose the community from which the standards will be selected"—as long as the community is in some way involved in the production or downloading of the porn—which frees the prosecutor to choose the community with the more restrictive standards (Cavazos and Morin, 94).[16] The space of the home becomes the site of a national standard of appropriate sex; as Kipnis puts it, "Net hounds around the country are faced with the task of ensuring that their fantasy lives conform to the community standards of the Bible Belt, or risk prosecution" (*Bound and Gagged,* 5).

Perhaps more significantly, computer technology remains open to a fairly limited number of people. Cyberspace is changing, but it is still mainly a white, male, wealthy preserve; a 1995 study by Nielsen Media Research and partners showed that two-thirds of the 24 million Internet users in the United States and Canada are male; furthermore, Internet usage by men accounts for about 77 percent of all online time logged. The Net is also governed by class: 25 percent of Net users have an income of more than $80,000 per year, compared to 10 percent of the general population (Cooper, "Caught in the Web," 32). The Internet has tremendous potential for democratic usage—including the potential "to break the pornographers' monopoly on sexually explicit expression and to formulate, through discussion, stories, fantasies, and pictures online, a new sexual 'truth,'" says law professor Carlin Meyer. "But lest it appear that the Information Superhighway will, without attention, be a panacea for all our social and sexual ills, it bears emphasizing that it is a roadway that belongs largely, at the moment, to relatively affluent, youthful, white males. And so long as that is the case, sexual communication and discourse on the Internet will be seriously skewed" (2,008). Meyer urges government to shift the funds from prosecution of porn to programs providing training in computer literacy to women, people of color, and older persons.

Content is to a large degree determined by who controls the means of production and who constitutes the primary consumer base. As documented in a 1997 *Wall Street Journal* article, sexually explicit sites on the Net have proliferated hugely in the last several years; they take in "millions of dollars" a month even as other Web sites are struggling and attract more customers than mainstream brands like Disney and CNN (Weber, A1). And there has been a certain democratization in the proliferation: "some of the biggest names in traditional pornography have only a limited presence in cyberspace," says Weber. But who is taking over? Computer nerds, says Bob Guccione, publisher of *Penthouse*. People like Seth Warshavsky, who at age twenty-three formed the Internet Entertainment Group, a company that produces various online adult sites. The most profitable is the live video site, which beams images of live exotic dancers out onto the Web; the dancers appear "in full color on the computer screens of users, who can even call on the telephone to chat with the performers in mid-gyration" (Weber, A8). Customers pay $49.95 for a thirty-minute show; nine customers can watch at any one time, generating $450 for the company. In one day, IEG makes about $25,000 from this site alone; it also has other sites that more closely resemble the pages of adult magazines; users pay $9.95 a month to subscribe to Club Love, for example, where they can access the hard-core photo archives and have the opportunity to spend more money—on massage lotion, taped bedtime stories, and other sex accessories. Weber argues that these adult sites have become so profitable because of their skillful marketing strategies; the *Wall Street Journal* reporter can barely contain his admiration for the ways the computer nerds have taken up the true mission of capitalism, where entrepreneurs can get started for as little as twenty dollars a month for a simple Web page and then gradually expand into a highly successful company. However, what the *Journal* article also makes clear is that this is a business expanding in a manner very similar to traditional pornography in terms of production and consumption: it's still mainly men making porn for men. The only woman Weber mentions is a former porn star named Danni Ashe, who started her own Web site, drawing on her fan club; however, she also clearly caters in conventional porn images and assumes that her clients are men. She tells the *Journal,* "I think a lot of these guys have never even bought an adult magazine" (A8). Ashe's comment underscores the similarities between pornography online and adult magazines; in fact, many adult bulletin board services merely scan their images from porn magazines rather than producing new ones (Meyer, 2,001, note).

Take, for example, Pixman's Vault: XXXCite PornoPix. I have a three-hour chunk of free time; I spend the first one and a half hours finding the service and following their directions for calling the 1-900 number in order to get my private access code—and get charged the $7.95 monthly fee. I get to the subscription page and type in my access number. I receive my User ID: "cunt342." Hmm. I finally get into Pixman's Vault, which advertises itself as carrying the "hottest porn on the Net," with "2,500 extremely hard-core porno pics and 50 video clips." There are about a dozen categories to choose from: anal, bdsm, bigboobs, blowjobs, celebs, cumshots, gaymales, lesbians, shitpiss, and so forth. I start at the top; a is for anal. Slowly, the image begins to appear; I can see two hairy legs and testicles, and, after a few more minutes, a woman's manicured nails holding apart her cheeks. But it's only the top fourth or so of the image, and there it remains—stuck, unfortunately, for the next hour. I realize I'm rapidly eating up the twenty hours per week of free online time that the university provides each user. I give up on this image and access a series of other shots that appear more quickly. Lesbian sex features two naked blonde women, engaged in an open-mouthed kiss. Under "bdsm," you can see a gagged woman tied with a series of crisscrossing ropes, or a woman tied spread-eagled to a bed, or a woman in a harness, mouth taped shut. Under "blowjobs," the subcategory "blueeyes" features a blonde woman sucking two black penises. "Cumshots" refers to male cum (even computer technicians haven't figured out to image a woman coming)—three penises cumming, for example, over the body of a prostrate blonde female. Under "pussies," two women lie side by side, legs spread to reveal their shaved genital areas.

Over two and a half hours of perusing the images, I find myself wondering how anyone can really masturbate to this very halting appearance of static images. It's hard to develop or sustain a fantasy. (Of course, some people undoubtedly have more powerful computers and modems, another matter of access.) There are other, more diverse sites; precisely because much cybersex is produced in connection with the broader pornography industry, it's not surprising that the same divisions between erotica and porn are occurring online. Women-friendly sites abound in the mainly print venues that are more democratic and accessible than the fairly expensive adult sites like those run by the Internet Entertainment Group. These sites include e-mail exchanges, encounters on chatlines, bulletin board services, and Usenet newsgroups.[17] In the next chapter, I discuss in more detail the potential for women to domesticate Internet porn, and the progress women have already made using these more alternative online spaces as aids to masturbation.

There are many local gaps in the governmental attempts to establish as antithetical the notions of domesticity and pornography consumption; in part, that's because governmental rhetoric remains, sometimes, at the level of rhetoric, and may actually serve to enhance sexual arousal (those Internet warnings could make cyberporn a more illicit/exciting activity for some users). Yet governmental policy and rhetoric on pornography work with and within other policies and social structures that produce situations that impede women's ability to domesticate pornography. Welfare repeal, generally lower levels of income for women, lack of child care resources, laws prohibiting same-sex marriages, and the domination of the pornography industry by male producers who make most of their profits from male consumers are just a few of the ways governmental discourse on and regulation of pornography end up working fairly effectively, because they overlap with these other conditions. Thus, although the pornography industry has increasingly targeted women as its audience, there are definite limits to that appeal and there is little impetus, after a certain point, for the industry to expand its conceptions of pornography precisely because men remain the primary audience, with more money, time, and places to consume it. As long as the resources remain unevenly distributed, we cannot really lay claim to a genre of pornography that is widely accessible to women consumers in the home.

The remainder of this book demonstrates why, in this context of governmental regulation and industry practices, the genre of domesticated porn is so important to consider. How have different texts aimed at women and couples tried to distance themselves from this history of regulation precisely to become more accessible in mainstream venues? To what degree are these distancing tactics, such as the labels "erotica," "adult programming," and "erotic education," mainly marketing distinctions (albeit important ones)? Using the safe space granted sexually explicit stuff that is not porn, how have these texts both redefined and reproduced conceptions of women, domesticity, and sexuality?

2

The Mainstreaming of Masturbation?

Making Domestic Space for Women's Orgasms

I don't want to sit around and tell people where their g-spots are. I'm more interested in sex and the mind. A lot of people think I'm some consumer advocate for sex toys; that was just opening the door. I couldn't care less about whether anyone buys a sex toy. It all happens in your head.
                                              —Susie Bright, interview

In the early 1970s Betty Dodson dedicated herself to teaching women how to liberate themselves sexually through the act of masturbation. Tired of consciousness-raising groups that "catalogued female suffering and social injustices" (73), she initiated an ongoing series of Bodysex Workshops in which she demonstrated how to reach orgasm through masturbation, eventually engaging all the women participants in the performance as an act of "selflove." In 1974 *Ms.* included her views on masturbation in an article, which was then published in a small but frequently cited book, *Liberating Masturbation: A Meditation on Selflove*. Indeed, in a 1995 article *Ms.* credited Dodson with being the primary feminist in helping women learn how to masturbate: "deserving most of the credit for helping women break free of the taboos about masturbating are feminists, especially Betty Dodson, whose Bodysex workshops enabled many to overcome shame or squeamishness" (Chalker, 50).

In 1995, after nearly twenty-five years of workshops, public performances, five reprintings of various versions of *Liberating Masturbation*, and a video called *Selfloving*, Dodson proclaimed her mission accomplished. In the 1995 preface to the latest edition, *Sex for One: The Joy of Selfloving*, Dodson says, "With this revision of *Sex for One*, I am releasing myself from a promise I made twenty-five years ago: my feminist commitment to liberating masturbation has been accomplished" (xiv). Studies seem to support Dodson's conclusions about the mainstreaming of masturbation for women: the latest Kinsey report (1990) found that 70 percent of the women interviewed said they masturbated, compared to 40 percent in the first Kinsey report, issued in 1949. Susan Quilliam's 1994 *Women on Sex* found that 81 percent of the women surveyed stated that they masturbated regularly (qtd. in Chalker, 50). Feminists, sexologists, and sex commentators like Nancy Friday and Shere Hite agree, to varying degrees, that masturbation for women in the 1990s has become an everyday practice—even a feminine one, for some. Victoria's Secret model Frederique says in an *Elle* roundtable discussion on "What femininity means now" that "I think orgasm by myself is much more feminine than the fuck thing. Being feminine for me is also about being sexual" (Soren, 149). Nancy Friday, whose groundbreaking 1973 book, *My Secret Garden: Women's Sexual Fantasies,* helped legitimize women's sexual fantasies, says in her 1993 *Women on Top: How Real Life Has Changed Women's Sexual Fantasies* that the mainly twenty-something women who responded to her requests for fantasies expressed no guilt about masturbation: "They have an ease with the subject of masturbation that is a pleasure to hear, a vocabulary so rich in description of when and how they masturbate that I am dazzled; their sexual fantasies soar into a realm of adventure that makes most of the reveries in *My Secret Garden* read like tentative stuff" (24). Shere Hite says in her 1994 report that 61 percent of the young women respondents had positive attitudes about masturbation, compared to 29 percent in the 1970s (73).

Yet statistics like Hite's also suggest that masturbation is not yet an everyday practice for some women; for example, 39 percent of young women do not have a positive attitude about masturbation. The 1990 Kinsey report indicates that a large percentage of the U.S. population— and more women than men—underestimate the number of women who do masturbate. When nearly two thousand Americans were asked in 1989, "Out of every 10 American women, how many would you estimate have masturbated either as children or after they were grown up," only 18 percent gave what the Kinsey Institute believes to be the correct answer of roughly 70 percent. Forty-seven percent thought that no more than 50 percent of girls and women have masturbated; furthermore, more women than men were likely to underestimate or simply say they didn't know the answer, suggesting, writes Kinsey director June Reinisch, that "a woman or girl who masturbates may believe that her behavior is unusual" (18). According to the University of Chicago's *Sex in America* survey, 47 percent of the women who said that they masturbated one to five times a year expressed feelings of guilt about it.[1] One must question the reliability of these studies: perhaps more women are masturbating but too embarrassed to tell the surveyor, but this hardly suggests a level of comfort with the practice.

Precisely because many women still do not feel comfortable masturbating or telling people they do masturbate, it would not seem wise, as some feminists would urge, for us to leave behind the more "mechanical" aspects of sex and move into the liberated area of the mind, as Bright suggests in her quote above. Similarly, Rebecca Chalker, writing for *Ms.*, suggests that "we" are ready to move beyond the masturbatory emphasis on immediate sexual pleasure and orgasm and posit the practice as part of a whole body sensuality and "an ongoing component of one's sense of well being" (50). Chalker quotes research by psychologist Gina Ogden, which shows that "more than 60 percent of the women said they could come to orgasm at will, solely through fantasy," without even touching their bodies, a process Ogden calls "thinking off" (Chalker, 50). The fact that many feminists seem ready to declare that the lesson of the clitoral orgasm via masturbation has been taught testifies to the very successes of a heterogeneous group of feminists, sexologists, and popular writers who in the 1970s helped make masturbation a part of women's everyday lives. Yet these successes are also vulnerable to other forces that constantly threaten to erode masturbation's everyday status. In the 1990s, U.S. Surgeon General Joycelyn Elders was fired for suggesting that masturbation be discussed in public schools, and Paul Reubens, the actor who played Pee Wee Herman, lost his children's television show after being arrested for public exposure for masturbating in an adult theater (as if any of the other patrons would have been offended).[2] Alan Bloom's best-selling book *The Closing of the American Mind* rails again the "onanistic" evils of rock-n-roll culture.

There are, thus, some important and still relevant lessons to learn by revisiting the masturbation discourse of the 1970s. Ranging from the Masters and Johnson report of 1967, which provided scientific proof of the importance of clitoral orgasm, to Nancy Friday's *My Secret Garden* (1973), which provided anecdotal evidence of women's desires for orgasm, this discourse worked to remove the shame of masturbation that had been fostered by parents (mothers usually get blamed), and helped women claim the material spaces where masturbation could occur in privacy and the mental spaces where it could occur without guilt. Masturbation was posited as a political act of individual liberation from confining social structures—the home, marriage, the family. Women needed to escape these structures in order to learn about their bodies and boost their self-esteem, and often this escape occurred in the context, either literal or symbolic, of communities with other women, in sex therapy groups and Dodson's workshops. Furthermore, the "home" as defined by these texts varied widely, from the more traditional home that sex therapists sought to redefine as a site of a married woman's pleasure to the implicitly radically reconfigured home of lesbians who championed the clitoral orgasm as the biological proof for the non-necessity of the penis. Thus, the fact that texts on masturbation and orgasm came from a variety of spheres—sexology (Masters and Johnson, Kinsey reports), sex therapy (Barbach and Helen Singer Kaplan), popular sex commentary (Hite and Friday), and different kinds of feminism (from Dodson to radical feminists to *Cosmopolitan*)—helped produce varying definitions of home that could in turn facilitate masturbation for women in—and out of—different kinds of relationships.

However, this "liberation" of the home as a site of masturbatory activity did not come without its own set of regulatory codes. The very emphasis on the female body and its pleasures as a matter of everyday concern contributed to a certain hierarchy of appropriate masturbatory activity and kinds of fantasy material, and it is here that we can see the seeds of the essentialism that characterizes some contemporary women's literary erotica. The essentialism derives not from the emphasis on the body but from the attempt to "normalize" desire; fantasy should be as egalitarian and liberatory as the bodily practices of sex posited in the pursuit of orgasm. Rape fantasies, for example, were represented as an impediment to true sexual desire. In other words, it was perhaps the very insistence on the body as part of women's everyday routines that contributed to the reconciliation of immediate bodily pleasures with the more abstracted realm of fantasy. Much as women could learn about their bodies, they could correspondingly educate their desires—a thesis predominant in Friday's solicitations of women's confessional fantasies. In this sense, popular texts intersected with the growing antipornography movement of the late 1970s and early 1980s: both insisted that women's sexuality was life-affirming and non-objectifying, that once women understood their desires as distinct from male pleasures, they would blossom into fully integrated individuals. In this sense, masturbation became a legitimate activity precisely because it was reconciled with the everyday—shown to facilitate women's health and well-being, to be a perfectly natural and normal thing to do. Essentialism, then, must be considered one of the conditions of access—albeit not unrestricted access—to certain materials that facilitate masturbation and orgasm.

Indeed, masturbation discourse laid the foundation for much of the women's erotica and couples' porn that appeared in the 1980s and 1990s; teaching women that masturbation was an accepted activity was a necessary first component to their consumption of erotic materials. Furthermore, masturbation discourse, especially as it valorized the clitoris, helped distinguish erotica from pornography, a genre connected to men's orgasms and masturbation. This chapter thus establishes some important concepts that I will pursue throughout the rest of the book—the valorization of the clitoral orgasm, the emphasis on the naturalness of female sexuality, and the reconciliation of fantasy and reality, all of which worked to differentiate erotica from porn. These common conventions of erotica are always defined somewhat differently, however—they are issues of struggle and contention, as I begin to demonstrate in this chapter through discussions of the domestication of the vibrator and the computer as masturbatory tools. Technology has helped women expand the categories of "reality" and "fantasy," to gain a certain distance from the insistence on the natural female body by proliferating the possibilities for pleasure within certain everyday routines. However, technologies have also met with some resistance, both because they often blur the distinctions between clearly defined male and female pleasures and also because they are not readily accessible for many women.

Seeking Sexual Liberation by Escaping the Home

Women's masturbation was only one of a number of sexual practices that gained legitimation in the early 1970s; numerous critics have documented the changes in social norms regarding sex and sexually explicit material throughout the 1960s and early 1970s. The advent of the pill and the increased dissemination of birth control information in general, the growth of the sex industry, the reduction of legal restraints on the publication of erotica and pornography, the liberalization of divorce laws, and the 1973 *Roe v. Wade* decision legalizing abortion are just a few of the changes that occurred in this period.

In this context, discourses about the body assumed a more open, mainstream position. Alex Comfort's book *The Joy of Sex: A Gourmet Guide to Love Making* became a national best-seller in 1972 and was followed two years later by *More Joy of Sex: A Lovemaking Companion to The Joy of Sex*. Hard-core pornography such as *Deep Throat* was becoming more mainstream (see chapter 1). Yet both *Deep Throat* and *The Joy of Sex* indicate what, for many women, was wrong with the so-called sexual revolution. The conceit of *Deep Throat* was that Linda Lovelace's clitoris was located in the back of her throat, which meant that the only way for her to achieve orgasm was through deep-throat fellatio. In this manner, the film recognized female pleasure as different from male pleasure yet, at the same time, brought the two together in a manner that obviously continued to valorize the phallus. Similarly, *The Joy of Sex* discusses in various of its dictionary-entry sections the importance of clitoral stimulation but continually prioritizes the phallus; the penis, for example, gets an entire entry and remains the central organ for both parties in the act of intercourse. Comfort describes the penis as having "more symbolic importance than any other human organ, as a dominance signal and, by reason of having a will of its own, generally a 'personality'" (78).

Shere Hite's respondents to her 1974 questionnaire were generally skeptical that a sexual revolution had even occurred: "Is there one?" asks one woman. "I hardly noticed. Talking a lot about sex hardly constitutes a revolution," said another woman. "Most 'swingers' are non-swingers. Most men have never heard of the clitoris. Boys are constantly looking to get laid, girls are constantly getting hurt—what else is new?" (310) Andrea Dworkin argued in her 1974 book *Woman Hating*, that the sexual revolution only made women more accessible to sexual exploitation—not only in the streets but also in the home:

> Rape is, in fact, simple straightforward heterosexual behavior in a male-dominated society. It offends us when it does, which is rarely, only because it is male-female relation without sham—without the mystifying romance of the couple, without the civility of money exchange. It happens in the home as well as on the streets. (83–84)

It wasn't only radical feminists condemning the home as a site of sexual oppression of women. Adopting a much more moderate approach than Dworkin, many scientific, sex therapist, sociological, and feminist texts of the late 1960s and early 1970s that focused on women and sexual fulfillment defined the home and traditional marital relationships as a site of impediment to orgasm. In her 1974 book, *The New Sex Therapy*, well-known sex therapist Helen Singer Kaplan noted that some couples in sex therapy are actually advised to leave home and stay in a hotel for the duration of their therapy. Her female patients had been so shaped by the notion that women should subsume sexual pleasures to their husbands' desires that they could not achieve orgasm out of various fears about the implications:

> Some women are afraid that they will die if they have an orgasm; some equate orgasm with a loss of control; other women fear that once they have had their first orgasm they will become preoccupied with sex, to the extent that they will become promiscuous; almost all patients believe on some level that their lives will change drastically once they experience climax. (389–90)

Of course, as is implicit in this example, the problematization of the home occurred often precisely in order to save the home and the couple; thus, the extrication of the individual woman from the home and its routines that dominates the recommendations in these texts is often posited as a preliminary step toward eventual reinsertion in a more (sexually) fulfilling home life.

There exists, in many of the popular sexological texts, an implicit albeit untheorized recognition that bodies get produced and defined differently in different locations, at different times. The way that bodies matter, in other words, depends on the material locations in which they gain meaning, and on the relationship between these places and other sites that help define those places. The sex therapy texts recognized that the home as a site of motherhood and housework often kept women from having both the physical time and the emotional self-esteem to understand their bodies and to see their bodies as sites of individual pleasure. "Liberating" women from these gendered and desexualized roles required an understanding that desire need not be fixed within a static conception of home; home could be redefined as a site of sexual pleasure—but this would mean a reconceptualization of a woman's duties within the home, a redefinition of the body as not only a site of performance of labor on behalf of husbands and children, but also a site of individual sexual pleasure.

Masters and Johnson's 1966 *Human Sexual Response* laid the foundation for a critique of heterosexual sex from a female perspective; the two researchers' work is widely cited throughout other genres because they were among the first to scientifically document the myth of the vaginal orgasm and the biological truth of the clitoral orgasm. Based on observations and interviews with 487 women, Masters and Johnson concluded that the dichotomy between vaginal and clitoral orgasms is false; "anatomically, all orgasms are centered in the clitoris, whether they result from direct manual pressure applied to the clitoris, indirect pressure resulting from the thrusting of penis during intercourse, or generalized sexual stimulation of other erogenous zones like the breast" (summarized in Lydon, 199–200). The Masters and Johnson work helped spawn a number of books that focused just on the clitoris and female orgasm, such as Seymour Fisher's *Female Orgasm* (1973) and a collection of essays by sex therapists and sexologists called *The Classic Clitoris* (1974).

The valorization of the clitoris served several functions. For one, it provided sex therapists with the ammunition they needed to argue that many women were not orgasmic in their relationships because their partners simply did not understand female anatomy and assumed that what gave a man pleasure simultaneously stimulated the woman (if indeed, the woman's stimulation was even a concern). As Lonnie Barbach writes in the introduction to her 1975 book, *For Yourself: The Fulfillment of Female Sexuality*, a 1972 study revealed that only 53 percent of women who were married an average of fifteen years achieved orgasm with intercourse 90 to 100 percent of the time, only a slight improvement, Barbach notes, from Alfred Kinsey's 1938–49 study, which showed that 45 percent of married women regularly achieved orgasm during intercourse (x). Sexual problems are not usually the product of some "underlying psychological problem," notes Barbach in attacking traditional psychotherapy. Rather, women and their partners need information about anatomy and sexuality in order to counter the culturally constructed myths about what produces pleasure and whose pleasure counts. Similarly, Shere Hite reported in her 1976 book, *The Hite Report: A Nationwide Study on Female Sexuality,* that only 30 percent of the women in her study (based on a 1974 questionnaire) could orgasm from intercourse. Like Barbach, Hite criticizes the notion that not having an orgasm during intercourse should be construed as a sign of failure or frigidity. "The questions should not be: Why aren't women having orgasms from intercourse?" Hite says, "but, rather: Why have we insisted women should orgasm from intercourse?" (139).

Furthermore, sex therapists argued that what kept women and their partners from understanding female pleasure was often a matter of traditional gender roles and duties within household routines. However, they did not use the debunking of the myth of the vaginal orgasm to make an institutional critique of heterosexuality or marriage, as did some other writers I will mention shortly. Rather, for Barbach, understanding female pleasure within an implicitly understood heterosexual relationship meant adjusting daily routines so as to give the individual woman time and space to learn about her body, to demystify the process of reaching orgasm. As Barbach says, "Orgasm, then, is a natural, normal, healthy process. No woman should be prohibited from enjoying the joy of sexual release in her own individual way. It can be as important and necessary for a woman to enjoy sex as it is for her to enjoy her work, children, environment, food, or recreational activities. It's just another potentially satisfying aspect of life" (4). Barbach frequently equates sex with the everyday: men "need to learn how a woman likes to make love, just as they need to learn how she takes her coffee" (7). Masturbating, says Barbach, is

> like the first time you baked a cake; it probably burned. If you had never tried again, you would have been a failure at cake baking. Perhaps instead you tried several times, went through a few trials before your cake was even edible; but now, it's probably pretty good. If you don't invent some real time in self-sexuality you won't get any results. (100)[3]

The notion that women need to "invent" the time to learn about their bodies—embedded as it is in the analogy to cooking—suggests that women need to be gradually encouraged to counter beliefs that go deeper than the immediate marital situation. Indeed, many sex therapists and sex commentators like Hite and Friday blamed parents—particularly mothers—for failing to educate their daughters about their bodies and/or actively creating a sense of shame about bodily self-exploration and masturbation. Thus, the definition of domesticity that needs to be changed is not only the immediate marital situation but also the whole concept of sex education within the family. In *My Secret Garden*, Friday describes the information void on girls and masturbation: "Little boys and masturbation are a normal, even charming part of the women's magazine stories as to how little boys are. . . . No one talks about girls masturbating, it was not a part of the prescribed myth of innocence, of growing up, of becoming a woman" (69). Friday elaborates this theme in her 1977 book, *My Mother/My Self: The Daughter's Search for Identity*; here she argues that girls learn from their mothers to distinguish between the roles of mother and sexual partner, largely because the former is so highly and visibly prized and the latter shrouded in mystery and shame. Says Friday, "We never 'see' her as the model from whom we learned our fear of our bodies as naturally as we learned to prize clean hair; we do not connect our anxiety when he tries to touch us 'there' with the same anxiety she felt when we, as babies, did it ourselves" (101). For Friday, the key to sexual liberation is uncovering the effects of a mother's socialization: "We cannot face the fact that our sexual anxieties today are inherited from mother" (101).

Barbach and Friday are tacticians of a sort, to use a term from Michel de Certeau's discussion of everyday life; they use the "vocabularies of established languages"; they "insinuate" themselves into the established places of domesticity, momentarily claiming the site of the home "without being able to tak[e] it over in its entirety" (xviii–xix). They aimed not to overthrow the traditional bourgeois configuration of a happily married couple with kids, but rather to gradually appropriate the space of the home in order to make it amenable to women's pleasures as well as men's, a process that begins with the mother (not the father) teaching her daughter (not her son) about her body. In the process of appropriation, there lies the possibility for building communities of women that could have a more long-standing effect on what it meant to reenter the home. Barbach's book, for example, continually stresses the importance of women sharing their feelings with each other, countering the isolation of the home that defined many women's roles. Yet in Barbach's anecdotes of women who were empowered in group therapy through each other's stories, the women deploy this empowerment to reconfigure their traditional relationships, using masturbation largely as a stepping stone to a better marriage.

In contrast, feminists like Betty Dodson drew on the techniques of consciousness raising to transform the individual and isolated act of masturbation into a group experience and critique of some of the main tenets of marriage. Says Dodson in the 1995 edition of *Selfloving*, describing what led her to start the workshops, "I thought compulsive [sic] monogamy, idealized romantic love, and dependent sex were the combined curse of womanhood" (47). In the workshops, women would sit in a circle and share various feelings and questions about sex, orgasm, anatomy, and so forth. They would also engage in "Genital Show and Tell," showing their genitals to each other in the interest of dispelling myths and misinformation about their bodies. Finally, the session would often culminate in a "guided masturbation ritual," in which all the women would masturbate together. Unlike Barbach, Dodson insists that masturbation be valued for the pleasures it can grant outside any relationship.

Other early second-wave feminists built on the biological documentation of the clitoral orgasm in order to mount a much stronger attack on the home as a site of the oppression of female sexual desire. Writers like Ann Koedt, author of "The Myth of the Vaginal Orgasm," were not concerned with saving or redefining domesticity but rather with ditching it altogether. Koedt, a founder of the radical feminist movement in New York, presented "Myth" at the first national women's liberation conference in 1968 in Chicago; it was subsequently published in *Radical Feminism*. Koedt's essay connects the perpetuation of the greater importance of male sexual pleasure to endemic male supremacy. In short, the documentation of the clitoral orgasm shows that women do not really need men at all—and thus also reveals why men are so anxious to retain the myth of the vaginal orgasm. Says Koedt, "Considering that the vagina is very desirable from a man's point of view, purely on physical grounds, one begins to see the dilemma for men. And it forces us to discard many 'physical' arguments explaining why women go to bed with men. What is left, it seems to me, are primarily psychological reasons why women select men at the exclusion of women as sexual partners" (206). The clitoral orgasm—now perceived as the truth of female sexuality—frees women from heterosexuality and paves the way for their resocialization as, perhaps, radical feminists. As Koedt elaborates, "The establishment of clitoral orgasm as fact would threaten the heterosexual *institution*. For it would indicate that sexual pleasure was obtainable from either men *or* women, thus making heterosexuality not an absolute, but an option" (206). Although Koedt shares some concerns with the sex therapists, one of them is clearly not the rearticulation of the couple/family, which was part of the heterosexual institution that radical feminism sought to overthrow.[4] In this discourse, "compulsory heterosexuality," to use Adrienne Rich's famous phrase, was used to explain why women *say* they experience pleasure in heterosexual relationships: the institutional structure of a patriarchal society is such that women do not even realize the falseness of their pleasures and the manner in which they are actually subsumed to male desire. Although it is not the point of this chapter to delve into the politics of the antipornography debates and feminist sex wars of the late 1970s and early 1980s, it is important to note that the discourse on healthy female sexuality was by no means particular to white heterosexual women; indeed, radical feminists often posited a particular kind of lesbian desire as the only true, politically correct desire. As Alice Echols writes in her history of early second-wave feminism, "it was generally assumed by radical feminists that female desire when liberated from male constraints and expectations would be untarnished by fantasies of dominance and submission" (290). African American feminist Audre Lorde's frequently quoted essay, "Uses of the Erotic: The Erotic as Power," argues that pornography and eroticism are "two diametrically opposed uses of the sexual"; erotica, she says, is "the assertion of the lifeforce of women, of that creative energy empowered, the knowledge and use of which we are now reclaiming in our language, our history, our dancing, our loving, our work, our lives" (80). The valorization of the clitoris can thus be linked to a definition of erotica that was distinct from any connection to male desire articulated through the phallus.

Intersecting with elements of both mainstream sex therapy and radical feminism, popular culture texts like *Cosmopolitan* urged women to find fulfillment outside marriage and children even as they perpetuated dominant standards of female beauty in a capitalist economy. Within the first six months of 1975, for example, *Cosmopolitan* ran four lengthy articles encouraging women to remain single ("The Challenge of Being Single"), consider separation as a means of deciding the merits of a marriage ("Trial Separation: Cop-Out or Marriage Saver"), embrace divorce ("Return to the Land of the Loving—Journey of a Divorcee"), and reject having children ("Marriage without Children"). Writes Nora Johnson in the divorcee article, "The truth is that once you have been disgorged by the legal machinery, once the decree is in your hand and the thing is over and done with, you have a truly wonderful opportunity to get yourself together, if you will only look at it that way" (xx). Other articles encouraged women to explore their sexual fantasies (an article by Nancy Friday, February 1975), and learn about how to achieve orgasm through oral sex (an interview with Dr. Wardell Pomeroy, a collaborator in the Kinsey studies). The encouragement of individual sexual liberation occurred, of course, within the contradictory context of ads for Mark Eden bust-enhancers and Frederick's of Hollywood lingerie ("How to be ALL Woman") and articles that valorized romance and heterosexuality both outside and within the confines of marriage. The traditional home, in other words, cannot be isolated as the only site of the production of rules about female sexuality and bodies; the bodies *Cosmopolitan* sought to produce were

both "liberated" from traditional relationships and home and "imprisoned" by conventional beauty standards.

Although we must recognize the differences across texts and social
sites, from *Cosmopolitan* to sex therapists and psychologists to radical
feminists, we can nevertheless identify a common skepticism of the home,
marriage, and family values and a desire to redefine sexual pleasure as
within the realm of the individual woman's immediate access and control.
I want next to narrow my focus, examining how the most mainstream
texts described the practice of masturbation such that it could fit within
a new yet familiar definition of domesticity.

Masturbation as Therapy

What were women to do once it became clear that their home situations
and partners were impeding sexual pleasure? If the people closest to
them, including mothers, husbands, and children, contributed to anxiety,
guilt, and misinformation about their bodies, then the obvious answer lay
in the individual pursuit of pleasure and self-exploration: masturbation.
Masturbation discourse was part of a larger discourse in feminism and
women's health that sought to reveal and politicize the social construction of the female body. For example, the Boston Women's Health Collective published the first of its many editions on women's health in 1971;
in it they proclaimed, "We can't write a book about men's bodies—that's
up to them" (12). They also declared, "We are our bodies" (39), a statement that seems to doom women to biological definitions. However, the
collective and other feminists writing about the body in the early 1970s
emphasized the materiality and specificity of the female body precisely to
liberate women from sexist beauty standards, traditional expectations
concerning motherhood and marriage, ignorance about their bodies, and
shame about sexual pleasure.

As Eithne Johnson writes, feminist self-care advocates taught women
how to examine their own bodies; using the very tools of clinical gyne-
cology, these feminists showed how the mirror, speculum, and flashlight
could help women enact a scene of self-representation and self-loving
(6–7). Several feminist documentaries on women's health produced in the
early 1970s—*Self Health, Taking Our Bodies Back,* and *Healthcaring*—
revealed "the spectacular scene as a means for female body-image production," argues Johnson (11). In addition, several feminists directed

experimental films on genital portraiture; Johnson describes how Anne Severson's *Near the Big Chakra* (1972) and Barbara Hammer's *Women I Love* (1976) and *Multiple Orgasms* (1977) emphasized the beauty and diversity of the vulva and clitoris as alternatives to pornographic representations of the female body.

In many respects, thus, learning about and claiming the body became the vehicle for the gender construction that would allow each woman to revel in her individuality—that would liberate her from the strictures of a patriarchal society. This belief in individual liberation through bodily pleasure characterizes Barbach's *For Yourself*: "This book, and the women's therapy groups, are both about liberation in the most basic sense: liberation from the social scripting which prevents women (and men, though perhaps in different ways) from taking control of their lives and expressing themselves as complete and autonomous individuals—free to act the way they feel despite the expectations of others" (197). Of course, "liberation" required an intensive disciplining of the body as well as the valorization of the belief in a woman's "unique individuality," especially in the sense that individuality signified distinctness from men and children. Both of these needs—knowledge and control over one's body and confidence about one's individuality—coincide in the practice of masturbation. Furthermore, masturbation offered sex therapists a manner in which to approach not the whole body but the much more manageable and politically significant clitoris. As Foucault writes in *Discipline and Punish*, control is a matter "not of training the body *en masse*, 'wholesale,' as if it were an indissociable unity, but of working it 'retail,' individually; of exercising upon it a subtle coercion, of obtaining holds upon it at the level of the mechanism itself—movement, gestures, attitudes, rapidity: an infinitesimal power over the active body" (137).

In Barbach's sex therapy groups, the first step toward masturbation was learning one's anatomy, in the process exploding myths about the female body perpetuated in a sexist society that assumed that male orgasm, with its very visible proof, was synonymous with female pleasure, which offered no visible, ejaculatory proof (although that too became the subject of debate). Women were advised to make knowledge of the body part of their everyday routine: stand in front of a mirror and examine yourself, advises Barbach. Learn that "an orgasm is an orgasm"; in other words, put to rest the red herring debate about the clitoral versus the vaginal orgasm and which is stronger proof of one's femininity (*For Yourself* 25). It is, as Foucault describes, "the meticulous control of the operations of the body"—a discipline encouraged by Barbach and (if learned correctly) internalized by her patients and readers. Consider this passage, for example:

> Label the parts of that special face [the genital area] by touching all the areas with your fingers; see if you can determine any differences in sensitivity. Notice the colors and textures of the areas. Place your fingers inside your vagina both to feel the pubococcygeal muscle that surrounds the opening and to see if some areas are more sensitive than others. (70)

Hite's 1976 *Hite Report: A Nationwide Study on Female Sexuality* similarly includes an anatomy lesson and a detailed description, drawing on respondents' answers, of various ways to masturbate. These variations are categorized into five methods, then described in minute detail that includes the exact positioning of body parts and the procedures used to bring one's body to orgasm.

Barbach breaks down masturbation into a series of steps dependent on women making the time and finding the place to feel comfortable practicing their masturbatory exercises in their domestic spaces. For exercises that take one hour each day, Barbach gives detailed instructions on how the women should proceed—where to rub, how hard to rub, what to do if the clitoris becomes irritated, how to counter feelings of disgust and shame, how to involve other parts of your body, and so forth. Here, as in other stages of the orgasmic process, women are encouraged to share their feelings with other women in the treatment groups Barbach supervised. Members of the group thus participate in the process of disciplining: "Evelyn complained that her hand got tired, so we suggested more movement of the fingers and less of the whole arm or vice versa depending upon the muscles which were being affected" (104).

Fueling this disciplining process is a potential contradiction: making masturbation and orgasm just a part of everyday life, a knowledge that every woman has easy access to, yet making orgasm the route to total happiness. Thus, on the one hand, Barbach advises, "Why not do away with the myth that there are better and worse ways of having an orgasm. Instead, acknowledge that having orgasms through intercourse without additional stimulation may not be possible given your unique physiological make up or the anatomic fit with your partner which may make sufficient clitoral stimulation impossible" (125). On the other hand, Barbach also says that finding the right kind of sex through which to achieve orgasm is a way to "escape the chains of myth and social stereotype and experience the freedom of expressing our authentic selves" (130). Thus, the disciplining of the body that Barbach encourages for the sake of liberation becomes the vehicle for wholeness, total personhood, a kind of freedom from the body based on the body. The possible regimentation and overdetermination that lurk around the orgasmic corner are avoided as orgasm becomes only a stepping stone to total happiness, including reinsertion in a healthy relationship.

One indicator of the insistence on the naturalness of female sexuality is the resistance initially posited to what has gradually become the most popular of women's sex toys, the vibrator—a domestic appliance if there ever was one, yet an appliance that also promised/threatened to disrupt the insistence on female sexual pleasure as naturally achieved, through coming to know one's own body without outside interference, including the interference of a machine. Herein lay the contradictions of the vibrator: it had actually been available since the turn of the century as a domestic appliance used for everything from furniture polishing to back massages and was thus highly accessible in the material sense; even though it was rarely advertised as a sexual toy, it was certainly used as one. Yet only in the 1970s did the vibrator come to be talked about somewhat openly as an aid to female sexual pleasure; this openness both increased access to the toy as information about its sexual uses proliferated and also raised the level of anxiety about its implications within everyday routines. We can see by analyzing the gradual domestication of the vibrator the manner in which technologies create anxiety precisely because they represent an expansion of certain categories that have come to clearly and reassuringly distinguish female from male desire. The phallic-shaped battery vibrator in particular raises all sorts of questions about technology, women, and pleasure: if the vibrator is intended to free women from reliance on men for their pleasures, then isn't there something ironic about using an artificial penis to get off? This debate has at times been particularly heated in lesbian communities, where the charge of "male-identified" has been leveled against proponents of vibrators and dildos.

The Vibrator as Domestic Appliance

Vibrators were first used in this country as a medical tool; historian Rachel Maines describes how in 1869 a physician named George Taylor patented a steam-powered massage and vibratory apparatus for treatment of female disorders, such as "hysteria." Medical and midwifery massage of the genital area had been a common practice since the seventeenth century for various female disorders, often categorized as "hysteria," a condition believed to result from the womb's revolt against sexual deprivation. The vibrator presented a more efficient way for physicians to treat hysteria, and by the turn of the century, they had access to dozens of vibrator models, including a portable battery-operated model invented by a British doctor.[5] By 1900, articles and textbooks on "vibratory massage technique at the turn of the century praised the machines' versatility for treatment of nearly all diseases in both sexes, and its efficiency of time and labor, especially in gynecological massage" (Maines, qtd. in Blank, 5). The portable vibrators turned house calls for hysteria into a more manageable task for busy doctors, and although an argument could be made here for the intersection of domesticity and eroticism, the sexual pleasure women might have derived from these visits has to be mitigated by the fact that the technology was used to pathologize female sexuality and to connect pleasure to illness.

Simultaneously, however, vibrators were advertised more widely as home appliances that could improve health and induce relaxation. According to Maines, a typical advertisement suggested the sexual uses: "All the pleasures of youth will throb within you," for example. Other inventors stressed more utilitarian applications; one 1906 invention "could be used on the face, head, and body; and 'in its larger or heavier forms for rubbing down and polishing all kinds of woodwork, furniture &c., that are given a rubbed or polished finish'" (Swartz, 58). The possibility increased, thus, that women could use vibrators for sexual pleasure not to treat illness but rather as an activity normalized through its advertisement as a home rather than a medical appliance.

This shift from the medicalization of the vibrator to its status as household appliance corresponds with the historical shift from women as sickly creatures in the late nineteenth century to managers of efficient homes in the early twentieth century; the ideology of domestic work as science included the professionalization of housework and the development of the field of home economics (Ehrenreich and English, 146). Indeed, many of the early vibrators were seemingly designed to look like other household appliances, as a trip through the Good Vibrations' "vibrator museum" reveals.[6] The "Ash Flash" battery vibrator, for example, looks very much like a flashlight, with a small suction cup attachment to the side; the electric "roller vibrator" resembles an iron on wheels. There is even a "Hollywood vita roll" that resembles a rolling pin.

The advertisement of vibrators as household appliances was interrupted, however, by two occurrences, according to Maines. First, in the 1920s, they began appearing as props for women performers in stag films, the underground pornography that circulated in brothels and men's clubs. Paradoxically, then, when vibrators became explicitly tied to sexual pleasure, it was for the pleasure of men—in an underground medium—which distanced them from even the subversive control of women. Although vibrators were still materially available, they had become symbolically linked to an illegitimate form of pleasure—illegitimate for women consumers, at least. Vibrators also largely disappeared from doctors' offices and magazine advertisements after the 1920s, says Maines, because physicians began treating hysteria with psychotherapy rather than through physical massage.

Vibrators did not begin to acquire relative mainstream legitimacy until the late 1960s, with the publication of the Masters and Johnson report and the other texts discussed in this chapter. In the 1970s the availability of vibrators increased both in mainstream markets like department stores and in more specific sex businesses, such as porn shops and mail-order catalogs. Their material availability and the knowledge about how to use them was thus expanding simultaneously—although not necessarily in the same venue. Sex therapists and sexologists often recommended them, with qualifications, and sometimes collaborated in their distribution by companies marketing them specifically as sexual products. The vibrator seemingly lent itself to this integration of the erotic and the everyday — readily available in department and drug stores as a quotidian household appliance, it promised to be efficient and productive, helping women achieve orgasm easily when they couldn't do it with their partners or their own fingers or when they felt squeamish about even touching their own bodies. Says Barbach in *For Yourself*, "Vibrators provide a consistent intensity that cannot be duplicated manually. As a result, the stimulation provided by a vibrator may be sufficient to bring you to orgasm one or more times with minimal effort on your part" (119). Joani Blank opened the Good Vibrations women's sexual aids store in San Francisco in 1977 and published the first edition of her book on how to use vibrators, *Good Vibrations,* the same year. U.S. companies, such as Norelco, Oster, Clairol, and Conair, introduced and/or expanded vibrator lines, hinting at their sexual uses to varying degrees. In 1980 *Esquire* ran an article entitled "For the Woman Who Has Almost Everything," documenting the decade-long growth in vibrator sales: from 700,000 pieces in 1975 (worth about $11.9 million) to 798,000 pieces in 1978 (worth $12.8 million) to 830,000 pieces (worth $13.3 million) in 1980. Industry representatives predicted sales of four million pieces a year by the mid-1980s (Swartz, 62).

The increasing venues of availability and sexually related information about vibrators and the emphasis on female masturbation and orgasm in the 1970s suggest a kind of unimpeded access. But the fact that the discourse generated was itself conflicted indicates that for many women, owning a vibrator—or at least owning up to owning a vibrator for sexual purposes—was an issue fraught with questions. As an appliance—sometimes a noisy one—the vibrator intrudes on the attempt to make sex seem "natural," part of the process of knowing one's body. Says Barbach, "Some women who object to the technological computer-instant-freeze-dried orientation of society may classify vibrators with frozen TV dinners, tape-recorded answering services, and microwave ovens. These women generally prefer a return to the more natural, slower, less complicated human functions. Thus, philosophically, they might be unwilling to use a vibrator" (*For Yourself*, 119). Indeed, the introduction of the vibrator into discourse on masturbation threatened to undo some of the gains masturbation had made in its accepted status for women. As *Redbook* magazine opined in March 1976, introducing two articles on vibrators,

> The following article may make a number of readers uncomfortable. Their feelings of discomfort or embarrassment are completely understandable and virtually inevitable. Until very recently, the subject—the use of vibrators for self-stimulation—has been considered unworthy of serious consideration. But in the past few years, on the basis of knowledge gained from studies of human sexual response, some of the country's most reputable sex therapists have reconsidered the matter and have come to new conclusions. . . . Because vibrators are being marketed on a nationwide basis, we believe that it is our responsibility, as editors of a magazine for women, to present appropriate and objective reporting on the subject so that readers can form their own intelligent opinions. (Safran, 85)

The editors may also have been prodded to consider the "legitimacy" of the topic when one out of five of the 100,000 women interviewed in their 1975 sex survey said they used some device during lovemaking, and for more than half of those women, the device was a vibrator (Safran, 86). Seemingly against their better judgment, the editors were forced to consider the legitimacy of a technology in conjunction with the always touchy issue of "self-stimulation"—they cannot even bring themselves to utter the "m" word.

Women's apprehensions about vibrators can be linked to the ways technology more generally has not worked in women's interests, serving only to create more work or to alienate women from access to leisure technologies, such as the television and, more recently, computers. One woman wrote Betty Dodson that after four years of marriage, in which she could not reach orgasm, she finally borrowed a "big electric vibrator from a friend, and after several painful weeks learned to have an orgasm. I hated myself and was ashamed that I had used a machine. I was sure that no other woman in the world was so sexually maladjusted that she had to revert to such perversity for her gratification" (181–82). Furthermore, alienation from technology contributed to women's fears that they would not be able to control their desire for the vibrator—paradoxically, given the fact that the vibrator is valorized precisely because it represents the potential for self-pleasuring. Barbach reported that "[some] women express the fear that they will turn into a 'vibrator junkie' and never be satisfied sexually by any other method of stimulation." She adds, only somewhat reassuringly, "To date, this has not been found to be the case" (119). In her *Redbook* article, "What's Good—*and Bad*—about the Vibrator," noted sexologist Virginia Johnson (of Masters and Johnson) gave a grudging endorsement to the vibrator—but only to stimulate a "physical release." Because they produce orgasms so quickly, Johnson worried that vibrators would impede women's ability to connect sex to emotions, words, and feelings, including fantasies. She wrote that "women who use the vibrator over a long period of time often report that they have lost much of their capacity for sexual thoughts, fantasies or daydreams. They feel that a great deal of the richness has disappeared from the ideas, thoughts, words, and gestures that once held such special erotic and emotional meanings for them" (136). Thus, although vibrator-induced orgasms may quickly solve the physical problem of climaxing, they may actually "create a whole new problem of dissatisfaction, since it can be a bit like convenience foods of the ready-mix, just-add-water variety; there is a usable product, but a lot is left out by the process" (136). Ultimately, says Johnson, the vibrator may even induce depression:

Over a long period of time, if a woman uses intense mechanical means to short-circuit her appreciation of the various stages of buildup to her release of sexual tension, it can diminish her ultimate joy. She may be left with a great yearning, a sense of restlessness or even depression, asking herself, like the old Peggy Lee song, "Is That All There Is?" (136)

Anthropologist Margaret Mead was one of the most severe critics of the vibrator as alienating technology, linking the tool to the broader mechanization of society. Quoted in the *Redbook* feature, Mead says, "Americans seem to prefer having machines to do everything. We have invented mechanical gadgets to substitute for what is natural. Machines alienate people from their bodies and from their emotions" (Safran, 85).

Technology thus came to represent the commodification of sex, something that women interested in defining a particular kind of female sexuality had rejected as characteristic of pornography but not of the new genre of women's erotica. Although the question was not always phrased explicitly, lurking beneath the vibrator anxiety was the issue of too much accessibility: should something that was so readily available, even in your neighborhood drug store, be used to define women's pleasure, especially when women were trying to distinguish their desires from the growing pornography industry? Would the progressive endorsement of vibrators by some feminists and sexologists interested in enhancing female pleasure get lost in the corporate rush to pad profit margins? Did the commodification of the vibrator as a sex toy indicate the commodification of the body, with sexual pleasure just another item in the profit margins? In a 1974 preface to his 1966 book on Victorian pornography, Steven Marcus comments disparagingly on the link in modern porn between "unlimited female orgasmic capacity" and consumer culture, singling out the figure of the masturbating woman, who achieves pleasure "with the aid of a mechanical-electrical instrument" (xiv). Mimi Swartz asks rhetorically at the end of her *Esquire* article, "Has the vibrator become a sort of microwave oven of the bedroom—a fast, efficient means of getting sexual pleasure? Is the most efficient orgasm the best orgasm? Is the bedroom really the place for a time-saving device?" (63).

The vibrator-wielding woman in this discourse occupied a role traditionally seen as masculine—able to come quickly, without engaging in any of the slow, romantic buildup that is supposed to characterize women's desires. Vibrators were implicitly linked to the pornography industry, in that they, like pornography, prompted quick, unfeeling orgasms—something supposedly identified with men. For lesbians, the debate about vibrators and dildos also centered on whether using a vibrator with a partner and enjoying penetration meant that you were overdetermined by heterosexual assumptions about what constituted good sex. Assuming the butch role through, in part, the use of vibrators and dildos was variously posited as a destabilization of the link between sex, gender, and sexuality and, conversely, as a patriarchal contamination of lesbian sexuality. Lesbian writer Dorothy Allison describes the baggage attached to the toys for much of the 1970s: "In 1979, the idea of using dildos was still anathema to most feminist lesbians. *Male-identified* was a bigger insult than ever" (132).

In both straight and lesbian communities, vibrators and dildos suggested a certain interruption in the purportedly natural flow between biological sex, gender, and sexual desire. Not surprisingly, then, marriage therapists—who usually rely on clear dichotomies between male and female desires—expressed some reservations about the impact of vibrators on heterosexual relationships. Helen Kaplan's endorsement was filled with cautionary notes about the vibrator's effect on the presumably male partner: "In therapy we suggest the vibrator as a last resort," she told *Redbook*, and "If your partner objects, you should not use it" (86–87). In her 1974 book, *The New Sex Therapy*, women were encouraged to use a vibrator only as an *initial* impetus: "To guard against the possibility that the woman will be limited to vibration-induced orgasms, we recommend the use of the vibrator initially only when less intense manual stimulation of the clitoris is not effective; in addition, we discourage sole reliance on the vibrator to produce orgasm and encourage exploration of alternative means of stimulation" (389). Even Ward Pomeroy, who worked on the Kinsey reports and helped finance a vibrator company started by an entrepreneur named Tex Williams, seemed resigned to the fact that many men wouldn't like the idea of their wives using a vibrator during sex: "Any self-masturbation in front of the spouse is probably the greatest taboo there is. So if a woman brings the vibrator into bed with her husband, it is anxiety-producing for both of them. The man often feels that she is married to a machine, and he's not needed anymore" (Swartz, 61).

Informing these anxieties is an early articulation of the fear of the cyborg, the paranoia that women using machines would turn into women *as* machines—robots addicted to endless orgasms, forgetting their household chores. The vibrator assumed the status of a household appliance run amok, complete with visions of women endlessly masturbating and eliding the romantic "process," which stereotypically distinguishes female pleasure from the quick male orgasm. Claire Safran warns in her *Redbook* article, "Reports are that over the course of an hour or so a woman can have as many as 50 consecutive orgasms using the machine" (86). The proliferating information about the vibrator thus began to include specific instructions for how to control one's pleasure, an interesting paradox given the endorsement of the vibrator as a way to "lose control," if achieving orgasm can be considered a temporary loss of control. Barbach recommends for her clients who became too dependent on the vibrator that they gradually lessen the amount of time spent using the vibrator before switching to manual stimulation, until eventually they wouldn't need the vibrator at all to reach orgasm (120). The vibrator marketed by Tex Williams's company even included this warning: "To guard against the possibility of some women limiting themselves to vibrator-induced orgasms, we encourage exploration of alternative means of stimulation after the initial phase of self-stimulation has been successful" (Swartz, 61).

Such advice did not render the vibrator obsolete, however, precisely because it is a multiuse household appliance—good for bursitis, backrubs, and clitoral massage. Not surprisingly, then, large corporations entering the vibrator market in the 1970s were reluctant either to focus on the sexual uses or to preclude them completely, and, in fact, they didn't need to choose in order to profit. The massager/vibrator is the perfect disciplining instrument—simultaneously breaking the body down into ever smaller parts and also promising a kind of whole body pleasure in the pursuit of general health because of its versatility. Corporations could enter the vibrator market confident that they would profit on the sexual uses without having to openly advertise them because this information was being disseminated elsewhere, albeit sometimes hesitantly. Mainstream publications were reluctant to accept advertisements for vibrators that indicated their sexual uses; *Redbook* ran ads for Tex Williams's Prelude three times, got one letter objecting to them, and pulled the ad (Swartz, 60). Even *Ms.* magazine, in 1979, would not admit to the sexual uses of the Prelude; its advertisement for the product showed a working woman massaging her neck with the vibrator as she takes a break from her drawing board, and promises relief and toning for thighs, skin, and feet. "The Prelude Experience . . . because it feels so good," said the ad (Swartz, 60). As long as the vibrator maintained its innocence, it could be openly marketed as a household appliance; in 1978 Prelude 3 was introduced at the National Housewares Exposition without any allusion to its sexual uses. Not surprisingly, dildos were much less accessible precisely because they were so clearly marked for their sexual uses. Allison describes how for much of the 1970s, lesbians, particularly in the South where she lived, simply had to be creative in devising dildos—using the fingers of rubber gloves stuffed with cotton, rubber devices found in pet stores, and vegetables.

In its potential to disrupt certain essentialist conceptions of gender and sexuality, the vibrator represented a link to women's fantasies: while knowledge about the body's anatomy was certainly important to achieving orgasm, the vibrator suggested that masturbation encompassed both bodily stimulation and mental imagination precisely because it introduced a nonbodily element. As such, the vibrator was a mediatory tool in the attempt to reconcile fantasy and reality, to introduce an "outside" element into the mechanics of masturbation. If liberation from the body was solely based on the body—as posited in the early masturbation texts—then women would indeed remain mired in limited possibilities for sex. But if the reconciliation of everyday life and sexual desire was seen as a constantly fluctuating negotiation, then technologies could help gently expand both fantasy and everyday life. And the popularization of the vibrator occurred at approximately the same time as the subject of women's fantasies became a topic of public discussion. *Cosmopolitan* ran a cover story in June 1973, the same month that Friday's *My Secret Garden* was published, quoting a prominent doctor who stated that "Women do not have sexual fantasies. The reason for this is obvious: Women haven't been brought up to enjoy sex. . . . women are by and large destitute of sexual fantasy" (February 1973, 9). Even some sex therapists suggested that, ideally, one would not need fantasies if the relationship was fulfilling. Helen Kaplan encouraged the use of erotic fantasies during masturbation as an effective distracting device; however, if treatment progresses as planned, the need for fantasy should diminish: "Thus, while erotic fantasy is the ideal distraction in that it is simultaneously a distraction and a source of stimulation, in the normal course of treatment the patient's use of fantasy diminishes progressively along with her sexual anxiety" (391). The unpredictable realm of fantasy was posited as unnecessary once the woman gains control of her body; it represented a threat to the woman's total concentration on the immediacy of the sex act with her partner. The antiporn movement was also beginning to exercise its influence, and its arguments that pornography enacts what it represents seemed to negate the possibility of a realm of fantasy (see introduction). Within this context, Friday's work was an attempt to legitimate the realm of fantasy yet also to define it in relation to everyday life; fantasy could not be too wild or anarchic, lest it upset the still nascent attempt to integrate sexual desire within everyday routines.

Everyday Fantasies

If sex therapists disciplined the body through their descriptions of the physical act of masturbation, Friday's solicitations of women's sexual stories represented the disciplining of the mind through the endorsement of certain kinds of fantasy. Friday elicited these fantasies by asking women to recount their guilty stories, encouraging them not to feel ashamed even as she incorporates into the book the idea that shame and repression breed particular fantasies, such as rape fantasies. Thus, even though Friday consistently says that women should feel no guilt about any fantasy, she simultaneously produces the belief that, in an ideal world, fantasy and reality would be reconciled—there would be no need for rape fantasies because only repression and shame breed those kinds of thoughts. As Friday says, "Forbidden things, locked away in tight, dark places, grow out of all proportion . . . the glimpse or idea that instantly sparked her imagination emerges as a fantasy, clothed in more outrageous gear and language than books, TV, films, or dirty jokes can offer" (201). In her 1991 book, *Women on Top,* Friday offers the proof for the implicit thesis of *My Secret Garden*:

> Here, for the first time [in *Women on Top*], these women's voices make it undeniably clear that our erotic fantasies have changed in juxtaposition to what has happened in the past years; they are not simply masturbatory diversions, derivatives of *Playboy* cartoons, but brilliant insights into what motivates real life—clues to our identity as valuable as the dreams we dream at night. (7)

Thus, for Friday, much as for sex therapists, the process of incorporating fantasy into one's everyday life—a life that is made increasingly "better" and more equal through the process of educating desire—eventually makes it likely that fantasy and reality will mesh, producing a whole and healthy sexuality. For Friday, possessing a healthy sexuality indicates that the woman is in control—able to construct her own fantasies from "real life" experience rather than resort to appropriating male fantasies.

Yet for Friday, the route to a healthy sexuality is more circuitous than it is for the sex therapists; she often celebrates a kind of "bad girl" liberatory quality of "naughty" fantasies. In *My Secret Garden,* Friday tried to counter the notion that "good" women did not fantasize because they were too busy being "good" housewives and mothers. Indeed, the conditions of women's everyday life actually were conducive to active fantasy lives:

> You could say that a woman's life was made for fantasy. All those idle hours, those boring repetitive jobs that her hands automatically do, the endless opportunities to reflect, construct and reconstruct. In a sense we were born to dream, to stay at home.... Even today's superwomen who leave the house to go to work have at least as much opportunity for the odd idle fantasy as the guy at the next desk (and more natural talent and practice at it!)—the tedious subway rides, the dull business conferences, hungover days when you just can't concentrate on anything except the erotic possibilities of the boss's moustache. (60)

In this manner, Friday legitimated the structures that constricted women's mobility, particularly in her essentialization of the stay-at-home woman, and yet rearticulated those structures to make them conducive to "nonproductive" work. While a man who wants to satisfy his desires can just "pick up the phone, go see someone, ask a girl out, or order one," a woman must use other strategies: "It is not so easy for a woman to reach out as readily and shamelessly for what she wants—to take his clothes off, take him to bed, take him from above, below, and if he won't take her from behind, take a whore to bed who will.... Instead women dream about it" (61).

Not surprisingly, some of Friday's respondents express an incorporation of the everyday with the erotic. Says Lillian, for example, "Sometimes, when I'm say, peeling potatoes, I imagine that Bill would come up behind me, bend me over and enter me, right there at the kitchen sink" (67–68). Or Esther: "I do my housework in the tops of baby-doll pajamas, stay in a half-hot mood most of the time, what with touching myself, or rubbing against different objects. The nozzle of the vacuum cleaner hose, for instance, played lightly over the pubic area is terrific and will bring on an orgasm if desired" (67). Or Viola: "My favorite daydream is of me cooking or washing dishes, my lover comes in, puts his arms around me, and as we kiss and press against one another and our passion builds, I just reach behind me and turn off the stove, the dishes are forgotten, everything left wonderfully unfinished" (68).

The material at hand is not just the daily routine of housework; it is also the manner in which domesticity and family life make sexual pleasure, particularly masturbation, a shameful and hidden issue. Friday wanted to denaturalize these domestic assumptions about masturbation by helping women articulate this shame and reach a level of sexual liberation: "it's the essence of what all this research boils down to: that women, once opened up and allied to other women, are indeed less ashamed, more adventurous, more accepting sexually than men" (70). Friday often frames women's confessions with the reassuring advice that guilt can be used as a stimulus to fantasy. Introducing a section where women confess their rape fantasies, Friday says, "It's worth repeating my conviction that fantasy need have nothing to do with reality, in terms of suppressed wish-fulfillment"; she elaborates that women who have rape fantasies insist they have no desire to actually be raped, and she believes them (109). Yet the reality of rape is not the only reality to which a rape fantasy might refer, and Friday says as much in her introduction to a section on masochism. Here she comments on the common use of the word "force" in women's recountings of fantasies: "They use 'force' liberally, almost involuntarily . . . even when the fantasy has nothing to do with rape or pain." The desire for pain, says Friday, "can become genuinely disturbing and shows to what ends—imagined though they may be—a woman will go to feel something at last, to feel at least something" (116). Thus, for Friday, fantasies of rape and pain are indeed tied to women's realities—the reality, for example, of not being allowed to express sexual feelings and thus, even in fantasy, refusing to claim responsibility for the desires. Friday wants to distance fantasy from reality in order to legitimate it, yet hopes for a day when women's fantasies will be based on a "healthier" reality, a reality that would eradicate the need for masochistic fantasies.

Women's literary erotica as it began appearing—almost a decade after the publication of *My Secret Garden*—took up where Friday left off, inquiring into the relationship between fantasy and reality in the pursuit of a specifically defined women's erotica that flowed out of the female body. There are clear connections between the women's erotica that began appearing in the late 1980s and the masturbation texts, connections that suggest that access to erotica was facilitated through the masturbation

discourse and through Friday's work. These nonfiction texts helped produce conditions of access—educating women about how to access their
own bodies, so to speak, and legitimating the consumption of erotic texts
that speak to the specific pleasures of their bodies and their minds. Quite
simply, without these nonfictional texts, literary women's erotica would
never have flourished; writers and readers needed to learn the biological
"truth" of the clitoral orgasm, find the time and the space to practice
masturbation, and foster an active fantasy life before the literary erotica
could claim an active (so to speak) readership. Women's erotica did not
gain the status of a literary genre by proving its ability to exist in a realm
of disinterested contemplation. Rather, women's erotica is a genre merit-
ing literary status precisely because of its grounding in the practice of
masturbation.

Technologies of Masturbation

I will turn in the next chapter to a closer examination of women's print
erotica, but before I do, I want to conclude this chapter by analyzing the
contemporary status of technologies of masturbation within domesticity.
One way of gauging feminists' claims that masturbation has been "liberated" is to ask whether access to technologies of masturbation has significantly increased over the last two decades. What conditions are
necessary for women to make the vibrator, the computer, and other sex
toys part of their repertoire of everyday pleasure tools?[7] In what specific
places are these technologies available, and how are the meanings of
those places constructed through various discourses?

Consider, for example, the ways the Illini Video Arcade in Champaign
helps construct the meaning of a vibrator. Entering the store, a customer
is immediately confronted with several rows of hard-core videos. Walking perhaps ten feet past these videos, she would come to the cash register and desk, where she might ask the salesperson for the location of the
vibrators. If she didn't want to ask, she might venture to her left, toward
the magazine section for both straight and gay men. Behind this section,
on the wall, are the sex toys, with a good selection of vibrators. There are
the basic Ladies Choice battery vibrators for $7.95, the Ms. Ultra Smooth
Vibrator for $15.25, and the more complicated Raquel Novice Kit, which
comes with four attachments, for $12.95. In fact, these vibrators are per-
haps the only items in the store with a specific address to women. This

address is undercut, however, by many of the products surrounding the vibrators, especially the blow-up dolls: the Felicia Fantasy Doll and the College Co-Ed doll. Asking for information about the different vibrators or even purchasing one might be difficult because all the salespeople, the manager, and the owner are men.

Recognizing the limitations of adult video and sex stores that cater mainly to men, a number of women have opened women-friendly sex shops in the last two decades. Located mainly on either coast, they include Eve's Garden and Come Again in New York, Good Vibrations and Romantasy in San Francisco, Love Seasons in Seattle, It's My Pleasure in Portland, The Love Boutiques in Los Angeles, and Grand Opening in Boston.[8] However, those locations still leave many women, in the Midwest and South, in rural areas and small towns, without physical access to sex toys other than the electric vibrator available at the mall. Seeing the opportunity here, many of the sex shops have started mail-order operations. Mail-order catalogs, especially those that supply information as well as advertise the products, seem to offer the ultimate in access: the availability of many products, information connecting the products to specific pleasures, and the privacy of choosing, ordering, and receiving goods in one's own home. This formula does not evade the issue of commodification; women are positioned as household consumers, in a manner that isolates them within a potentially insularized, self-sufficient home. However, women are addressed as consumers for their own pleasures rather than for the needs of other household members; using vibrators, they will be both consumers and producers, if one can consider orgasms a product. Furthermore, the catalogs, unlike most women's magazines and catalogs, do not play on women's insecurities and attempt to make them buy in order to conform to certain standards of beauty, a notion of consumerism I take up more in chapter 4. The catalogs feature only rather abstract drawings of female figures; the products are sold in a manner that emphasizes their pleasure-enhancing rather than their beauty-producing qualities. Furthermore, the catalogs provide information alongside the products, emphasizing, for example, the importance of practicing safe sex—something for which vibrators and dildos are potentially very useful. Although ideally women's mobility could be enhanced by trips out of the home to women-friendly sex stores, catalogs may be the next best thing given the lack of access to such places, especially because many of the catalogs try to replicate the shopping experience of a woman who actually visits the store. In the Good Vibrations catalogs, for example, different kinds of vibrators are advertised with information describing the advantages and disadvantages of each of the three types: coil-operated, electric, or battery-operated. The information given—the power and speed of vibration, noise level, portability, durability, and price—encourages women to connect the product's features to her body's pleasures and to the conditions in which she will use it. Possibilities for pleasure have proliferated since the days of Tex Williams's Prelude 3; for example, coil-operated vibrators come with four to six plastic attachments, at least one of which—the Clitickler—is specifically designed for clitoral stimulation. There is also the Twig, which is designed for simultaneous clitoral and vaginal stimulation, and various four- to five-inch shaft-like attachments that can be used for vaginal or anal penetration. The G-Spotter Plus attachment is a curved, four-inch rod designed to reach, obviously, that tricky g-spot. Lest the information provided next to the sex toys is insufficient, Good Vibrations offers a separate catalog listing all the texts in its library, including several books and educational videos on how to use sex toys as well as fictional texts that incorporate sex toys as props in the story lines.

Sex toys and texts are demystified, made integratable into everyday routines, often in a humorous way. A 1997 catalog is even organized around the theme "A Day of Erotic Pleasure." "Instead of hitting the snooze button on your alarm clock, why not reach for a vibrator instead? Meet your lunch date for an afternoon quickie or attend your next staff meeting wearing one of our quietly vibrating toys," says the opening page. The rest of the catalog features various toys for different times of the day: vibrators for that 8 A.M. alarm clock, a butt plug for that long car commute, a set of three Black Lace novels to read on the subway, even a silicone dildo that adheres to glass or tile, "leaving your hands free to seek other pleasures" during that 11 A.M. erotic phone call. The Auto Arouser vibrator plugs into the cigarette lighter of a car. And the Orbit is a remote-controlled vibrating egg that "allows you to tickle your lover's fancy from across a crowded room."

Yet anxieties about vibrators have not been put to rest. Ongoing concerns indicate the continued relevance of debates about the relationship between technologies and female bodies. Even in the *Herotica* series, which has over the last decade included many stories that valorize the use of the vibrator, some of the vibrator-phobia of the 1970s is repeated. In *Herotica* 4's "Real Pleasure," the lesbian protagonist learns a lesson about the fallibility of her set of sex toys. From the start, the protagonist is presented as tough and unemotional; she seems capable of loving only her collection of sex toys. Asked to help conduct a safe-sex workshop in Paris, she packs her suitcase full of toys, which are unexpectedly searched at the customs stop. Narrating the story, she describes how she "lovingly undid the straps [of the suitcase] and lifted the lid." There were her thirteen vibrators, thirteen dildos, and assorted "ass plugs in varying shapes, sizes and colors. A real rainbow coalition. I was proud to be an American, proud to be a dyke, and very proud to be an impeccably accessorized butch top" (Blackwell, 70). The very sexy female customs officer, however, confiscates the toys, saying, "I wonder why you think you need these *accessoires* to inspire the love of *femmes francaises.* You are cheating yourself. You need a *femme francaise* to show you what real pleasure is" (71). The officer, Marie Antoinette, then unexpectedly shows up at the sex workshop and volunteers for the demonstration. She straps on a harness and inserts the biggest dildo, tells the protagonist to close her eyes, and pretends to penetrate her with the dildo. Only later does the protagonist realize that she has been fooled—Marie Antoinette actually penetrated her with two fingers, but was so skillful at this more "natural" technique that the protagonist never realized she wasn't being penetrated by a dildo. However, the protagonist still hasn't learned her lesson; she rejects Marie Antoinette's overtures at a further relationship, assuming that the French woman wants something permanent. Only after talking to her does the protagonist realize she has tried too hard for too long to be cool and unemotional—a repression that is linked to her reliance on inanimate sex toys. Says Marie Antoinette, "Just because I have emotions doesn't mean I want a relationship. It only means I'm not a machine. That shouldn't scare you, it should reassure you—unless you fantasize about robots" (80). The story issues a final critique of technology when the two women, leaving the sex workshop together, reject even the metro. "Let's walk," is the last line of "Real Pleasure."

This story represents the kind of "technophobia" described by Carol Stabile in her book on the technology debates in feminism. Technophobia, she says, "seeks definition in some mythic matriarchy that defines (and has historically defined) itself in opposition to a patriarchal, technologized present"; technomania, on the other hand, "seeks to efface or transcend history through the construction of new myths for the future" (27). These debates are certainly being played out in relation to cybersex in a manner that overlaps with the vibrator debates of the 1970s. While the vibrator represents the coupling of women with machines in a manner that emphasizes the materiality of the body, computer sex represents, more problematically, a kind of disembodiment. Although it is precisely this disembodiment that has been celebrated for its ability to provide relief from restrictive identity categories, it also has sometimes elided issues of the real bodies who have access to computer technology. Who owns the means of production of sexually explicit materials on the Internet? And who has the financial resources, technological knowledge, and time to access these erotic sites? I have already dealt in some detail with these issues in chapter 1; my point here is to specifically address the possibilities of computers as an aid to female masturbation in the context of feminist debates about technology.

For some feminists—the technophobes—computer sex is anathema to the natural female body; in fact, it represents the disappearance of the body. In her "(Dead) Bodies Floating in Cyberspace," Renate Klein links "virtual sex" to other postmodern strategies of "dismemberment and disembodiment," lambasting the computer games that allow players to "kill off" one of their multiple selves: "With the click of a button dead bodies are floating in cyberspace: the ultimate bodily obsolescence, mind rules supreme. And people are saying, just as they do with pre–virtual reality pornography, that this has no impact whatsoever on what you do in 'real' life—who are they kidding?" (357). Klein's argument is consistent with the tenets of the antiporn movement, which disallows any distinctions between reality and fantasy and which also homogenizes all kinds of porn under one condemning rubric. In this conception of computer porn, women who use the online sex as a stimulation to masturbation are victims of false consciousness, as are women who seek access to any kind of porn.

In more moderate critiques of computer technology, some feminists argue that there is nothing *essentially* masculine about computers; rather, computers have been constructed as a masculine leisure toy. Computer nerds are more likely to be boys/men who have for years been encouraged to dabble in computer technology, an educational factor that is only now being taken up in many public schools. Karen Coyle argues in *Wired Women* that women's access to computers is limited not by their inability to master the technology but by the social construction of the computer, which still links it to men, especially in terms of its potential as leisure rather than work technology. Although "some statistics show that as many as 30 percent of Internet accounts are held by women, they're not necessarily taking up a third of the bandwith" (52); thus, even women with the financial resources and technological know-how do not spend as much time on the Internet, either because they don't have as much leisure time or because, as Coyle suggests, it's "obvious to women who make their first forays into cyberspace that it's mainly men out there" (52). The disjuncture is particularly obvious in relation to sexual representations on the Internet, says Coyle, citing for support the ads in the back pages of many consumer computer magazines, such as *PC Magazine, Computer Currents, and MicroTimes.* Coyle does not cede the computer to men; rather, like other contributors to *Wired Women,* she argues for a true democratization of the technology, which can happen only if more women are encouraged through the various social constructions of computers and the Internet to become active users.

The technomaniacs in this debate are represented by the Net Chicks, a group of brash young "post-feminists" who scoff at the idea that the Internet is a masculine domain. In *Net Chicks: A Smart-Girl Guide to the Wired World,* Carla Sinclair describes who can belong to this "stylish, post-feminist, modern grrrl culture":

> you certainly don't have to be a technical expert to be a Net Chick. What you *do* need is a sassy-ass attitude and a sense of adventure. Net Chicks realize the power of the Internet. They aren't afraid to explore the digital jungle, finding that this medium actually facilitates communication and offers unlimited avenues to new information and entertainment. They don't buy into the myth that the Net is a male dominated area. Because it's not! (6)

Sinclair concedes that maybe "the world of computers used to belong to men, but that was only because women gave it to them" (6). In one easy move, then, Sinclair elides the issues of material access: how does one increase women's access to the Internet? One simply has a "sassy-ass attitude" and cyberspace is yours. Although the guide is indeed full of good, "lay girl's" advice about how to understand and use the Net, women-friendly sites, and what kind of software to use, the various contributors never do take up the question of class as it prevents many people, both women and men, from gaining access to cyberspace.

Yet the Net Chicks are sometimes savvy about connecting the freedom of the Net to the realities of women's bodies: "Enjoy the oddness of being judged only by the quality of your ideas and self-expression, not by your looks," says contributor Marjorie Ingall (31). Despite their rather privileged perspective, then, the Net Chicks suggest what is necessary if computer sex is to become a technology that more women can use for sexual pleasure: connect real, material bodies with the momentary freedoms from bodily identity experienced in Net surfing.

Online sex can represent access to women as both writers and readers of erotica, in somewhat the same manner as the authors and readers of literary erotica that I am about to discuss.[9] Because virtual sex is anonymous and lends itself to role playing, women can write their bodies; as Shannon McRae puts it in her essay on sex in *Wired Women*, "the eroticism of netsex has as much to do with the play of language as the play of bodies" (258). Netsex is thus a way of writing one's own erotica/ fantasy and then conveying that fantasy to a, or many, desiring reader(s). As McRae says, "Netsex allows two (or more) people to simultaneously write themselves and each other. The convention is that one person describes, in the third person, what she is doing to her partner, whom she addresses as you," as in this example:

> "Amaela slips her fingers gently across your collarbones and kisses your mouth slowly, lingering, as if tasting something delicious for the very first time."
>
> Amaela's partner might respond: "Jamie shivers, tongue slithering over yours, hands sliding down your back and pulling you hard toward him."
> (259)

Virtual sex encourages the production of literary erotica; this production is immediately put into circulation, becoming a potential masturbatory aid for another person and creating a kind of virtual masturbation community that recalls Betty Dodson's circles of women masturbating.

At its best, virtual sex does not ask women to ignore their bodies but rather involves "a constant phasing, simultaneous awareness of the corporeal body at the keyboard, the emoting, speaking self on the screen, and the existence of another individual, real and projected, who is similarly engaged" (McRae, 260). Consider this example from Bianca's Bedroom, a free Web site that offers users a chance to share masturbation fantasies. Writes "Jessica" on a Friday morning in May 1997,

> I am masturbating my brains out today while the kids are at school . . . I have cum 5 times all over this house . . . I have been fantasizing about getting caught by the kids as they come home. god i feel guilty but so hot and horny . . . I can't believe how many times I've cum today fantasizing about it. Any other mothers have this fantasy or been caught real life . . . I hope I am not the only one here . . . Please no guys . . . I only want to talk with mothers . . . I don't need your put downs.

Seven minutes later, "mom" responds with this reassurance: "I do it all the time, all over the house while my kids are at school, but I fear getting caught, if I hear them coming in, it does make it more intense though, almost getting caught . . . have lots of different fantasies." And a few minutes later, Thoran responds—despite the original sender's injunction against males—"I would never think of putting someone down because they like to masturbate." Jessica is thus connected, almost immediately, to a small community that validates her masturbatory fantasy and practice; it all occurs within the material space of the home but in a manner that expands Jessica's sense of home, where she is apparently restricted by material conditions of housework and child care. Of course, Jessica could very well not be a mother, which adds another layer of complexity to the manner in which masturbation for mothers gets legitimated. (If she is not, the issue of domesticity and eroticism nevertheless remains—for whom does the image of a masturbating mother carry an erotic charge?) Jessica becomes a writer of erotic fantasies, with an immediate and responsive audience; there is, however, a literal cost to pay for the possible masturbatory thrill. Online services charge a flat monthly fee, ranging from $10 to $20 a month, then an additional cost per hour, ranging from $1 to $2.95. Like the (usually male) consumer in a private booth at an adult video arcade, Jessica likely pays by the minute for her satisfaction.

For women with the money, time, and education to access it, the computer represents the culmination of thirty years of women's work on masturbation and fantasy. It is a technology that claims the material site of the body as one of pleasure, within the privacy of home, yet allows one to escape the body and the home momentarily. It is both situated and liberating, placed and (momentarily) placeless; it expands women's paths outside the home even when they are tied to that material site. Masturbation via the computer has been facilitated by the (partial) resolution of the vibrator debates and by the proliferation of women's erotica I am about to discuss, both of which helped produce the venues in which women could become producers and consumers of sexually explicit materials. There is still considerable resistance, however, to women's domestication of computers for erotic use—not only by the feminists discussed above but also by the governmental representatives discussed in chapter 1. For these critics, the computer represents a threat to domesticity; this demonization of the computer in turn helps produce a safe space within everyday routines for women's print erotica.

3

Aesthetics and Access

On February 9, 1996, an episode of the popular television show *Picket Fences* featured the story of twelve-year-old Zach's unfortunate escapades with cyberporn. The boy morphs the head of his teacher onto a lingerie-clad female image on the Internet; then, much to his chagrin, the teacher discovers his deed. A bad situation gets worse when, unbeknownst to Zach, his friend uploads the image onto the World Wide Web, prompting "600 hits a minute around the globe," according to the teacher's lawyer. Zach's parents, especially his mother, chastise themselves for failure to monitor their young son. The school principal advises the mother during a recess in the court hearing (the teacher sues the parents for "negligent supervision" and the two boys for sexual harassment), "Read to your children." The teacher eventually settles out of court, and the episode ends with the mother dutifully reading to her child from a volume of some weighty classic.

The injunction "read to your children" signifies the privilege of the printed word; contextualized, as it is in this scenario, in relation to pornography, it represents the legitimated status of the literary—broadly defined—as juxtaposed to the threat of the image, particularly images disseminated within the home by media technologies like the Internet and television. This episode followed by one day President Clinton's signing into law of the Telecommunications Act, including the Communications Decency Act discussed in chapter 1. In Champaign-Urbana, the local nightly news (whose jingle is "At Home with You") that followed *Picket Fences* included a report on computer software that helps parents keep children from accessing sexually explicit materials.

This media event illustrates the way women are warned about the appropriate materials for their homes—visual technologies are dangerous, the printed word is family-friendly. We can safely assume that no judge, televisual or otherwise, is advising parents to read *Story of O* to their children; nevertheless, the safe space granted literature broadly defined has helped legitimate the production of a genre of women's popular literary erotica that stands in contradistinction to visual and computer technologies of porn. Although literary erotica has been sanctioned through juridical proceedings for much of the twentieth century, only in the last twenty-five years have women used this safe space to create their own erotica, sharing some of the cultural purchase granted to canonical works by authors like James Joyce and Henry Miller but significantly revising erotica's conventions in order to reflect a "woman's way of writing." The act of writing erotica in the 1980s became another venue for distributing the information about women's bodily pleasures and sexual fantasies that was produced in the masturbation discourse discussed in the previous chapter. In fact, literary erotica has provided a way for women to explore, under the legitimating auspices of aesthetic discourse, the many different ways to reconcile reality and fantasy, the everyday and the erotic. Much women's erotica has historically tried to include different kinds of pleasures under the rubric of a woman's way of writing; furthermore, different identity groups have produced their own volumes of erotica: African American, Latin American, Latina/o, and Asian American collections of erotica have all appeared in the last decade, making claims about desire that are connected to a collective racial or ethnic group. More than the other technologies of pornography and erotica discussed in this book, print erotica has proven to be a highly democratic and accessible venue for women, gay men, and people of color, even serving as a component of political movements for groups for whom sexual desire is often the cause of social ostracism.

Print erotica's claims to aesthetic value and the discourses that help produce this value outside the text facilitate the process of domestication through which women gain control over sexually explicit materials as readers within the spaces of their homes. As argued in the introduction, domestication is a potentially progressive practice that nevertheless is also partially produced by conservative conceptions of the relationship between "home" and porn consumption. Women's erotica benefits from its association with a conservative political agenda on pornography, as illustrated in my opening anecdote, because it markets itself as distinctly "not pornography." Furthermore, erotica relies on the politically suspect realm of "highbrow" aesthetics; as numerous cultural studies critics have argued over the last decade, aesthetics is often deployed in the interest of legislating class distinctions rather than opening access to different groups of consumers.[1] Tony Bennett, for example, proclaims in *Outside*

Literature that "To announce a requiem for aesthetics *in toto* would, no doubt, be premature inasmuch as . . . it still has undeniable political use-value—but only for the right" (148). Following Bennett, we should simply dismiss the whole genre as colluding with a conservative agenda, for nearly all of it relies, to varying degrees, on the claims to whole subjectivity that he criticizes. With the editors acting as moral guides, the texts as literary artifacts of depth and complexity promise to resolve the problems of female sexual identity, to bring the politics of fantasy into line with the politics of reality. Bennett's criticism of aesthetics coincides with the criticism by some feminists of the attempt by other feminists to prescribe female desire through the use of the erotica/porn dichotomy as one that is at least partially based on aesthetic value. Women's erotica often claims to be using the literary form to capture the more complex nature of women's desire, setting it apart from the crasser representations of pornography and its appeal to a quick masturbatory fix.

What, then, are we to do with a genre so clearly defined through its claims to aesthetic value? We should not follow the fashionable trend in cultural studies to dismiss such claims as universal and homogenizing, for to do so is to refuse to examine the *effects* of the claims to aesthetic value. The question to ask concerning aesthetic discourse is not how it ensures a universal subjectivity, for no single discourse could ever achieve such an objective, even if it purports to. Rather, we should ask what aesthetic discourse effects at particular times and places; for example, how does the deployment of the claim to aesthetic value facilitate circulation, and in what places? Does aesthetic discourse itself get redefined as a more differentiated discourse as it is deployed from different sites? How does aesthetic discourse intersect with other discourses of value? We must define aesthetic discourse through the question of place—where the erotica is produced, sold, and consumed—in order to understand how and why it assumes a particular aesthetic value and how, in turn, this value is connected to questions of accessibility.

Although "erotica" has a long history of claiming a certain class distinction based on its aesthetic value, I show in this chapter that the writing, publication, and distribution of women's literary erotica combine to produce a much more complex notion of aesthetic value than one of clear, upper-class distinction. The popularization of women's erotica is one indication that erotica is no longer tied to a specific class and that it circulates broadly even as it retains a certain cultural purchase.[2] As Kerri Sharp, editor of the British series of women's erotica, Black Lace, says of this commercialized line (2 million copies sold as of spring 1997), "Black Lace appeals to women from all classes and incomes. We've taken erotic publishing out of the hands of sleazy porno merchants or elitist publishers and put it in shops in every high street in Britain. That's populist."[3] Black Lace is also distributed throughout the United States, perhaps most prominently in Borders bookstores. Aesthetic value thus facilitates a broad circulation, which in turn redefines the traditionally elitist associations of "aesthetic value."

Furthermore, I challenge the common academic assumption that a broad circulation indicates a loss in the transgressive value of works previously deemed literarily and/or sexually radical; indeed, I show through a case study of the career of radical lesbian writer/activist Susie Bright that the very categories of mainstream and center are inadequate for understanding the politics of popular erotica. Although there are limits to what popular erotica can include and still be distributed within mainstream venues, the genre of women's erotica has grown increasingly explicit, such that, at times, it seems that the label "erotica" is more a marketing strategy than a clear indication that the content is less explicit than pornography.

At the same time, women's erotica represents "explicit" sex in a much different manner than pornography traditionally has; women's erotica often relies on traditionally upheld literary qualities, such as the development of plot and complex character portrayal, in order to create a story in which women's everyday concerns are represented as part of the same world in which explicit sexual desires and fantasies occur. This integration of the everyday and the erotic stands in marked contrast to the fantasy world often represented in hard-core pornography, which historically has not been concerned with fleshing out its characters (in any multidimensional way, at least) or complicating its plots. This may sound like the tired high art/mass culture distinction; however, I mean something much more specific here about the uses and effects of the aesthetic value conferred by intricate plots and character complexity. Because women's erotica deploys these literary features in the interest of making erotica relevant to women in the contexts of their everyday lives, it produces a much more *located* sense of sexual practice than does most pornography. Women have careers, return home to spouses or partners and/or kids, pick up potential lovers in bars, and have sex in relation to all these sites. In contrast, in its emphasis on sexual numbers to the exclusion of other aspects of everyday life, pornography represents a much more dislocated kind of sex—although there are increasingly exceptions to that convention as well, as I discuss in chapter 5 regarding couples' porn.

Cultural Studies and Aesthetics

Because I situate my project within the field of cultural studies, I wish first to take issue with the anti-aesthetic argument; this will lay the groundwork for my position against poststructuralist feminists' dismissal of any identity-based politics, particularly one grounded in texts. Both positions hamper an engagement with the popular spheres in which an invocation of aesthetics is strategically important for the political effects desired— and these are not political effects desired by the Right.[4]

"Aesthetics" is defined variously in different disciplines; I am referring here only to the specific charge in cultural studies that aesthetics is a discourse that relies on textual interpretation as a means of establishing a didactic relationship between critic and reader. For Bennett, Ian Hunter, and Lawrence Grossberg, all of whom have been influential in shaping a particular strain of anti-aesthetic cultural studies, the criticism of aesthetics is related to their desire to distance cultural studies from methodologies that rely on textual interpretation as a kind of basis for identity politics. Rather, they argue, identity should be formulated—if we should even still be concerned with identity—in relation to theories of place and space. Although I agree with their emphasis on the importance of place, we need not oppose aesthetics to place; rather, we should analyze the ways aesthetic discourses and the places they circulate are mutually determining.

Many of the criticisms of aesthetics are formulated through a critique of one of cultural studies' founders, Raymond Williams. Common to these critiques is the belief that Williams privileged literature, literary criticism, and cultural history as the means for understanding and shaping class consciousness, which in turn led to an understanding of society as a whole. Williams "purport[ed] to contextualise aesthetic cultivation, describing the transformations undergone during its supposed embodiment in a movement to cultivate society as a whole" (Hunter, 89). However, Hunter argues, Williams's belief that art, particularly literature, could represent culture as a whole put him in the same position as dehistoricizing aestheticians. Other critics have agreed with this accusation; Lisa Jardine and Julia Swindells say that although Williams sought to anchor his reading in social and political history, his "continued commitment to reading and texts took younger left critics equally firmly in the direction of more sophisticated techniques of text analysis," thus producing "a left criticism which in the crucially formative early years once again isolated the text from history" (112–13). Williams purported to be "offering an alternative reading of texts generally treated as bourgeois, to reveal, in their inner conflict (the textual version of struggle), democratic values and attitudes"; however, his reliance on this very textual analysis to the exclusion of a complex historical situatedness only reproduced the aesthetic belief that meaning inheres in a text (Jardine and Swindells, 112).

If meaning inheres in the text, then its discovery depends on a passive and appropriately valuing subject. As Bennett argues, one of the effects of construing value as inhering in the object is to produce a subject that is "marked out from other subjects by his/her ability to recognize the value which such objects are said to embody" (151). Thus while Williams purported to be democratizing culture, these critics point to the ways his reliance on aesthetic ideals set up a hierarchy of readings and readers that excluded elements that would disrupt his ability to define a whole way of life via authentic, holistic interpretations. As Stuart Hall asks about Williams's positing of a "whole way of life": "Whose way? Which life? One way or several? Isn't it the case that, in the modern world, the more we examine 'whole ways of life,' the more internally diversified, the more cut through by complex patterns of similarity and difference, they appear to be?" (359). In the use of cultural texts to produce a whole way of life, Williams elided, through the power of a totalizing narrative, a range of complicating factors that these critics point to: gender, race, ethnicity. In other words, Williams was able to find in certain cultural texts a certain embodiment of working-class culture and to produce interpretations of this authentic class consciousness that ignored complicating factors. As Jardine and Swindells argue, "the production of authenticity was facilitated by the narrative voice that sought to shape and validate its own authored/authorized version of experience" in the language of authenticity (122). Most important, it seems, for Hunter and Bennett, Williams ignored the "institutional underpinnings" of cultural studies, namely, the technologies of public education and its intersections with government and economics. This institutional specificity locates the purportedly universal critic.

Williams occupied a privileged position, not exactly as a universalist, but achieving somewhat the same effect by valorizing his Welsh marginality to the degree that it allowed him to "acquire an understanding of British culture as a whole in view of his lived experience of the relations between the culture's dominant and resistive elements," argues Bennett in "Being 'in the True' of Cultural Studies" (218). Cultural studies has naively accepted a self-history that accepts this view, rather than acknowledging its institutional locations. The historical reliance of cultural studies on the personal qualities of the intellectual, such as Williams, produces a conflation of moral life and work that serves, Bennett argues, to legitimate cultural studies through "charismatic closure," the moral authority of the intellectual. This reliance on personality helps to constitute cultural studies as a never-definable field that can heal the fragmenting effects of intellectual specialization; it's a manifestation of a nostalgic desire for culture as a whole way of life.

Hunter argues that Williams differs little from the man of letters who purports to be representing a universal class, to be telling readers how to become a whole person. The universal appeals provide the venue for the critic to engage in the moral self-shaping of the reader; but, says Hunter, there's nothing universal about the appeal:

> Instead it must be seen as a product of the specific ethical practice through which a minority of ethical athletes have shaped a relation to the self as the subject of moral action. It is simply not the case that "cultivation" or "culture" could restore the sum total of human capacities to their home in experience or class consciousness because the figure of a complete development of human capacities is nothing more than a talisman of ethical cultivation itself. (99)

Drawing heavily on Foucault, Hunter advances an alternative conception of subjects, in which he argues that all subject formation is a matter of technique, that the kind of moral shaping sought by cultural critics puts the subject into a "mode of subjection" through which the individual "is led to recognise moral obligation" and to attempt to shape himself or herself in the proper, moral manner ("Culture," 96–97).

Thus the critique of aesthetics becomes a means of advancing a particular argument about subjectivity, such that aesthetics is inflated to cover all theories of subject formation that rely on theories of consciousness and interpretation; indeed, any kind of textual analysis becomes suspect. Such is the case in Bennett's analysis of Laclau and Mouffe; initially, he sympathetically explicates their theory of a political criticism based on rhetorical strategies:

it is possible to see how their arguments might secure a place for a radical concept of criticism's function that is not dependent on, nor serves as a means for, band-aiding a holistic Marxism back into place: namely, that of so reading cultural texts as to introduce discursive relations of antagonism into a limitless array of social relations while also assisting in organising a chain of equivalences between all the democratic demands to produce the collective will of all those people struggling against subordination. (*Outside*, 260–61)

Here, then, we have a notion that cultural criticism that reads texts *could* be engaged in the shaping of subjectivities in a manner that is not congruent with a universal subject formation but rather draws on a complex and conflictive array of relations and positions. However, Bennett ultimately makes the same critique of Laclau and Mouffe's rhetorical/textual analysis as he does of aesthetic discourse: they are "unable to offer any convincing account of the social, of the mechanisms through which rhetorical constructions of political interests and subjects are able to connect with and concretely influence differently constituted spheres of political relations" (*Outside*, 264). We are back, then, to a decontextualized form of rhetorical/textual criticism that relies on the individual as ideological subject rather than, as Bennett wishes, individuals as "functionaries of institutions and organizations" (*Outside*, 267–68). This is the politics of consciousness, which is reminiscent of, though not exactly equivalent to, the kind of moral shaping engaged in by aesthetic critics. Like Hunter, Bennett endorses instead a Foucaultian model in which critics are concerned not with the psychological struggle for consciousness but rather with "the politics of truth peculiar to particular regions of social management where such politics are understood as concerning the ways in which distinctions between true and false, existing in the form of institutional routines rather than abstract propositions requiring consent, fashion human conduct in ways which operate quite pre-consciously" (*Outside*, 270).

What Bennett and Hunter share with the work of Lawrence Grossberg is a frustration with a kind of identity politics that has partially defined cultural studies and that they see based in the politics of consciousness. Much as Bennett critiques the privileging through marginalization achieved by Williams and its ongoing influence in cultural studies, Grossberg criticizes models of identity based on difference, which, quoting Kobena Mercer, he says invariably give rise to "the mantra of race, class and gender" (89–90). These theories of identity are grounded in a politics of representation, which, for Grossberg, "sees identity as an entirely cultural, even an entirely linguistic, construction" (90). Although my summary here necessarily involves some simplification, it is fair to say that Grossberg links representation with consciousness; in his view, this "privileging of consciousness" in the conceptualization of subjectivity is a leftover of romanticism that survived poststructuralism as a *temporal* construct: "identity is entirely an *historical* construction" with "subjectivity as internal time consciousness; identity as the temporal construction of difference; and agency as the temporal displacement of difference" (100). And, much as Bennett counters the politics of consciousness with the politics of truth particular to social management, Grossberg proposes a spatial theory of subjectivity to replace the purely temporal: "subjectivity describes the points of attachment from which one experiences the world" (101). In this model, subjects gain agency through their movement—their ability to gain access to particular places of empowerment:

> If subjectivity constitutes "homes" as places of attachment, temporary addresses for people, agency constitutes strategic installations; these are the specific places and spaces that define specific forms of agency and empower specific populations. In this sense, we can inquire into the conditions of possibility of agency, for agency—the ability to make history as it were—is not intrinsic either to subjects or to selves. Agency is the product of diagrams of mobility and placement which define or map the possibilities of where and how specific vectors of influence can stop and be placed. (102)

My goal in the remainder of this chapter is to use this very notion of agency to show how identity claims made through aesthetic discourse can be mapped in precisely the way Grossberg outlines above. Identity, in other words, need not be posited in opposition to place; claims to be shaping identity, as occur in the erotica anthologies, have particular effects only as they begin to circulate in certain places, such as bookstores and homes. Agency is indeed a matter of subjects' mobility between different sites, but this mobility is partially determined by texts, not based on their intrinsic value but rather on their circulation, which is partially shaped by their content. Interpretation of the content is thus one component of understanding questions of access and mobility. On the one hand, I want very much to agree with these critics: the editors/critics of women's literary anthologies have acted precisely as moral exemplars (to use Bennett's phrase) or ethical athletes (to draw on Hunter), who have worked to shape the consciousness of women readers by advancing a particular relationship between critic and text: Read these erotic stories as reflecting the truth of your sexual identity, and you will find the truth of your overall identity.

However, we cannot merely leave the aesthetic claim at this point, as Bennett does. Because he dismisses aesthetic discourse upon proving its moralizing tendencies, Bennett never asks how aesthetic discourse *circulates* differently, in different situations. *Outside Literature* falls into the very trap it critiques, presenting a series of textual analyses of various Marxist critics' approaches to literature, showing the moralizing and decontextualizing tendencies of aesthetic approaches but never asking how these approaches circulate in particular historical circumstances. Bennett thus positions *himself* as a moral exemplar standing in judgment of such deployments, reading texts and shaping the readers' consciousness about those texts without connecting them to broader and probably conflicting discourses.

Many of the women's erotica anthologies are ripe for Bennett's critique. Consider this comment by Luisa Valenzuela, which the editors of *Pleasure in the Word: Erotic Writings by Latin American Women* quote in their introduction:

> Pornography is the negation of literature because it is the negation of metaphor and nuance, of ambiguity. It seeks a material reaction in the reader, a direct sexual excitement; eroticism, on the other hand, although it can be tremendously brazen and strong, goes through the filter of metaphor and poetic language. Pornography does not enter into literary disquisition. I think that as women, we have to rescue erotic language because in the final analysis it is dominated by male fantasies. Every one of us must tell one's own truth, trying to express the other's desire, because the last thing that wants to be expressed is desire. (Fernandez and Paravisini-Gebert, 28)

The editors thus attempt to set up a correct way of reading the stories that follow; they position themselves as the moral exemplars deploying the particular features of literature, which stand in opposition to a discourse of lies—pornography—that women need to unlearn in order to find the truths of their sexual identities. But we must ask how this claim helps the collection circulate as a literary text, meant especially for women, how—regardless of whether individual women readers take the editors' advice or not—the very act of claiming aesthetic value, which is produced in the material artifact of the book, *helps* shape but does not exclusively determine the conditions under which women consume the erotic stories. We must ask under what particular social and historical conditions this aesthetic claim is produced, and why it is critical for women, in this case Latin American women, to make a claim about sexuality that is grounded in aesthetic validation.

Bennett's critique of aesthetics and my critique of Bennett are useful in understanding the importance *and* the limitations of feminist critiques of the erotica/porn distinction, insofar as that distinction is partially based on aesthetic claims. Contemporary erotica varies in the degree to which it retains this strict distinction, but nearly all the anthologies do still draw a clear line between erotica and pornography, often in aesthetic terms: erotica is complex, concerned with developing characters and plots in a manner that shows the struggle between mind and body, eventually resolving it; pornography is predictable, stock, concerned solely with bodies and penetration. In setting up these norms, the erotica collections function as what Judith Butler describes as a "regulatory practice." These practices produce notions of identity—social definitions of "intelligible genders," which Butler defines as "those which in some sense institute and maintain relations of coherence and continuity among sex, gender, sexual practice, and desire" (17).

The normalizing appeal to a category of Woman that *seems* coherent is precisely what has fueled arguments by feminists critical of the attempt to distinguish between erotica and pornography. Paula Webster critically describes a Women Against Pornography presentation positioning erotica as the alternative to pornography:

> [Erotica] was good, healthy sexual imagery—the standard against which pornography and perhaps our own sexual lives were to be judged. . . . What is defined as pornography and what is defined as erotica no doubt depends on personal taste, moral boundaries, sexual preferences, cultural and class biases. . . . There are no universal, unchanging criteria for drawing the line between acceptable and unacceptable sexual images. As feminists, we might question the very impulse to make such a rigid separation, to let a small group of women dictate the boundaries of our morality and our pleasure. (32)

We must acknowledge Webster's main point here—that the erotica/porn distinction entails a certain amount of judgment, a kind of moral boundary that is, indeed, somewhat exclusive and that tries to set up a correct relationship between reader and text, mediated by the critic, or, in the case of erotica anthologies, between the editor and the reader. Indeed, the erotica anthologies offer an excellent example of the mediation of the critic because the editor *is* the critic, present at the start of each anthology, prescribing a certain way of reading the stories.

The production of identity erotica based on stable identities functions, following Butler, as a regulatory practice that maintains gendered binaries and renders "unintelligible" those sexual practices that do not fit within the matrix of intelligibility. In fact, Butler is unrelenting in her critique of any use of categories of identity, even strategic uses:

> The suggestion that feminism can seek wider representation for a subject that it itself constructs has the ironic consequence that feminist goals risk failure by refusing to take account of the constitutive powers of their own representational claims. This problem is not ameliorated through an appeal to the category of women for merely "strategic" purposes, for strategies always have meanings that exceed the purposes for which they are intended. In this case, exclusion itself might qualify as such an unintended yet consequential meaning. (*Gender Trouble*, 4–5)

Bennett's critique of the use of aesthetics to produce a universal subject is here supported by Butler's critique of strategies within feminism, of which we could here include the invocation of the aesthetic, to build a unity around identity, a unity that is necessarily exclusive and normalizing. And while I generally agree with the political goals of Butler's argument, I disagree with her suggestion that the effects of "strategic" invocations of identity will be predictably exclusive. We must examine such invocations as they circulate in order to understand their many different effects, some of which will be exclusive, but in unpredictable and contradictory ways; and, after all, it is hard to imagine an articulation of identity that is not in some manner exclusive. We must ask how the preservation of a category based on identity, articulated through aesthetic distinction, circulates in a manner that might bring the text into contradiction with discourses that articulate identity differently. The rest of this chapter illustrates how aesthetic value and notions of identity are produced at various sites—authorship and consumption, publication, marketing, circulation, and textual content—in a manner that reveals the limitations of these criticisms.

Literary Production and Access

As John Guillory argues, the anti-aesthetic critique inflates aesthetic discourse such that it becomes the sole indicator of value, divorced from its relation to "other domains of the social" (281). He adds, "The dismissal of aesthetics, as the discourse of 'universal' value believed to suppress differences, has thus had the paradoxical effect of removing the basis for apprehending the work of art as the objectification not of subjects or communities, but of the relations between subjects, or the relations between groups" (282). Following this argument, we could begin to understand how aesthetic value is produced through women's erotica by inquiring into the *relations* between women as producers of erotica and women as consumers of erotica. In this brief history of women's literary erotica, I show the gradual democratization of the author function for women writers of erotica, a process that has diffused aesthetic value throughout more popular circles even as it has retained the cultural purchase attached to the "literary."

Literature is one of the discourses "endowed with the 'author function,'" says Foucault: "the author's name indicates the status of this discourse within a society and a culture" ("Author," 107). This phenomenon is clear in the obscenity trials of the twentieth century, where the literary reputation of many male writers was produced in part through decisions that legislated distinctions between art and obscenity. We are perhaps accustomed in literary studies to consider the evolution of the author function in a manner similar to the one Michael Bérubé traces in his book on the politics of canon formation. While all texts in print assume some degree of the author function, says Bérubé, only "(a) small number of texts assigned author functions are also assigned the 'aesthetic function,' which (borrowing from Mukarovksy) means that they are authorized to be read 'as literature' (and not as diet books)." Furthermore, says Bérubé, "(a) still smaller number of literary texts qualify as [Richard] Ohman's 'precanonical' works; and very, very few of these ... are licensed for exegesis by the entire profession of literary studies" (59). A text's value thus seemingly increases from the mundane (diet books) to the canonical, from widespread accessibility to a level where the text can be understood only if properly interpreted by a credentialized group of professionals; this is clearly a process that occurred in court hearings on the canonical male writers of erotica. The wording of legal decisions made it clear that the works were intended for only certain, highly educated readers; literary critics were often called as expert witnesses at the obscenity trials of works by writers like Henry Miller, James Joyce, and D. H. Lawrence. However, women's erotica has enabled a different trajectory of aesthetic value; when aesthetic value is popularized even as it retains a certain literary cultural purchase, aesthetic value becomes a means of expanding rather than contracting access to erotic literature.

For Anaïs Nin, access to the means of literary production was generally more difficult than it was for her male counterparts in the 1940s in Paris; indeed, she saw her erotic writing as a potential liability to her other work. In the 1977 preface to her collection of erotica, *Delta of Venus*, Nin recounts how she started writing erotica in the early 1940s in Paris because friends, including Henry Miller, needed money. The collector for whom she was writing liked her stories and continually asked for more. Even as late as 1977, Nin apologizes for succumbing to the demands of the market, which she says tainted her work, especially because the collector exhorted her to "leave out the poetry and descriptions of anything but sex," suggesting links to pornography. However, in recovering her work thirty years later, in a different political climate, she finds in them a suppressed woman's voice and uses this recognition of difference to make a literary claim about her erotic stories. Thus, it is not until 1977, due to many of the conditions discussed in this book, that Nin's erotica can coincide with rather than contradict her author position. At the risk of exaggerating the effects of a single text, we can say that the publication of *Delta of Venus*, with Nin's preface, became one of the conditions facilitating the claim by other women erotica editors and writers to occupy the author subject position; many editors cite Nin in their introductions for contributing to the legitimation of women's erotica through its specifically literary status. As Foucault says, the author's name assumes a classificatory function:

> the fact that the discourse has an author's name, that one can say "this was written by so-and-so" or "so-and-so is its author," shows that this discourse is not ordinary everyday speech that merely comes and goes, not something that is immediately consumable. On the contrary, it is speech that must be received in a certain mode and that, in a given culture, must receive a certain status. ("Author," 107)

The more often canonical women writers like Nin are ascribed that function in relation to erotica, the more likely it is that other authors will find sanction to write sexually explicit materials that count as literature.

Several of the specifically literary erotica anthologies take up Nin's challenge to the canon of male erotica, participating at the same time in the more general feminist project of canon revision and expansion. Editors of the women's erotica anthologies that stress literary recovery claim to be writing a different history of literature's representation of sex, a history that includes women writers who, despite attempts to repress them, have succeeded throughout the years in subverting social conventions in order to represent female sexuality. *Erotica: Women's Writing from Sappho to Margaret Atwood* argues that all the stories included in the edition have in common a certain set of literary characteristics that have been overlooked in the patriarchal construction of canonicity. Writes Jeanette Wintersen in the foreword:

> *Erotica* is a wild plunge into mostly overlooked territory. It accepts that women have not always been able to write directly about sex or desire but that they will have done so through nuance, suggestion, poetic device, and allegory. The *Lais of Marie de France* are a good example of this and what else was Christina Rossetti doing in *Goblin Market*? Dr. Reynolds [the book's editor] is not so simple-minded as to assume that the authors of her extracts will, in every case, have been aware of what they were doing. Most of us, even now, do not have that kind of self-knowledge. (Reynolds, xxi)

Wintersen suggests that once properly trained by the critic who herself has awoken to the realities of the literariness of the female-authored erotic text, the (female) reader will recognize the true literary, and thus erotic, nature of these texts. Yet the notion of a stable definition of "literature" is eroded when one considers the texts included in the anthology—stories from authors as diverse as lesbian s/m advocate Pat Califia and William Wordsworth's sister Dorothy.[5] Califia's stories, which in other contexts have been labeled pornographic (a label to which she herself would not object), circulate here under the rubric of erotic literature. Access through aesthetic claims becomes in this case a means of expanding the canon of literature and the definition of "women's desires."

The concept of the author function speaks to the ways the author is constructed in discourse in a manner that does not necessarily coincide with the individual writer's intentions. This is aptly illustrated by the example of Pauline Réage, the pseudonym of the French woman who in 1954 wrote *Story of O,* a novel that describes one woman's consensual decision to participate in sexual practices that increasingly bring her under the control of her male "masters." The novel was published in the

United States by Grove Press in 1965, and although Réage still did not reveal her identity, the novel has, throughout the 1980s and 1990s, inspired many women to write erotic stories roughly based on O. These stories claim literary value through references to O's reputation, even as they rewrite O's story to make it more realistic for contemporary women (Réage's O made almost no references to O's life outside her sexual experiences, even though she is introduced as an independent woman with a career as a fashion photographer).[6] Anne Rice's *Exit to Eden* is a retelling of O that explores multiple sexual roles for men and women (the back cover advertises it as the contemporary sequel to *Story of O*: "And just as *The Story of O* [sic] shocked the sixties by speaking aloud what had only been whispered, *Exit to Eden* gives voice to the sexual secrets of this decade"). In a 1992 collection of women's erotica, *Slow Hand: Women Writing Erotica,* writer Lisa Tuttle's "Story of No" uses the *Story of O* to explore situations in which "no" may actually mean "yes." Tuttle apologizes in a brief note that follows her story for her failure to find a "new way of writing about sex"; she seems embarrassed to have relied on what she calls "literary inspiration"—suggesting that she knows the arguments, such as Andrea Dworkin's article on the novel, that assignations of literary value mask O's pornographic reality. Nevertheless, Tuttle's story is quite unabashed in its pursuit of the ambiguities of masochistic pleasure. Despite Réage's reluctance to be associated with her novel, the fact that *Story of O* was widely received as a literary masterpiece—perhaps most famously in Susan Sontag's 1967 essay, "The Pornographic Imagination"—contributes to the ability of other women writers of erotica to occupy the author position, even to appropriate and rewrite the text of a perceived canonical figure. Literary value is diffused throughout popular circles, increasing the access of both writers and readers.

Moving into the author position thus serves as a way for women to write things they wouldn't be able to write if the texts did not then circulate as literature; women are indeed domesticating pornography (broadly defined) by laying claim to a genre of sexually explicit writing that historically has been legitimated as erotica by male writers. Marjorie Agosín argues in the preface to *Pleasure in the Word: Erotic Writing by Latin American Women* that "eroticism, love and sensuality have been masculine reserves where intellectuals, historians, and sexologists wrote—and still write—about women's sexuality and eroticism, telling them how to think and feel and giving them recipes for making love" (Fernandez and Paravisini-Gebert, 15). The anthology allows women to "give shape to the interactions among the real, the imaginary, and the symbolic; [the writers] dare to describe pleasure, sensuality, and women's eroticism not as strangers to the language of love but as bold mistresses of their own words" (15). Beginning with the erotic poetry of the seventeenth-century Mexican nun Sor Juana Inés de la Cruz, the editors construct a tradition of Latin American women's erotica representing a wide variety of desires, expressed through genres including poetry, short stories, and excerpts of novels.

As is suggested by Agosín's preface, the question of expanding and revising the literary canon should not be perceived as simply an issue of representation of previously excluded writers who should now be considered worthy of study; rather, "the problem of what is called canon formation is best understood as a problem in the constitution and distribution of cultural capital, or more specifically, a problem of access to the means of literary production and consumption" (Guillory, ix). Interestingly, U.S. and British literary anthologies do not foreground this question of access to literary production, suggesting that women writers have begun to take for granted their ability to write sexually explicit materials that count as literature. The struggle, rather, is to challenge cultural stereotypes about female sexuality as portrayed in pornography. No mention is made of anything other than the attempt to define a feminine erotic language, as if language itself could transform women's lives. As Wintersen says, "Crucially, we need to remake the language of sex. Language is power" (xxiii). In its emphasis on women as a homogeneous category, united in sisterhood against a patriarchal history, these volumes elide other questions of access. In contrast, editors of the numerous anthologies linking sexual desire to race and ethnicity continually stress the connections between literary access, sexuality, race, and political empowerment. The editors of *Pleasure in the Word* connect the politics of representation to a broader politics of access; they describe the stories and authors in relation to the political situations of their countries in order to emphasize how sexual expression is shaped by structures of power that include not only sex and gender roles but also class and race struggles in the specific cultural contexts of many of the writers.

For people of color, gaining access to sexually explicit materials involves countering the stereotypes that intertwine sex and race in pornography and popular culture more generally. In race-identified anthologies for both men and women, such as *Under the Pomegranate Tree: The Best New Latino Erotica, Erotique Noire/Black Erotica,* and *On a Bed of*

Rice: An Asian-American Erotic Feast, the editors assert aesthetic value as a way to distance their work from these stereotypes; the specifically literary nature of the writings legitimates the work for skeptical members of the identity group who fear that writing on sexuality could reinforce popular stereotypes. For example, the editors of *Erotique Noire,* all academics, describe the uncomfortable reaction of many colleagues when they began soliciting contributions for the collection: "'You're compiling a collection of *what?*' Raised eyebrows all over the place. 'Is there any literary merit to erotica?' Pinched noses in the air. 'Do Black people actually *write* that?' Disbelief everywhere. And in two months—one submission" (xxiv). Contributions started to flow, however, after Charles Blockton, a bibliophile and collector of erotica, helped legitimate erotica because of his association with the literary world; thus began a process of recovering a history of black erotica as an "art form" (xxxi) that counters myths about the sexual proclivities of black women and men. To help in their selection process, the editors devised a list of seven criteria, many of which coincide with this one: "conform to high aesthetic standards" (xxxiii). Erotica from prominent writers like Alice Walker, Audre Lorde, Gloria Naylor, Dennis Brutus, and Ntozake Shange help legitimate the literary value of erotica by lesser-known writers, contributing to the conditions of access for readers turned off both by pornography's racist stereotyping and by other erotica's refusal to recognize the importance of articulating race and sexual desire.[7]

Identity erotica relies on the power of aesthetic value to create a kind of imagined community based on sexual desire and race. The process of building community is contingent on the aesthetic value's potential to circulate widely, outside the immediate community of writers and into potential communities who may not yet claim their identity, for example, lesbians and gays who have not come out. In this sense, identity erotica relies on the definition of literacy put forth by Guillory: "I will define literacy ... not simply as the capacity to read but as the systematic regulation of reading and writing, a complex social phenomenon corresponding to the following set of questions: Who reads? What do they read? How do they read? In what social and institutional circumstances? Who writes? In what social and institutional circumstances? For whom?" (18). Those are the questions addressed by Jewelle Gomez in her introduction to *Best Lesbian Erotica, 1997:* "This is a country where African Americans have fought to be allowed the right to read, where women of color are still routinely victimized by media misrepresentations, where our sexuality is used against us. The sexual stereotypes about women of color still abound and not just on television and movies but ... also in lesbian bars, businesses, and activist organizations" (Taormino, 15). Gomez asserts the power of writing to reshape these social and institutional conditions as it produces alternative communities: "writing is about community. Telling our stories ... to pass down history, to open up new paths for others" (15). It would seem that Gomez is indeed functioning as Bennett's moral exemplar—making claims about the power of literature to shape personal and political consciousness. However, the claim to aesthetic value here intersects with claims about other discourses, such as racism and homophobia; furthermore, aesthetic value is situated in relation to material conditions, such as where lesbians can get erotica. Thus, it becomes impossible to claim at this point that aesthetic discourse shapes a universal subject, cut through as it is with many other discourses.

The legitimation of women as writers of erotica contributes to, though does not exclusively define, the legitimation of women as consumers of erotica within the conditions of their everyday lives—that is to say, conditions that do not require them to see their sexual selves as hidden or shameful but rather as part of a community. Marcy Sheiner, editor of *Herotica 4*, makes this connection in her introduction: "Our stories are sold in national chain bookstores, promoted at international book fairs, and distributed through mainstream book clubs. The more we publish, read, and talk about what we think and feel concerning sex, the more the boundaries of our sexual imagination expand" (xii). Furthermore, the relationship is circular—more women publishing erotica prompts more readers, which, in turn, prompts more writing. Black Lace's Kerri Sharp estimates that she receives about twenty-five manuscripts a week from women wanting to be published under her imprint, which is part of Britain's Virgin Publishing. Black Lace, which by August 1997 had published a hundred books in its four-year history, restricts authorship to women; the books are marketed as "erotic fiction by women for women." In *Playgirl* magazine, readers are encouraged to become writers by contributing short erotic stories describing their fantasies to the "Readers' Fantasy Forum"; the fantasy of the month receives $100, all others $25. In a collection of these fantasies, *The Fifty Best Playgirl Fantasies*, contributing editor Charlotte Rose advises women that writing erotica will help them see the erotic nature of each aspect of their everyday lives, even a trip to the dentist (imagine a piece of dental floss tied around a taut nipple, gently pulled on during oral sex). Emphasize the details; "place the characters in a sexy locale," which "adds dimension to a story that may fall flat if it's *just* sex"; and develop the character's motivations, focusing on the woman's perspective, says Rose. With this advice, any woman can write erotica, using her own response to gauge if it's any good: "The more you come, the better it will sell. It reminds me of a title of a *Playgirl* article we once ran on erotic writing: 'Write It and *You Will Come*'" (Rose, 25). Writing, reading, and masturbation merge in one climactic moment.

In the history I have just traced, the domestication of erotica has been facilitated by the diffusion of aesthetic value throughout more popular spheres; I want to show next how the process can also work in reverse, illustrating further the complexities of aesthetic value, its simultaneous production in both literary and popular spheres. Susie Bright's status within popular spheres helped move her into a more canonical status; even in this process, however, "canonical" cannot be associated with narrowing circles of accessibility but rather with a democratization of the audience licensed to read literature. Furthermore, this "progression" does not involve a deadening of the potential for political critique; aesthetic value can converge with a progressive sexual politics and still help produce a popular circulation.

Susie Bright: From On Our Backs to Simon and Schuster

In 1984 Susie Bright and Debi Sundahl started the raunchy lesbian sex magazine *On Our Backs*; it was a takeoff on the politically correct Washington, D.C., feminist antiporn newspaper *off our backs*. *On Our Backs* was hardly a magazine that prided itself on aesthetic value or worried about making distinctions between erotica and pornography. As Bright remembers, "We would make fun of the word 'erotica.' The only time I used the word 'erotica' was if I thought people would be frightened of the word 'pornography,' like not saying a bad word in front of your grandmother."[8] We might say at this point that Bright occupied the position of author, but that such a function was largely irrelevant to a journal unconcerned with mainstream legitimacy acquired via aesthetic claims.

At the same time she edited *On Our Backs*, Bright was working at the Good Vibrations sex toys and bookstore in San Francisco, where she saw women consumers avidly buying books by Lonnie Barbach and Nancy Friday. "There's an incredible market for this, I told Joani [Blank, cofounder of Good Vibrations]," says Bright. "I would sell Barbach and Friday and say don't read the psychological stuff—it's just a guilt trip."

Good Vibrations is part of Open Enterprises, which also owns Down There Press, a small feminist publishing house that specializes in sexuality/self-help books. *Herotica* would become the first—and only—fictional series that Down There publishes as Bright and Blank began soliciting stories for an edition of women's erotica. Bright says, "[we] begged our friends to write something, and then we edited the hell out of it. We tried to create a voice and a feeling that hadn't existed to that point." Finding good fiction for *Herotica* was much more difficult than finding stuff to publish for *On Our Backs*, says Bright. "Lesbian fiction was easier to find than straight women's erotica. We didn't want anything apologetic or deferential; it had to have some imagination and verve, some confidence. That confidence didn't really exist in a widespread way. We tried to cultivate it as we acquired the work."

Bright here articulates the double legitimation on which the series draws: literary distinction (imagination and verve, facilitated by "editing the hell out of" the writing) and sexual identity (confidence in expressing desire). This emphasis on identity meant initially excluding some aspects of desire that Down There Press felt would inhibit women consumers from buying the series, such as expressions of sadistic or masochistic desire. The fact that such an exclusion is normative in a way that *On Our Backs* rebelled against did not escape Bright; however, she acknowledges now that the emphasis on a woman's way of writing that set itself apart from pornography was necessary in the late 1980s and is still necessary, for some women consumers, today. "Joani [Blank's] view was that we were trying to reach your typical woman who is isolated sexually. The very word 'pornography' is for men, against women [according to the general perceptions of porn]. Everything about porn is going to make women turn away from it. She was absolutely right, although that has changed somewhat since the late 1980s."

Beginning with the first *Herotica*, Bright used the platform of literary legitimacy to push for an expansion of what would constitute women's desire. In the introduction, she criticizes the tamer kinds of "erotica": "At its worst, erotica is a commercial term for vapid femininity, a Harlequin romance with a G-string." She also takes a cut at those feminists who she says have tried to dictate desire. Bright suggests that she would like to call the collection "women's pornography," but admits that this is a "contradiction in terms for many people, so convinced are they that pornography represents the darker, gutter side of lust" (3). As such, Bright—more than many erotica editors—acknowledges that "erotica" is a necessarily strategic term but one that does not rigidly define all female desire. In fact, Bright refuses to characterize as victims of false consciousness those women who like pornography; rather, she characterizes pleasure in male-produced porn as a kind of subversion, based on the kinds of materials women have had access to in the past. "Subverting men's fantasies and using them for our own arousal is the foundation of every woman's under-the-bed bookshelf" (3).

Yet even as this "right" should be protected, Bright upholds the need for women to write their own erotica and argues that there are real differences from male-authored porn: "The most obvious feature of women's erotic writing is the nature of the woman's arousal. Her path to orgasm, her anticipation, are front and center in each story" (4). Bright refers here, obviously, to the emphasis on the clitoris, a carryover from the masturbation discourse of the 1970s. This attention to the body is then connected to a particular way of writing: women's erotica's "uniqueness lies in the detail of our physical description, our vulnerability and the often confessional quality of our speech in this new territory" (3). As does much women's erotica, *Herotica* claims a particular set of textual features in order to establish its aesthetic distinctiveness; the editor thus sets up a relationship between text and reader that tries to ensure the reader's appropriate self-formation. The introduction is a strategic attempt to begin establishing women's erotica as an accessible, legitimate, yet inclusive genre. "With any luck," says Bright at the end of her introduction, "this anthology will find its place not only under the bed but on a few coffee tables and in a few libraries as well" (5).

Herotica made a major step toward the coffee table when it attracted the attention of Plume, a division of Penguin Books, which in 1990 bought the publishing rights for the second *Herotica*. The contract linking *Herotica* and Plume has continued throughout the fifth edition, which is expected out in 1997. Plume doesn't agree in advance to any volume. Rather, Down There Press collects the stories, signing contracts with writers and assuring them that if Plume rejects the collection, Down There Press will publish it. Then Down There negotiates a contract with Plume; as yet, Plume has rejected no collections. *Herotica*'s ability to claim aesthetic value was clearly crucial in attracting and maintaining Plume's interest, and it continues to be important as women's erotica carves out a niche that is distinct from the popular women's romance, another genre that has proliferated in terms of both women writers and readers. Deirdre Malane, the Plume editor in charge of the *Herotica* series, says that even though erotica has gone mainstream, it doesn't approach the sales of the romance and doesn't want to: "The romance is plot driven. There's not as much appreciation of the text itself. There's a lot of attention to the writing in the *Herotica* series."

Going mainstream (by way of these claims to both aesthetic value and identity politics) did not produce concessions from Bright or the series in terms of the explicitness of the stories. In fact, each *Herotica* anthology has become more explicit and experimental, seemingly less concerned with clearly defining a woman's desire even as the book continues to be marketed as reflecting and producing that desire. Plume packages each volume in identical format, using the same titles and subtitles for the second and third *Heroticas* as the first collection used and altering the subtitle of the fourth collection only slightly. The second, third, and fourth editions all have variations of the same artistic rendering of a woman. Thus, the material artifact of the book remains the same even as the content of the erotica expands to encompass more kinds of desire. "Brand identification is very important," says Malane, "so that somebody can recognize that they're going to get the same quality experience that they've gotten before."

Bright and the current editor, Marcy Sheiner, consistently—albeit strategically—uphold the need to distinguish women's erotica from pornography. However, a defining quality of women's erotica seems to be the impossibility of defining a particular desire, and, for Bright, lesbian erotica becomes the marker of this experimentation: "Lesbian erotica writers have grabbed gender-bending by the genitals, taken the whole spectrum of masculine/feminine eroticism by storm" (*Herotica 2*, xv). Much more than in the first edition of *Herotica*, the second volume includes stories that integrate elements of the *On Our Backs* philosophy—although that is certainly not their only moment of origin. Bright describes the stories that violate gender norms: "In 'The Journal,' a lesbian novelist sets her hand to gay male porn, while in 'There's More of You,' one woman lover reads to another from a heterosexual bodice ripper" (xv). Furthermore, straight women writers take on masculine roles; in "Taking Him on a Sunday Afternoon," the female protagonist explains how her male lover is worried about her smelling his anus:

I slip my hands inside the shorts and trace circles on his muscular cheeks, letting my thumb dip down to the space between the balls and buttocks, then sliding a finger up to explore the puckered mouth of his bum. He clamps up to prevent me from rubbing there, but aggression has risen in me and I press on, massaging a moistened finger at the entrance. It's slick there, and I can imagine the smell, which excites me; I know he's concerned about the smell, too—how I'll find him—and this excites me more. (19)

Bright and the *Herotica* series push at the boundaries of what constitutes women's erotica by expanding the sexual roles women characters are seen to occupy; yet the stories are said to nevertheless constitute a particular female language. Thus, even though *Herotica* is still characterized by a claim to establish a particular relationship between critic and reader, aesthetic discourse here intersects with discourses of difference, such as race, class, body type, age, and sexual preference, that undercut the attempt to tie a specific way of writing to women as a homogeneous category. Furthermore, even as *Herotica* draws on a language of literary pedigree, it prides itself on a democratic appeal to a popular yet complexly constituted audience. As such, the volumes make no claim to the status of a noncommodified form of high culture; rather, part of their value lies precisely in their unabashed appeal to a wide audience, albeit one that can appreciate the value of "literature."

Its reliance on the "erotica" label notwithstanding, the *Herotica* series increasingly flirts with its proximity to pornography. Sheiner begins her introduction to *Herotica 4* with the phrase "The first time I wrote a pornographic story," and although she goes on to make the familiar distinctions between erotica and pornography—erotica is more complex, more about context, better written, and so on—Sheiner also draws on certain aspects of pornography to define erotica. "Pornography is not polite—that's one of the reasons it's continually under attack," she says (xiv), suggesting that this *Herotica* has learned some lessons from pornography's forays into forbidden zones. Indeed, some of the stories actually raise the possibility that *Herotica* could contribute to women's access to *pornography* by demystifying it—domesticating porn, to return to the premise of this book. Thus, one of the conditions of everyday life that is increasingly referenced in *Herotica* stories is the antiporn movement; stories debunk the antisex messages of the antiporn movement and thus help women reconcile their desires for erotic fantasy with the messages they may have received that such fantasies place them in the realm of false consciousness. *Herotica 4*'s "Porn Flicks" describes how two lesbians watch a heterosexual hard-core porn video as part of a sex game. "Every time a woman gets something in her cunt, you get something in yours," says one lover to another. One woman, watching heterosexual porn for the first time, concludes that "women in this thing . . . weren't as bad as I feared . . . I decided that from their necks to their ankles, all the women in the film were damn hot, if only they'd lose the stupid shoes, makeup and the Farrah Fawcett hair" (Tan, 21).[9]

Another story in *Herotica 4* describes a woman's desire to be humiliated by two male lovers:

> They were being way too polite. I had to tell them to talk filthy to me. They started out pretty tame, but they ended up whispering things like "Come on, bitch, come for us. You know you want to. Let's hear you come. You like having two cocks in you, don't you? You like getting fucked by two dicks at once, you slut. Oh, you're such a little whore. What a sweet little snatch you have. Your ass is so hot and snug." (Reed, 13)

Later in the story, the protagonist, Madison, asks another lover to handcuff her and spank her, calling him "Daddy" as he brings her to orgasm. The story recalls *Story of O* in its unabashed focus on Madison's masochistic desires, portrayed in a manner that emphasizes her self-awareness of these desires: "Madison's most biting desire was thus her most humiliating secret. She dreamed that Jack would dissolve her identity, crush her faults, distill her down to a small pure lump he could slip into his pocket with his keys" (16).

What, exactly, has identity erotica facilitated? Are we returning to the claims made on behalf of erotica, including *Story of O*, by Susan Sontag in 1967, where erotic literature counted as literature precisely because of its ability to "plumb the depths of human consciousness," in a state removed from the specificities of identity? Bright indicates as much when she describes her transition from editor of *Herotica* to editor in 1993 and subsequent years of Simon and Schuster's literarily marketed annual compilation of *Best American Erotica*. Says Bright of her relief from the burdens of identity erotica, "I don't have to say 'I'm sorry, you're a man, you can't write about that.' Anyone can write about whatever they want—my only criteria is the quality of writing." As the erotica assumes at least a popularized form of canonical status, it seems to absorb the categories of identity that facilitated its inception and that helped bring erotica into the mainstream by proclaiming its benefits for particular identity groups.

Yet Bright also excerpts stories from identity erotica and cites their contributions in her introductions in a process that redefines "general" erotica as a genre more sensitive to the particularities of desire than the "universal" work of Miller and Lawrence. In her introduction to the first *BAE,* for example, Bright describes the notion of "femmchismo," quoting her own introduction to *Herotica 2*; she also reprints one of the *Herotica 2* stories. She cites the influence of gay men's erotica, especially the volumes edited by John Preston, and of lesbian erotica, citing specifically Pat Califia's fiction. Says Bright, "*BAE* wouldn't be here today if it weren't for the desktop revolution in lesbian and women's writing" (xix).

So has this lesbian sex radical, outspoken proponent of s/m, lost her cutting-edge status? Or has she succeeded in redefining the center, her own progressive sexual politics intact? Neither, I would say. Rather, we might say more accurately that Bright's career indicates the inadequacy of notions of margin and center to capture the complexities of the politics of erotica. Even though *BAE* foregrounds its literary transgressiveness in a seemingly universal manner, the stories conscientiously represent a spectrum of desires that references all identity groups: straight, gay, lesbian, bisexual, and within those categories, vanilla and sadomasochistic desires, a mix of ages, races, and so forth. The writing celebrates not universality, recalling Sontag, but rather the proliferation of desires tied to many different aspects of identity.

As such, identity erotica enters the "center" both to redefine it and to be redefined itself; a story previously published in a gay zine and reprinted in *BAE* does not lose its radical edge but rather circulates differently, facilitated both by aesthetic claims, gay identity claims, and the demands of the marketplace in bookstores like Barnes and Noble. Identified as one of the most well-written erotic short stories of the year, it acquires a kind of aesthetic value that facilitates a different kind of circulation, among different readers, or among similar readers but with a different cachet. My central point here is this: because it is impossible to clearly define mainstream and center, we would do better not to focus on the transgressiveness of desire but rather to ask how texts circulate in a manner that makes them more or less accessible to different groups of readers. In the case of Bright's movement from the *Herotica* series to the more "literary" *Best American Erotica*, we can say that her recognized status as an editor of popular women's erotica and radical sex spokeswoman facilitated her movement into a more specifically literary category. Although Bright says she feels freed from the restrictions of identity politics and can now focus purely on the aesthetic value of the texts, the collections emphasize, rather, that identity politics has infused aesthetic discourse, making them mutually (re)defining discourses of value.

Superstores and Aesthetic Value

Aesthetic value is further produced at the sites where the erotica is sold; as an example of this production, I turn to the superstore chains Barnes and Noble, which with $1.35 billion in sales in 1995 was the leading book retailer in the country, and Borders, which was second, with $683.5 million.[10] I have been arguing that the writing and publishing of erotica produce an aesthetic value that both reproduces certain class associations of a literary pedigree and rearticulates those in a more democratic and accessible fashion. The bookstore chains further represent this argument, which is well stated by John Frow: "There is no longer a stable hierarchy of value (even an inverted one) running from 'high' to 'low' culture ... 'high' and 'low' culture can no longer, if they ever could, be neatly correlated with a hierarchy of social classes" (1).

The superstores distance themselves from the shopping mall, both geographically and in terms of the internal environment they try to create. The non-mall location seems to be a strategy to recover a bit of the public coffeehouse appeal, to keep one foot in the past of literary pedigree, standing apart from the crass commercialism of the shopping mall. Here is a place where people with time to indulge their intellects can browse and lounge in comfortable overstuffed chairs. In Champaign, for example, both stores are located within a mile of each other, just off Interstate 74, in an area populated by various megastores and fast food restaurants: Target, Pier I, McDonald's, Taco Bell. Even as they distance themselves from the mall mentality, the superstores strive for accessibility and convenience, locating themselves within easy reach of the tasks that might be included in a day of errand running. Both stores have cafés that similarly suggest a nostalgia for a time when reading literature was considered an indicator of bohemian intellect, even though each store stresses its multimedia availability—CDs, computer software, books on cassettes, and so on. Barnes and Noble is more nostalgic: its Starbucks cafe is decorated by artistic renderings of the likes of Virginia Woolf, T. S. Eliot, and James

Joyce; the plastic bags used for purchases bear likenesses of literary canonical figures. In contrast, Borders' café is decorated with drawings and paintings—artsy but not specifically striving for the highbrow literary appeal.

There are further indications of the complexity of cultural value. As you enter Barnes and Noble, a large display greets you: hardcover books that make the *New York Times* best-seller list, a symbol of cultural capital that seems to suggest limited access, are sold at a 30 percent discount, thus broadening access (Borders has a similar discount policy). The sense of cosmopolitanism offered by a large magazine and newspaper section is offset by regular appearances at both stores of local artists, musicians, and authors designed to create the impression that the superstore is part of the community. Vying for the family values vote, the Champaign Barnes and Noble announced in May 1997 that it was joining *Parenting* magazine to launch "Family First," a "nationwide initiative designed to raise awareness of and funds for family issues." In conjunction with this effort, Barnes and Noble sponsored "How to Read with Your Children," led by a woman who began her fifty-year teaching career in a one-room schoolhouse in Cullom, Illinois. Another family event featured author Susan Post talking about her book *Hiking Illinois* and explaining why hiking is "one of the most enjoyable activities a family can participate in."

There's another indication that Barnes and Noble may be going for the more conservative consumer: if you are looking for the erotica section (and are too shy to ask), you will not find it. The Champaign manager says there is no erotica section because there has been no specific demand for it—a tautology that emphasizes the importance of display to access. The erotica is located either in the literary anthology section or the gay and lesbian fiction section, which is in an entirely different part of the store. In contrast, Borders has a rather large erotica selection—roughly four hundred volumes—in a single section specifically called "Erotica," directly next to the literature shelves. This difference raises an interesting question about the policies of display and access. It may be harder to find erotica at Barnes and Noble, but once you find it, is it easier to skim the pages, looking for the good stuff, without being noticed than it is at Borders? In either store, the comfortable chairs invite a long perusal of a book that does not proclaim too loudly its status as sexually explicit. In fact, at Barnes and Noble, the anthology section is located just next to the children's section, a juxtaposition that is clearly frowned upon in relation to visual pornography: zoning regulations in many cities have stipulated that adult video stores be sufficiently distanced from schools, churches, and residential areas.

You will find all kinds of erotica in both stores, both the highly literary stuff published by major houses and the more alternative stuff published by independent houses, such as two volumes by the Kensington Ladies' Erotica Society—a group of middle-aged women in San Francisco whose editions were published in the late 1980s by Ten Speed Press. The independent presses are represented in both stores, perhaps even more at Borders: Masquerade Books, with its Rosebud imprint of specifically lesbian erotica; Cleis Press of Pittsburgh, which also specializes in lesbian and gay erotica; Carroll and Graf, which has published a large number of Victorian and pseudo-Victorian erotic texts. The chains can afford to stock the alternative texts, even those with relatively small expected sales, in part because they buy most texts in such huge quantities that they get considerable discounts. Ironically, alternative bookstores that cannot afford to buy in such large quantities may have to be more selective about which "alternative" books they buy, since they do not attract such a wide range or quantity of consumers. The superstores' contribution to erotic accessibility must be measured against its potential for contributing to the closure of smaller, independently owned bookstores, many of which have explicitly marked erotica sections. Although the main alternative, locally owned bookstore in Champaign that stocks erotica, Pages for All Ages, is surviving, local bookstores in other locations have closed when the superstores have opened.[11]

Accessibility is also a question of cost. The average price of an anthology of erotica is perhaps thirteen dollars; a Black Lace novel at Borders costs about six dollars, roughly the price of renting an adult video. The book will travel more easily than an adult video, of course, especially at Barnes and Noble, where the plastic bag imprinted with the image of a canonical literary author offers the final stamp of cultural capital. Returning home with a volume of erotica, a woman can feel fairly comfortable leaving it out—there are no pictures, and there is a relative sublimation of sex to literature that occurs in the title, packaging, and introduction to each volume if not the stories. Publishers recognize the importance of packaging to sales; in reader surveys reprinted at the back of each novel, Black Lace asks readers how they acquired their copy (personal purchase, borrowed, or bought by a partner) and whether the cover of the book is too explicit or about right or not explicit enough in terms of their level of embarrassment in purchasing the book. Also, the survey asks, "Would you read a Black Lace book in a public place—on a train for instance?" The possibility exists, thus, that women might read erotica on their paths between home and work, home and leisure activities, home and child care centers. There is nothing essentially liberatory in this reading of erotica in public, or between private and public spaces, for it might indicate that women have very little time for their own pleasures. It does indicate, however, that the erotic spaces within the home may be expanded by contact with more public spaces, and vice versa.

Unfortunately, there is no way of gauging exactly how many women read erotica in their homes; neither publishing companies nor bookstores will release sales or demographic figures. My argument on the widespread accessibility of women's erotica posits a coming together of economic capital and cultural capital: erotica represents a means for accumulating cultural capital—a kind of literary authenticity—that does not require a large amount of economic capital and thus does not exclude working-class women. At the same time, reading is itself a practice dependent on institutional privileges, and a more detailed study of this question would need to address questions of educational access and broader issues of literacy in the United States.[12]

We can at least say that women are the (sometimes homogeneous) class targeted most intensely by major publishing houses; roughly three-fifths of the American reading public is composed of women under fifty. Book club fliers distributed by the major publishing houses help legitimate reading as an activity congruent with women's everyday routines; furthermore, by locating the image of women within the home, often performing traditional tasks such as cooking, caring for children, and gardening, they support dominant conceptions of women's roles. However, by valorizing women's rights to the leisure activity of reading, they revise the expectation of uninterrupted domestic labor. "Go right to the top of the bestseller list—without leaving home!" proclaims a Doubleday advertisement flier for its book club. The flier contains only images of *women* reading; underneath one such photo, the caption reads, "One less errand to run. One less trip into town. There's nothing like the luxury of escaping with a best seller you've chosen from your own home." The selection of books represents the seemingly heterogeneous pleasures of an audience that is represented largely as white middle-class women: romantic mysteries, romance novels, Stephen King thrillers, beauty and diet advice manuals, career and finance books, home and garden texts, his-

Figure 1. Doubleday's book club fliers appeal to women as readers within the space of the home.

tory, and dictionaries. Women are shown lounging on couches, applying makeup, working on computers, buying groceries, serving a meal to children, and soaking in a bubblebath.

The Doubleday flier also includes a full page of books on sex and relationships. These include some predictable heterosexual texts, such as John Gray's *Mars and Venus in Love*, Graham Masterton's *203 Ways to Drive a Man Wild in Bed* and *How to Make His Wildest Dreams Come True* as well as Susie Bright's *Best American Erotica*. Each of the volumes on this page contains variations of the warning "Explicit sex, language and subject matter"; however, they are clearly legitimated by their inclusion in the overall catalog as texts that can be integrated into women's everyday routines. Furthermore, the images in the flier seem to mildly undercut the heterosexual expectation: not a single image includes a woman with a man, although one image shows two women friends conversing and several show women with children. Reading is often a solitary activity, but one that facilitates your interaction with other women and with children.

The book club fliers support the notion that women deserve to read as a break from everyday routines—reading is an "escape" from these routines, yet it keeps women located within the space of the home, serving to validate women's labor and recognize the need for relief from it at the same time. In this sense, reading represents a form of somewhat subversive agency, as Janice Radway describes in her study of women romance readers. These readers described how the very act of reading in isolation angered their husbands, who resented the fact that their wives chose to read alone rather than watch television with them. For these women, reading represented an escape from daily routines and even the particularities of their bodies—through identification with the glamorous heroines of the romances. Yet when "escape" involves sexual fantasy and masturbation through the reading of erotica—which relies more on horny heroines with ordinary bodies than on glamorous ones—reading carries an extra charge, one with the potential for momentarily claiming material spaces in the home as sites of embodied pleasure.

Aesthetic Value and "Responsible Publishing"

In her 1967 essay, "The Pornographic Imagination," Susan Sontag made an influential argument about the distinction between literary "pornography" and baser forms of pornography; she says that the latter "disdains fully formed persons . . . and reports only the motiveless tireless transactions of depersonalized organs" (37–38). In contrast, literary pornograpy, such as Réage's *Story of O,* shows the complex development of character. She says, for example, that O's journey into sexual slavery is not a passive journey of victimization and degradation but rather a "quest" whose goal is the "transcendence of personality" (55). Sontag argues that truly literary pornography qualifies as such because it refuses to reconcile reality and fantasy and rather drives a wedge between the sexual psyche and the healthy person.

Contemporary women's erotica retains the emphasis on plot and complexity in distinguishing itself from pornography; however, rather than arguing that such qualities work *against* a reconciliation of fantasy and reality, editors and writers are much more likely to deploy these literary characteristics to show that sex and everyday life can indeed be reconciled—in part through the complex portrayal of women's lives. Women's erotica takes up where the masturbation discourse of the 1970s left off, finding ways to make clitoral orgasm and fantasies mesh with the other elements of women's identities within their everyday routines. Thus, literary qualities are invoked not for their intrinsic aesthetic value—as Bennett would argue is necessarily the case with aesthetic claims—but rather for their usefulness in creating a context in which to situate sex. This is not to say, however, that women's erotica avoids the kind of prescriptiveness based on interpretation to which Bennett, Hunter, and Grossberg object; in fact, women's erotica is in many ways much more engaged in making value claims about how readers should integrate sex and everyday life than is pornography, with its rather timeless, placeless world of multiple sexual configurations. But given the history of pornography's greater access to men, as I describe in chapter 1, it behooves us not to condemn women's erotica for attempting to reconcile fantasy and reality through the shaping of consciousness, but rather to understand why such an attempt is a critical component of legitimating women's consumption of sexually explicit materials.

The popular British line of women's erotic novels provides a good example of the politics of access as it is produced by the perceived need to reconcile fantasy and reality. Black Lace editor Kerri Sharp says the series is the product of "responsible publishing," which involves a negotiation between the liberatory realm of the sexual imagination and the regulatory realm of women's rights.[13] For example, Black Lace guidelines for au-

Figure 2. Black Lace novels often feature strong female protagonists who are looking for ways to express their masochistic desires.

thors state that "all the activities should be between mutually consenting adults—no matter what's happening, how kinky, or how depraved, it must be clear that the character is enjoying it, that it's being done with her consent." Yet Sharp also opposes the notion that fantasy should be dictated by feminist criticisms of pornography: "A lot of feminist criticism of explicit works of erotica has been based on the old chestnut that it's demeaning to women. That's an unreconstructed view. It also denies the marvelous machine that is the human imagination. Whatever may be politically correct in real life, you can't really apply to fantasy." Sharp thus tries to have her cake and eat it too—to hold up Black Lace as a series that does not police the imagination and yet to say as well that they are "responsible" publishers, in other words, not anything goes. Finding the balance between these two positions is the key to mainstream distribution. Says Sharp, "We want to be seen as responsible publishers, appealing to a mass market. There are other imprints which explore the extremes. We want to be sold in W. H. Smith [the large British book chain]."

Black Lace conducts reader surveys that help it write the author guidelines and thus become the basis for what constitutes a sort of national conception of the appropriate range of female fantasies. At the end of each novel is a reader survey, which includes questions about what kinds of fantasies the readers most desire. For example, readers are asked to specify their ideal Black Lace heroine and given a choice of fourteen characteristics, including such traits as "dominant," "submissive," "glamorous," "ordinary," "bisexual," "kinky," and "naive." A similar question concerns the male character, with traits listed including "caring," "cruel," "sexually dominant," and "sexually submissive." Sharp says that this research shows that a majority of women want sexually dominant but caring male characters: "The fantasy male is someone who knows what you want without you having to ask for it. It's nice to give up responsibility in fantasy. It's purely sexual." But it's not "purely sexual" in many of the novels; rather, authors attempt to integrate the sexual with the everyday in a manner that retains the charge of the sexual without making it seem completely unrealistic within the everyday lives of women readers. The novels clearly struggle with the issue of how even the partial reconciliation of fantasy with everyday life might produce a regulation of desires that would seem to work against the appeal of reading erotica—as an escape into what might be experienced as an unregulated realm of fantasy.[14]

This negotiation between fantasy and reality becomes particularly complicated given the fact that many women readers of erotica turn to this fictional genre for *information* about sex, indicating the historical investment in the sexological discourse of the 1970s. For example, what are the writers' responsibilities in terms of representing safer sex practices if indeed the erotica represents a primary source of information about sex? Very few stories represent condoms or other practices of safer sex, an elision that suggests that women writers may be minimizing the risks of HIV infection, perhaps rationalizing the elision by falling back on the claim to be writing fantasy, a genre purportedly distinct from the discourse of sex education. Black Lace novels, for example, print this reminder at the beginning of each text: "Black Lace novels are sexual fantasies. In real life, make sure you practise safe sex." Gabriele Griffin addresses this conflict as it occurs in lesbian erotica in "Safe and Sexy? Lesbian Erotica in the Age of AIDS," in which she criticizes Pat Califia and the Sheba Collective for not going to greater lengths to eroticize safer sex. Basing her argument on her belief that lesbian erotica is often used by readers who are looking for information about lesbian sex, Griffin suggests that lesbian writers incorporate safer sex practices within the narratives rather than ignoring the issue completely or setting it off in the introduction or conclusion, as does the Sheba Collective in its volume *Serious Pleasure*. The editors include their notes on safer sex in part to justify the fact that none of the contributions reference safer sex practices: "*Serious Pleasure* is in no way a lesbian sex manual. In the same way that fantasy is no indication necessarily of what any individual will do in 'real life,' neither are the stories in *Serious Pleasure* what either the authors or the readers necessarily 'do.' Safer sex is a case in point" (11). Yet in their next statement the editors contradict their belief in this gap between reality and fantasy: "Do lesbians in general still believe that AIDS is not a significant reality for them in terms of sexual transmission? We would guess that this is so and may be the primary reason for the absence of any mention of safer sex in these stories" (12). In fact, then, the lack of reference to AIDS is an indication of a "real" problem, not a conscious decision to bracket practices of safer sex in the interest of writing better fantasy material.

The incorporation of safer sex into erotica is impeded by the fact that much lesbian erotica relies on the conventions of romance, which "demand the construction of an object of love/desire which is perfect in a variety of ways, including perfectly healthy," argues Griffin (151). Griffin thus confronts a seemingly irresolvable conflict: which "reality" should lesbian erotica attempt to reconcile with fantasy? The reality that lesbians are susceptible to AIDS and should practice safer sex? Or the reality that counters homophobic refusals to acknowledge lesbians in romantic, coupled relationships? For heterosexual women as well, condoms seem to represent an interruption of the romantic ambience that erotica is supposed to create as a context for sex. A *Redbook* review of a Candida Royalle Femme Productions video, *Sensual Escape,* which shows a couple using a condom, has this to say about condom representation: "they're kissing, they're undressing, they're licking, they're—oh no! He's reaching for a condom. We decide it's as much a mood killer to watch as it is to experience." Although the reviewer wants to distinguish fantasy from reality, she inadvertently connects them, indicating that she doesn't like to use condoms in "real" life and neither does she want to have fantasies about them.

Some women's erotica remains very much invested in linking fantasy to the reality of romance, defined as women's need to connect sex to emotional security and contrasted, again, to men's desires for a quick orgasm—we see here, again, one of the dichotomies distinguishing erotica (the purely emotional) from pornography (the purely physical). Lonnie Barbach makes this distinction, for example, in *The Erotic Edge: Twenty-Two Erotic Stories for Couples* when she describes the differences in how men and women view affairs. For women, she says, "an affair is more than a sexual liaison. The emotional relationship is as important as the sexual one, and concerns about consequences are addressed from the beginning" (140). In contrast, "Men are more able to isolate the sexual and emotional aspects of a relationship and create an encounter that is based entirely on sex" (140). The one-night stand, says Barbach, "is a predominantly male theme" (142). The couples' porn discussed in chapter 5 relies, to varying degrees, on this rather stereotypical notion of romance based on traditional gendered roles. However, much contemporary erotica redefines romance through its emphasis on raw sex from the woman's point of view; it may still be invested in portraying coupled sex (as opposed, for example, to the group sex scenes common in porn), but it's sex rather than love that conquers all, with the clitoris leading the way.

Romance is being redefined in the late twentieth century by feminism and the gay and lesbian rights movements, as the editors and contributors in *Romance Revisited* argue. Editors Jackie Stacey and Lynne Pearce emphasize the instability and diversity of articulations of romance, but also argue for a "recognisable set of concepts which suggest that many women no longer accept their place within classic narrative trajectories (seeking to challenge men, transgressing the taboos of interracial relationships or exploring the possibilities of 'deviant' desires)" (36). Romance has come to be recognized as a cultural construction, capable of being altered, not a biologically inevitable state. Defining this new kind of "postmodern romance," Stacey and Pearce say,

> If classic romance can be characterised as the quest for love delayed by a series of obstacles which desire must overcome, then postmodern romance might be conceptualised as the condition in which romance itself has become *the obstacle* which the desirable love relationship must overcome; surely everyone knows too much these days really to expect romance to last and has no-one to blame but themselves if they thought otherwise. Thus, the knowledge (and yet the disavowal) of the impossibility of "true romance" can both be called upon with equal conviction in a culture in which the rhetoric of individual rights vies with that of self-sacrifice. (37)

Thus, one of the conditions of everyday life that women's erotica must deal with is the desire for yet the skepticism of romantic love. This dilemma confronts many of the women in the adult cable series *Red Shoe Diaries* that I analyze in chapter 6. Similarly, many of the women protagonists in the Black Lace novels are independent career women for whom romance is very much of a struggle; having gained their autonomy through their public sphere activities, they are redefining their personal relationships in a similarly independent manner. Yet they are also very nostalgic for a time when romance did rely on more clearly gendered roles. In a common strategy for representing this conflict between reality and fantasy, several Black Lace authors turn to representations of female masochistic desire. In several of their novels, integrating the erotic with the everyday means showing how the everyday world of work and ambition has made it hard for women to feel they can truly "be themselves" in sex, which means relinquishing control and enjoying the skills of a confident, sometimes even sadistic lover. Consider the Black Lace catalog blurb for *Wicked Work* by Pamela Kyke: "At 28, Suzie Carlton is at the height of her journalistic career. She has status, money, and power. What she doesn't have is a masterful partner who will allow her to realise the true extent of her fantasies. How will she reconcile the demands of her job with her sexual needs?" Another Black Lace novel, Frederica Alleyn's work *The Bracelet,* provides an apt illustration of this negotiation.

In what appears to be another contemporary rewriting of *Story of O*, *The Bracelet* tells the story of Kristina Masterton, a successful twenty-six-year-old literary agent who has gotten bored with her four-year relationship with Ben, an advertising copywriter who faithfully honors Kristina's feminist sentiments about what constitutes a good relationship. Through her journalist friend Jacqueline, Kristina learns about a secret bondage group called the Society, composed of wealthy men who want to dominate successful career women. Kristina decides she wants her friend Jacqueline, who has been "chosen" by a diamond trader, to put her name up for membership, and she is eventually chosen by a famous psychologist, Dr. Tarquin Rashid. When they are together, Kristina agrees to wear a bracelet, signifying membership in the Society and her willingness to do whatever Rashid commands.

Like O in *Story of O*, who is a successful photographer, both Kristina and, to a lesser degree, Jacqueline agonize over their desires to be dominated; unlike O, however, whose struggles are mainly internal and not articulated to her career, the women in *The Bracelet* couch their conflicts in terms of feminism and their careers. For example, Kristina initially struggles to understand why Jacqueline joined the Society: "But you're a modern, liberated woman," protests Kristina. "What's the point of women's new-found freedom if you end up getting some blond-haired South African hunk to tie you up and use you for his own pleasure? Don't you think you're rather letting the side down?" Jacqueline answers, "Haven't you stopped to think that perhaps because we're successful career women we've trapped ourselves in a life where we're always in control? Don't you long for someone else to make a decision for you?" Kristina answers, "Of course I do!" Jacqueline responds, "And so do a lot of other highly qualified, intelligent, high-profile women. This society . . . is intended for people like us. The 'have-it-all' women who find they haven't got it all" (30).

Kristina finds herself increasingly attracted to Tarquin; she breaks up with her partner, Ben, and becomes obsessed with Tarquin, even letting her career slide in order to fulfill her insatiable desires to be had by her new lover. The story stresses Kristina's consent to the various forms of humiliation and bondage; she has only to remove the bracelet and the role playing stops (O also consents but is increasingly "marked" in ways that are not easily removed, including genital piercing and branding). Tarquin orders Kristina to give him a blow job while attending the opera as a competitor of hers in the publishing industry watches; she consents. There are several bondage and whipping scenes, and one interrogation scene where Kristina is "punished" in various ways each time she misses an answer to Tarquin's quiz on Shakespeare's plays.

The novel refrains from either endorsing Kristina's decisions or condemning them; rather, it presents her desires as a struggle about what it means to be "in control" of your sexual life as it relates to the rest of your life. At times, Kristina seems to be losing control of her career: "She was in truth a prisoner of the bracelet, forever waiting for the call that would summon her to escape and ecstasy" (120). Yet the struggle to determine the relationship between fantasy and reality is a constructive one for Kristina, with her ability to completely relinquish control in sex presented, eventually, as the ultimate marker of her self-confidence and autonomy. She pursues what she wants and gets it: "I wanted a man who wasn't afraid of my success, who was able to take the lead in bed and then step out of my life and let me take the lead in all other respects" (218). This is, indeed, what Kristina gets: she and Tarquin decide they want to live together, even as Kristina wins a prestigious award from the Publisher's Association. Yet the novel also resists devolving into monogamous romance: after six months, Kristina realizes that although she still wants to stay with Tarquin, boredom is beginning to seep into their relationship. She suggests that they renew their membership in the Society, this time with a female client of hers whom she thinks Tarquin will find attractive. As they ponder the *ménage à trois*, their passion is rekindled and Kristina has "one mind-shattering climax after another" (267). At the end, Kristina does "have it all," with fulfillment presented as a high-powered career, a dominant but caring man, and the promise of new sexual partners within the "security" of a relationship. This novel appears quite representative of the Black Lace line's reluctance to simplistically link sex with romance, in the process redefining the place of sex within coupled relationships.

In the competition between "the rhetoric of individual rights" and that of "self-sacrifice" to which Stacey and Pearce refer above, the Black Lace protagonist most certainly chooses individual rights. She is in many ways the same "New Woman" to whom much contemporary consumer culture appeals. She is the woman Hillary Radner describes in *Shopping Around: Feminine Culture and the Pursuit of Pleasure* as the unabashedly narcissistic professional woman. This "New Woman" is hailed by feminine cultural texts as a consumer who shops not to fulfill her husband's pleasure but as a means to "externalize her self-worth as properly her own.... The woman as subject is invited to take control of the process whereby she represents herself. At the same time, she is constantly reminded that she must submit to a regime that externalizes figurability through product usage" (64). The New Woman's struggle over the relationship between fantasy and reality is how to have it all—both the consumerist lifestyle in which professional careers guarantee endless pleasures and the ideal sexual relationship, in which a nostalgia for more clearly gendered times can be played out in the "privacy" of one's home. This is, in fact, the woman featured in the United States' most profitable lingerie catalog, Victoria's Secret, and it is to her that I now turn.

4

The New Victorians

Lingerie in the Private Sphere

Sexuality in Victorian England, Foucault tells us, was "carefully confined" within the home, and the home was the site of reproduction, where the "couple imposed itself as model, enforced the norm, safeguarded the truth, and reserved the right to speak while retaining the principle of secrecy" (*History*, 3). There seems to be a remarkable nostalgia for this conception of Victorian England in the 1980s and 1990s, a harking back to a time when sex was more domestic in the contained sense of that word, when boundaries between public and private were more clearly defined, and where certain rules of class and etiquette were more rigidly enforced. Such boundaries make it easier to claim to be keeping a secret—all the while, as Foucault says, participating in the production of ever more rules for maintaining secrecy.

True to the precept of proliferation, the concept of such a Victorian period has generated even more claims about sexuality in the 1990s. Antifeminists like Katie Roiphe, Camille Paglia, and Rene Denfeld accuse a seemingly homogeneous group of feminists of Victorian prudishness. In her book *The New Victorians: A Young Woman's Challenge to the Old Feminist Order*, Denfeld says feminists have "embarked on a moral and spiritual crusade that would take us back to a time worse than our mother's day—back to the nineteenth-century values of sexual morality, spiritual purity, and political helplessness. . . . This is the New Victorianism. And this is why women of my generation are abandoning the women's movement" (10–11). Simultaneously, right-wing conservatives like Charles Murray and William Bennett would like to see us return to "Victorian values," implicitly arguing that feminism, among other liberal forces, has been responsible for the freeing of female sexuality, which has caused problems such as welfare and "illegitimacy." The cloistered couple in the procreative bedroom appeals strongly to this camp, as I explore more in the next chapter. The fascination with Victorian culture has also manifested itself in film: the last two decades have seen an unprecedented number of films set in Victorian times, including screenplays based on Victorian novels, such as *Jane Eyre, The Age of Innocence, Howards End*, and *Little Women*. Garrett Stewart says that such films "concentrate on that zone of domesticity, and that culture of privacy, which the Victorian novel helped both to invent and to advertise" (153–54). As such, they "advert to a world freer than ours from siege by body or machine, less plagued, on either side, by sexual threat or advanced technological encroachment" (154). The films unite the audience in a kind of nostalgic fondness for the "sureties of the Victorian era, especially for the period's different understanding of the erotic body and its social commerce" (154). The contradiction between the explicit sexual representations in some films and the sexual prudishness of the Victorian films is really not a contradiction, says Stewart: "Each media form is preoccupied with corporeality, with the weight and curve of the flesh, whether intriguingly draped or tantalizingly unwrapped. Underwear that barely covers the body and gowns that scarcely expose it operate equally as fetishistic displacements" (167). He notes the ironies of the multiplex couplings: *Sliver* showing next to *The Age of Innocence, Basic Instinct* alongside *Howards End, Disclosure* with *Little Women*.

The film couplings resemble in some ways the odd mix of volumes in the erotica section at many bookstores: a First Ballantine Book's reprinting of the famous Victorian pornography magazine *The Pearl* next to *Herotica 3*, a Carroll and Graf reprinting of the pornography memoirs of a Victorian gentleman, *My Secret Life*, next to *The Best Lesbian Erotica, 1997*. The very accessibility of the contemporary erotica helps produce a desire for a time when sex was indeed more private, when there were more rules to follow, when pornography circulated underground, almost exclusively among upper-class men. Victorian pornography violated the rules of sexual morality in its time; it was easy to be naughty and still share your secret with a community of like-minded readers who garnered public respect. Contemporary reprintings of Victorian erotica offer the pretenses of secrecy, privilege, and inaccessibility within the open venues of a Borders bookstore.

There is perhaps no better example of a nostalgia for a more contained body and a more "secret" sexuality within the trappings of Victorian, imperialist England that is, all the while, articulated through contemporary notions of sexuality and advertising than the Victoria's Secret lingerie catalog. Throughout its twenty-year history, the company, which is owned by the huge apparel conglomerate the Limited, has been careful to sell its sexuality under the guise of privacy.[1] It's a "secret," consumed within the privacy of one's home, whose products are delivered to one's doorsteps in the name of a model, Victoria, whose identity is shrouded in mystery.[2] VS legitimates itself through its insistence that lingerie is a decorous product, in the Victorian tradition rather than in the mold of that other, "trashy" lingerie mail-order catalog, Frederick's of Hollywood, which connects itself to a public place of stardom and glitz. This deployment of Victorian trappings in the interest of selling women lingerie has made the company the object of some feminist criticism; in her widely read *Backlash: The Undeclared War against American Women*, Susan Faludi argues that Victoria's Secret participates in the attempt to recontain women's advances by locating them within a setting of demure, Victorian femininity and by reinstating a fascination with restrictive undergarments. Are underwire push-up bras all that different from tightly laced corsets and rear bustles? Says Faludi, "In every backlash, the fashion industry has produced punitively restrictive clothing and the fashion press has demanded that women wear them" (173).

One can certainly find in Victoria's Secret the feminine images Faludi describes: a model wearing a delicate, floral-patterned chemise and another in a "sweet, feminine, charming cotton bustier." The popularity of the company and other Victorian enterprises would seem to testify to the successes of the conservative definition of domestication, in which the private sphere is reasserted in a manner that generally isolates it from public sites in the interest of restricting women's mobility. However, Victoria's Secret and the sale and consumption of lingerie more generally also illustrate the contradictions and gaps in the attempts to reassert a bounded private sphere; for VS, the emphasis on privacy is undercut by the appeal to women as consumers in pursuit of their own pleasures— versions of the New Woman introduced in the previous chapter. On the page following the "charming cotton bustier," the sultry supermodel Stephanie Seymour flaunts a revealing lace bodystocking, buttocks thrusting out in a hardly demure manner. Several pages later, a model in a red jacket and skirt strides down a sidewalk, her cellular phone and briefcase indicating her professional status. Then a woman lounges in cotton leggings and a sweatshirt; the catalog is alternately practical (cotton panties, four for $20) and luxurious ("Experience the sheer luxury of Victoria's Secret lingerie," over an image of sheer bras and panties). Faludi's argument does not begin to capture the contradictory brand of femininity Victoria's Secret represents, or why it is so profitable right now: Victoria's Secret stores and the catalog operation grossed $1.8 billion in 1994; the company plans to expand from about six hundred stores to a thousand, adding about fifty stores a year, according to a 1995 article in *Forbes*.[3] Appealing to the independent, mobile woman, the VS catalog references places—the workplace, sites of leisure and exercise, and various rooms in the home—and thus shows a relationship between the erotic and the everyday that suggests a more fluid kind of domestication than pure Victorian backlash. A new advertising campaign for a line of sheer bras and panties called "Angels" in spring 1997 self-reflexively foregrounds this play of private and public, good girl and bad. "Good angels go to heaven," says the catalog cover, "Victoria's Secret angels go everywhere." True to the ad's suggestion of mobility, the lingerie-clad, cavorting angels appeared in a television commercial, the first time the company has advertised on that medium.

Into this contradictory mix we must add the fact that so many people, both women and men, receive the VS catalogs in the mail weekly that is has come to function as a kind of free soft-core porn available for domestic use independently of the ordering of merchandise. To bring together the (soft-core) pornographic with the everyday in a text that appeals to women as consumers suggests a certain potential for deconstructing the private-public division that has worked, as many feminists have documented, to contain female sexuality within a traditional definition of home. It is perhaps because the danger for this deconstruction exists that Victoria's Secret posits itself as upholding this boundary; the company's insistence on its private, intimate image functions to maintain a proper kind of femininity that distinguishes itself from pornography even as the catalog builds its profits on its pornographic overtones. The company rhetoric, not surprisingly, does its best to distance itself from the male gaze, the presumed defining quality of heterosexual porn. As public relations official Stacie McCall told me in an interview, "Our main appeal is for women. We are not for men to look at but for women to feel good about themselves." In the 1980s, she says, the company decided to stop representing men in boxer shorts alongside women in lingerie because of consumer complaints that such images hinted too strongly of porn. One can only wonder how company officials felt when Seymour posed for *Playboy* in 1993 (were they secretly delighted?). In fact, *Playboy* sold Seymour's image almost exclusively through her VS reputation; reprinting covers of VS on which Seymour appeared, the magazine explained, "So

Figure 3. Victoria's Secret's recent advertising campaign features mobile "angels."

vivid are Stephanie's portrayals of feminine fire in her Victoria's Secret catalogs ... that many people think Stephanie is Victoria. But there is nothing Victorian about Ms. Seymour" (71). *Playboy* furthered the associations between Victoria's Secret and pornography when, on the cover of its June 1997 issue it featured its Playmate of the Year, named Victoria, under the headline "Victoria's Secret"; the model holds a finger to her lip as if saying "shh." Of course, antiporn feminists have pointed out these very connections between pornography and advertising; for them, the VS images are pornographic because they objectify women within a certain convention of beauty that relies on the endless consumption of products such as lingerie. However, with the representation of lingerie in women's erotica as my guide, I show how the uses of this product exceed the intentions of the producers, indicating how the erotica domesticates lingerie in a manner that may not correspond with the lingerie producers' intentions but that is nevertheless facilitated by the visual and textual appeal to the female consumer.

Frederick's in the Home

In order to gauge the charge that Victoria's Secret and lingerie more generally participate in a conservative backlash, we might first consider a short history of VS's predecessor and ongoing competitor in mail-order lingerie, Frederick's of Hollywood, which, in a manner more true to Faludi's criticism of lingerie, did begin its operations with a decided focus on women pleasing men. Frederick's began its mail order operations in 1946, targeting American "housewives" with the message that these beauty products would save a marriage, regain your man's desire, or catch you a husband. This appeal is aptly illustrated in an article by Frederick himself, Frederick N. Mellinger, published in a 1973 retrospective celebrating and recording twenty-seven years of business. Mellinger begins his article by reprinting a letter he received from a customer in which she recounts a recent evening out with her boyfriend. While at a restaurant, her boyfriend, George, left the table and approached a woman wearing "a top that looked like two G strings tied together over a long skirt with a slit way up to her thighs." Initially mortified, "Marion S." is relieved when her boyfriend returns not with the other woman's phone number but with a Frederick's catalog. Asks Marion S., "What did you do to make that girl look so good?" From there, Mellinger espouses his philosophy of femininity, which, as he says, is all geared toward helping every woman "dress to please the MAN in her life." Says Mellinger, "I BELIEVE I OWE IT TO ALL WOMEN . . . to help them proportion and reproportion their bodies so that their appearance in our fashions is perfect and in proportion" (9).

Mellinger thus acts as the patriarch through whom masculinity is reasserted, a prevailing cultural concern in the post–World War II years as men returned from the war to find women managing without them in both the workplace and the home, as Elaine Tyler May argues in *Homeward Bound*. On the pages of the catalogs reprinted in this retrospective, Frederick's face often appears as a small cutout, looking rather dashing with a slight, knowing smile, overlooking the women represented in the drawings (no photos were used in these early catalogs). In one cutout, a balloon issues forth from his mouth with these words: "I believe you MUST look truly feminine to enjoy life. Our aids to nature assure that look INSTANTLY! Order yours now." He lauds himself as the expert on women's figures, in collaboration with other men; as one page from 1957 showing glamorous evening gowns says, "Date fashions selected by our male jury."

Although the catalogs suggest that female consumers may be transformed through this apparel, it contains the threat of overt and perhaps mobile sexuality (outside the home) by its frequent references to Hollywood stars and Paris fashions, places clearly not within the realm of possible travel by most consumers. A 1957 catalog proclaimed, "Paris Points the Way . . . in French Follies Bras"; the bras, shown alongside a toweringly phallic Eiffel Tower, are named the "French caper," the "French fantasy," and the "Bou-Bou," which "plays 'French-y' tricks—separating and lifting busts." "The French scandal," advertised in a 1954 catalog, featured cups cut out to reveal nipples: "Wear it if you dare!" challenged the copy. Another 1954 catalog featuring the headline "Hollywood Bust Lines" advertised bras like the "Hollywood Push-Up," assuring consumers that "Now you can have a real Movie Star bosom!" Photos of movie stars and models appeared on some pages, with endorsements like this one by "Miss Hollywood 1962": "Frederick's changed me to a celebrity—over night. It's these sensational Frederick foundations that did it. They make a girl a woman, and a woman all the more so."

The lure of consumption worked, thus, through an appeal to fantasy places, linking lingerie to the glamour of a Hollywood and a Paris represented in movies and on television. This transformation could be performed only with Mellinger's expertise on the female body; "Frederick is a genius at figures!" said one 1957 catalog, which advertised elaborately constructed panty girdles with complicated zippers and inset panels designed for ultimate control. In the introductory article, Mellinger presents the female body as the site of engineering: "We can bring up a droopy bust, suppress the stomach, pull the waist in to achieve proportion in a woman's figure. If a woman is short we can add 5 inch heels, put a dome on her head under a wig, and re-distribute her figure so that she looks taller, slimmer, more in balance." The padded push-up bras are elaborately constructed and explained with a series of intricate, arrow-supplemented drawings that show exactly how the construction of the bra enhances cleavage, an important marker of femininity during the 1950s. "It's later than you think!" warns a woman pointing to a clock on a page advertising a variety of push-up bras, perfect for "drooping" breasts. "Set back the clock: Youth Insurance!" urges a 1955 advertisement, again for bras, such as the "Empire Line: Give yourself a new lift for the new Empire Look with this special youth-up shaped cup." Frederick's of Hollywood thus worked to represent erotic lingerie as something that kept women quite firmly fixed within the security of heterosexual romance, within the home; wearing the male-engineered fashions would transform women into something approximating Hollywood stars and Paris models. Although I do not mean to argue that the female consumers of Frederick's products or images were merely passive, for consumption is always productive and complex, I do believe that the very distance between Hollywood and home and the constant intrusion of Frederick with his bits of advice foregrounded the way female sexuality, particularly when overtly celebrated, was best articulated to the home as a relatively fixed and contained place, not intersecting with other sites, not suggesting women's mobility. To this extent, Frederick's did little to suggest mobile subject positions for its female consumers to occupy outside traditional home-bound roles; we can scarcely argue that compared to Frederick's, Victoria's Secret engages in any kind of unmediated nostalgia.

Throughout the 1960s and 1970s, Frederick's gradually lost its reliance on the figure of Frederick, and its lingerie became increasingly daring, appealing less to housewives and more to "sexually liberated" women with such items as leather body suits and nipple-revealing bras; indeed, Frederick's problem today may well be that it has linked lingerie too much to a public sphere rather than to the propriety of the private sphere. When Victoria's Secret entered the market in the early 1980s, the distinctions between the two catalogs became readily apparent in terms of the intersections of class, aesthetics, and femininity. Frederick's breaks the rules as to what constitutes "proper femininity" with its more forthright appeals to an uncontained female body. Take, for example, this ad for bras: "Double padded push-up bra with heavy fiberfilled, underwired cups plus removable push-up pads make the most of even the smallest bustline." Frederick's lacks the sense of propriety that Victoria's Secret establishes through its appeals to privacy, British sophistication, and a more refined, classically beautiful femininity. For the moment, it appears that Victoria's Secret has successfully negotiated its closeness to yet distance from porn: as its profit margins soar, Frederick's struggles to break even—in 1994 Frederick's closed twelve stores and reported a loss of $903,000.[4]

Circulation

I want next to consider Victoria's Secret as a text that circulates in a manner that makes it widely accessible as both an erotic text and a mail-order source of lingerie for women consumers within the home. Circulation, as I have argued throughout this book, is a critical component of access, and the catalog's mail-order status guarantees that both men and women have "every week" access to a text that for some, functions almost exclusively as soft-core porn. To distance itself from this association with a mass culture form even as it retains contact with the "masses," VS employs several strategies that facilitate its circulation as an aesthetically sophisticated, classy text, strategies that are likely obvious to mail carriers, consumers, and various household members. Each cover features the word "London" prominently, in the upper right-hand corner—even though the catalog's headquarters, as part of the Limited, are in Columbus, Ohio, and public relations officials will say only that there is a "buying office" in London. The price of the catalog, in the bottom left-hand corner, is listed in both pounds and dollars—even though the company only charges for the catalog in its stores, and never in pounds! In stressing its exclusivity through an articulation to British sophistication, Victoria's Secret invokes the high art/mass culture distinction that has worked historically to distinguish art from porn, and in that sense relies on some of the same aesthetic privileging that women's literary erotica does.

But Victoria's Secret is indeed a mass culture text; its free catalogs are so frequently and widely distributed that its very mail-order ubiquity renders it a public artifact, one that is often cited in other mass culture texts. The February 20, 1996, episode of the TV show *NYPD Blue*, for example, opened with a female detective telling the precinct secretary that she just purchased some lingerie—from Victoria's Secret—in anticipation of her date that night with a (male) detective. Working hard to distance itself from such commonness, Victoria's Secret refuses to reveal distribution figures; it will say only that a "good" customer receives up to thirty-five catalogs a year; the *Forbes* article on the company estimates that between 200 million and 240 million catalogs are mailed to 10 million people annually, with some receiving as many as 45 catalogs a year.[5] To further construct the myth of exclusivity, VS regularly foregrounds the specialness of its catalog recipients: "PRIVATE SALE: As one of our most valued customers, we're sending you this exclusive private edition."[6] These appeals to intimacy and privacy rearticulate the "pornographic" image on the front cover, distancing the catalog from porn that circulates without the overtures to class and aesthetic distinction yet retaining the explicit nature of the catalog.

These strategies of display linked to circulation are similar to those deployed by publishing companies, including Blue Moon Press and Carroll and Graf, who have issued compilations of Victorian erotica, laying claim to their "private" yet daring status. Carroll and Graf has published about forty volumes of Victorian erotica, including a four-part volume called *Eroticon*; *Eroticon I*'s back cover contains this blurb: "This glorious erotic periodical shocked our Victorian forebears. It is a compendium of lustful writing that includes complete novellas as well as provocative stories, 'inciteful' poems and salacious yarns. In its daring and delightful range, this long suppressed book captures all the randy flavor of the Victorians at play in the privacy of the bedroom." *Eroticon II* suggests that readers can inhabit a similar world: "This volume reveals even more of the rich and bawdy seam of sexuality that thrived beneath the face of 19th century respectability." Blue Moon Books has reprinted *The Boudoir*, an underground pornographic journal that was originally published only six times (according to Blue Moon); the reprint includes this back-cover blurb: "Circulating from hand to hand, this daring assortment of erotica was at one time enjoyed only behind closed doors. Now, at last, it can be read by all." The packaging thus tries to replicate the cultural purchase of the original erotica and the manner in which it circulated—"from hand to hand," in the "privacy of the bedroom." As Steven

Marcus notes in *The Other Victorians*, his study of Victorian pornography, the underground circulation of pornography carried over into intensely private reading practices. The texts were read "not merely in the privacy of one's study or closet, but behind locked doors, and are kept in locked drawers or cupboards; they are consulted in a silence beside which the unmoving air of a library reading room is as the din of market places" (Marcus, 247).[7] Yet, much as the literary erotica described in chapter 3, the Victorian erotica also posits itself as more democratic and accessible, while still retaining the cultural purchase that accompanies "literature"— in this case, previously illicit literature. Similarly, Victoria's Secret capitalizes on an aesthetic distinction in order to circulate ever more widely, including, now, on television; at the same time that new legislation has been passed requiring television networks to rate each show for sex and violence, Victoria's Secret has introduced a new level of sexual explicitness into the television commercial.

Reproducing Racism

"Hello, and thank you for calling the Victoria's Secret catalog sales center." The recorded voice is a woman's with a sultry British accent, providing a series of options to access. Press "two" for ordering and you'll likely hear a woman with a flat midwestern voice take over, all efficiency and intimidation, asking for catalog, page number, size, color, then, after taking your first order, "And what else for you tonight?"

In terms of place and origin, Victoria's Secret works hard to construct a sense of Victorian England as home, belying its boring heartlands locale and its dependence on international labor; it plays on a nostalgia for clearly defined and bounded locations in these post-fordist times of globalization, high-technology communications, and decentralized production. Although it proclaims that England is home, Victoria's Secret products are made all over the world; the Limited's 1994 annual report states that during that year the company, which owns twelve businesses, "purchases merchandise from approximately 4,000 suppliers and factories located throughout the world. Approximately 57 percent of the Company's merchandise is purchased in foreign markets and a portion of merchandise purchased in the domestic market is manufactured overseas." Capital's mobility masks the conditions of production, the particularities of the working conditions of the women and men who labor in factories around the world, in conditions that Victoria's Secret consumers are unlikely to think about.[8] Labels in panties and underwear indicate the places of labor exploitation: Sri Lanka, Guatemala, the Dominican Republic, Mexico.

The stark juxtaposition of references to Victorian, imperialist England as home and the realities of the (colonized) workers suggests a fondness for the days of empire, when, as Anne McClintock has written, commodities helped carry out the "civilizing work." Describing advertisements for teas, biscuits, tobaccos, cocoa, Bovril, and soap, McClintock shows how the representations appeared at the same time that the British empire was threatened, and thus served to bolster the sagging imperialist ego: "Late Victorian advertising presented a vista of the colonies as conquered by domestic commodities" (142). Victoria's Secret both continues this work—in that its use of Third World labor perpetuates a sort of neo-imperialism—and is nostalgic for a time when there was a more clearly defined imperialist role. Commodity racism, as McClintock calls it, also functioned through the representation of black people in ads as a means of consolidating white identity. In an advertisement for Pears' soap, for example, a young white nursemaid prepares to bathe a little black boy; in the next panel, the maid looks happily at the effects of the soap: where it has been applied, the skin has turned white (132). In a less obvious but still present way, Victoria's Secret engages in commodity racism; black models rarely appeared in the catalog at all until the last two or three years, and when they did, it was to model not lingerie but rather sportswear and street clothes. One of the most prominent representations of black women clearly positions them as exotic Others who reinforce the white subject identities and, furthermore, suggests a continued need for the white civilizer. The 1994 "Christmas Dreams" issue of the catalog, headlined the "Collector's Edition" and slightly larger than most catalogs, offers consumers the possibility of buying one of five Christmas dream vacations: London ($43,300), the English Cotswolds ($36,200); the Caribbean island of St. Barthélemy ($26,840), Aspen ($46,000), or New York City ($60,000). In each clearly bounded location, models advertise the appropriate attire (the package also includes a daily delivery of VS lingerie). The special edition begins with London, valorizing it as a site of civilization: "An English Christmas is a quintessential celebration of tradition. Victoria's Secret begins our magical journey in London, bringing you a collection of gifts that draws upon our English heritage of luxury, style and elegance." The product descriptions similarly celebrate "our" shared tastes: a black lace teddy is "classic lingerie" and a silk nightgown "draws upon our heritage of luxury." Stephanie Seymour, the only model in this "Christmas in London" section, is featured in lingerie and evening gowns, lounging on sofas, standing seductively by a Christmas tree wearing a sheer black beaded bodysuit and a long tafetta skirt, tied at the waist with a big Christmas bow. The next section advertises a holiday in the English Cotswolds, where models represent another kind of "classic English style" as they stroll in the sheep-specked countryside wearing a camel hair coat and a "beautiful handknit" sweater in the "English Christmas tradition." The lingerie here is decidedly conservative: a Canterbury flannel nightdress (another "English classic") and a blanket plaid robe that is "So English . . . so inviting." Then, we turn to St. Barth, "a distinctly French island frequented by the world's most discriminating travelers," where blonde models cavort on the beach and lounge in sidewalk cafés, suggesting that this Caribbean island has been successfully civilized for tourists.

The last vacation represented occurs in New York, the location of least tradition, which works to consolidate the identity of the white models and to present blacks as exotic "natives" of an urban "jungle." The headline, "A city of great energy and individuality, the New York look has a style all its own," sets the location distinctly apart from England; it represents not tradition but "a place where anything can happen . . . and does." The first model in this section is black; in the first set of images she wears a jacket described as "camouflage for the urban jungle," with leopard faux fur on one side, black velvet on the other. The next model, also black, wears a black leather vest, black mesh shirt, skin-tight black jeans, a silver chain belt hanging down around her hips, and high-heeled black boots, with fingernails painted black, and long, straightened hair. The lingerie in this section, also modeled by a black woman, is the most exotic in the catalog—or indeed, in any Victoria's Secret catalog: a velvet bodysuit, a metallic chemise. The emphasis is on a more decadent, unrestrained kind of pleasure: "she looks to unwind in the most sybaritic of fabrics she can find," says the caption next to a model in a silk/cashmere tunic. The representation reproduces stereotypes of black/native sexual prowess linked to less civilized but more sexually knowing cultures, a common tactic in Victorian erotica and contemporary rewritings of Victorian erotica as well. The Black Lace novel *The Seductress*, set in Victorian England, shows how Lady Emma Longmore gains her sexual knowledge in a time when women were protected from such information:

she reads her husband's book, written by an anthropologist, *Mating Habits of Some South Sea Islanders*: "Emma glanced again at the detailed portraits of dusky-skinned women with large, pendulous breasts and extraordinary protuberant behinds being serviced in all manner of ways by men with phalluses the size of cucumbers. Emma felt herself growing wet again as she surveyed the lewd pictures" (LaFay, 7). Lady Longmore is, in every other way, a remarkably progressive and enlightened woman; after discovering that she can't bear children and being rejected by her husband, she travels throughout Europe, initiating young men and women alike into the practices of sex.[9] The novel thus functions in a manner similar to the Victoria's Secret catalogs, emphasizing the independent, sexually sophisticated woman whose identity is partially defined through her (British) whiteness. Although the catalogs increasingly represent black women, they are always light-skinned and still not fully integrated into the positions that white models occupy. In its special "bridal collection," for example, the model is very blonde, as is the cover girl for the new Angels line of lingerie. Her long blonde hair blown back, her eyes closed in rapturous delight, the model rests on a fluffy cloud, with wings sprouting behind her.

Victoria's Secret also legitimates its lingerie through the settings; most of the lingerie is represented within the private confines of the home—a particularly luxurious home, sometimes with plush, Victorian backdrops, often including ornate, high-backed sofas in deep reds and burgundies, the softly curving frames mirroring the models' curves. Models are rarely shown on beds, which may be too suggestive, but are more likely to be represented lounging seductively on chairs or sofas or standing; there are occasional lingerie shots in gardens. In contrast, Frederick's wastes little time on settings and artistic ambiance, although it still bears the historical imprint of its first three decades' emphasis on the public places of Hollywood and Paris. One common image, for example, features a woman in leather standing next to a motorcycle. For Victoria's Secret, the private places set the proper context for the classically beautiful body, linking place and body in a manner that distinguishes the catalog from the public and tasteless. The body is "a refined, orifice-less, laminated surface—homologous to the forms of official high culture that legitimate their authority by references to the values—the highness inherent in this classical body," as Laura Kipnis describes it (*Ecstasy*, 225). The models are thin, with shapely but not enormous breasts, wearing minimal makeup, most often with unpainted, blunt nails, little jewelry, and moderate heels.

Frederick's models tend to be fuller-busted, and the catalog is not shy about appealing to various body types, even if they're not directly represented. Says an ad for swimming suits: "Lose an inch . . . Gain the Glamour with Slimsuits . . . an instantly toned look of smooth perfection for non-perfect bodies with these gorgeous slimsuits." Many clothes are available in "plus sizes." Models are less contained than the VS models: hair full-blown and tousled, more makeup, higher heels, bosoms and hips threatening to burst from their tight clothes. In less exaggerated ways, Frederick's represents the kind of class transgressions that Kipnis ascribes to *Hustler* magazine, in which, she says, representations of the body as "insistently material, defiantly vulgar, corporeal" operate as a critique of dominant ideology, an ideology that tries to contain and mark off the out-of-control body, thus defining its own, tasteful and contained, seemingly non-material body (223). Victoria's Secret is eager to distance itself from its raunchy competition: "We represent beauty and artwork," says McCall. "We're not as explicit or cheesy as Frederick's."

The New Woman

Even as it asserts its private image, however, Victoria's Secret reveals its dependence on spatial relations: the catalogs appeal to working, independent women who return to the home but cannot be fixed there, and who desire a home where *their* needs and pleasures are fulfilled. The text regularly speaks to the needs of the busy working woman to relax after a long day. The pleasures of looking slide into the pleasures of buying in a manner that does not coincide with the conventions of pornography as they appeal to male spectators. The Victoria's Secret consumer is positioned not as a caretaker of a husband and children, or someone who must shop to beautify her home, but rather as someone exclusively interested in her own pleasures and desires. The domestication of desire—its practice through reading, consuming images, and ordering from the catalog—occurs in the "privacy" of the home, but a home that is constantly connected to the public sites at which women earn the money they need to make their purchases and to which they will go, wearing their lingerie.

  The catalog integrates certain tenets of feminism when it represents women constantly going out—in casual sportswear, evening gowns, athletic gear, and swimming suits—illustrating relationships between the private and the many publics represented. Any single issue shows the same models in multiple locations, appearing in the opening pages in lingerie, then later in casual pajamas, sportswear, jeans, evening wear, and workplace suits and dresses. The summer 1997 "City" catalog introduced a line of signature athletic wear, including sweatshirts, bra tops, T-shirts, and baseball caps, all with the Victoria's Secret insignia. A svelte model is shown working out on various machines and lifting weights with the help of a male trainer. In contrast to Faludi's argument that VS fixes women in traditional roles, the message seems to be mobility, which, as Doreen Massey argues, is a "gender-disturbing message, a threat to a settled patriarchal order" (11). Models climb mountains, wade across streams, and even wear glasses while reading the newspaper. The fact that the models move freely through the pages in various kinds of attire, juxtaposing the erotic with the everyday, suggests that lingerie is not necessarily a means of confinement within a particular role or place but rather may facilitate movement, within the kinds of class and race privileges suggested.[10]

Erotic mobility, in other words, is tied to class mobility, with the career woman positioned as someone who can freely cross boundaries of public and private, able to discern what is appropriate in which sphere because she has experienced both. The catalog foregrounds this concept of public/private in its summer 1997 issue. Describing a series of very sheer pieces of lingerie, the catalog says, "Sheer defines the season. Whether it's lingerie or clothing, a private moment or a public one, there's a degree of sheer for everyone." In appealing to the mobile career woman who has earned the right to wear extremely sheer lingerie in either private or public (this catalog is the first one in at least the last five years that allows the viewer to see the shadow of a nipple through the gossamer gowns, teddies, and robes) the catalog invokes the image of the New Woman that I introduced in the previous chapter. Hillary Radner argues that the New Woman is accorded a considerable degree of agency, albeit within the strictures of a consumer culture that makes her constantly reassess herself. The New Woman performs femininity as a kind of masquerade:

> The reader is recognized as complicit in the system of consumerism that constitutes her as a subject. But she is actively rather than passively engaged in the process of her own constitution of subject. She is that subject who represents herself for herself, but she is also another subject who consciously creates, manipulates, and compensates for the figurability of an imaginary subject that projects cohesiveness as the founding assumption through a fictional body. (178)

The Victoria's Secret catalog always appeals to the female consumer, never referencing men: "Treat yourself to a new look of luxury" and "Pamper yourself daily with the personal luxury of our beautiful bras." And, advertising comfortable cotton sleepwear: "No work. No stress. It's your time. Style at home." This concentration on female pleasure does not preclude the possibility that women consumers are concerned about "looking good for him," but the appeal is sufficiently distanced from the male gaze so as to leave open the possibility that female pleasure, of various kinds, will be pursued. As Radner argues, in many appeals to the New Woman, the masculine gaze "is no longer the linchpin in the mechanisms whereby she produces identities" (xiii).

The exclusivity that the catalog tries to ensure is contradicted by its textual appeal to working women, *all* of whom deserve luxury and pampering; in this gap lies the possibility of articulating together the practical and the pleasurable—the cotton leggings, two for $52, and the black lace teddy. "Treat yourself to a new look in luxury: our beautifully designed sandwashed lounging pyjamas," says the headline on a page advertising silk pajamas, $29 for the top, $39 for the pants. If the silk is too impractical for some women's tastes, there's a sale on cotton thermal knit pants and sweaters: "Cotton thermal knits to relax in after work—and all weekend long."

In its narcissistic appeal, Victoria's Secret is ambiguously nostalgic, contradicting Faludi's emphasis on a backlash that seeks to return women to some previous, pure notion of femininity. The catalog wants to claim *both* a tradition and a rearticulation of femininity. Its 1996 spring preview catalog, for example, promotes its new line of silk plaid lingerie: "The return of ladylike and sophisticated epitomizes this season's glamour. Whether it's a retro plaid on silk pyjamas, a classic blazer outlined with contrast piping or the daytime jacket dress that transforms by night, Spring Preview 1996 is a celebration of everything feminine and new." The "new" may be read, in part, as the erasure of the patriarchal gaze common in the early history of Frederick's; "ladylike" has to be rearticulated through the mobility of working women.

In Victoria's Secret, different representations of femininity exist side by side, inviting viewers to examine the contradictions between, for example, a revealing push-up bra and its "everyday" name (albeit a slightly sophisticated everyday name). There's the Michelle bra, the Melissa, the Elizabeth, the Madeline, the Julia, the Natalie, the Emma, and so forth.

In contrast to the subject positions Frederick's constructed throughout much of its history, which asked women to identify with movie stars and French models, and to its current subject positions, which are constructed through fashions labeled "Playmate," "Hot fun," and "Silver studs," VS encourages women to identify with sexual, sultry images of leisure that are filtered through the everyday associations suggested by the practical and the everyday, the cotton panties and high-necked flannel nightgowns juxtaposed with the lace bodysuits. The point is that the "pornographic" is normalized through its associations with everyday attire and activity; even though the models are hardly "everyday" women in terms of their bodies, the catalog represents them in ways that encourage "everyday" women to identify with them through an association with her everyday life, perhaps enhancing the possibilities of purchasing as well as making their "pornographic" consumption a mixture of the erotic and the everyday.

Victoria's Secret further indicates the gaps in femininity's constructions with its fluctuating appeals to both the comfortable, "natural" body and the constructed, clearly engineered body. In contrast to Frederick's, which consistently represents the female body as a site of complex engineering, Victoria's Secret offers alternatives. In its "Private Sale '95" issue, for example, the catalog leads with two pages of "Body Blushers," bras and underwear described as "practicalities that feel like luxuries in next-to-nude tints. An amazingly soft, body-conforming knit that follows every nuance, every curve." Adds a headline on the facing page, "The next best thing to wearing nothing at all." This appeal recalls the bras of the 1960s and 1970s, when, as Elizabeth Ewing describes in her history of lingerie, the trend was toward "increasingly natural shaping . . . improving on nature without exaggerating natural curves or introducing any artificiality" (168). Then, five pages after the "body blushers" in the same issue, the catalog features its famous Miracle Bra collection, including three versions of the bra that gives you those curves "you just can't get from working out." The Miracle Bra belongs to the genre widely advertised in 1994, the year of the Wonderbra, a highly engineered bra that received top billing even from *Newsweek* in its "1994 in Perspectives" issue. Its headline asserted, "It was a bad year for Bill Clinton, baseball, and Marlon Brando's biography. But it was great for defense lawyers and push-up bras." The summary of the Wonderbra, headlined "The Year Fashion Went Bust," featured a photo of a woman displaying the cleavage-producing bra. In its emphasis on the Miracle Bra, then, Victoria's Secret participates in a certain nostalgia for the highly engineered breast, referencing the 1950s as well as, perhaps, the Victorian emphasis on the bosom, which, as Ewing describes, "was provided with artificial aids to curvaceousness when nature failed," including "remedies" such as false busts and "camisole-like garments with elaborate structures of whalebone or a series of wire springs built into the underside of the front" (86). However, to the extent that VS also recognizes the attraction for a so-called natural breast, it rearticulates and diffuses the nostalgia, placing it within a context that is more complex than merely a "backlash," incorporating notions of comfort in lingerie from the 1960s and 1970s into a contradictory and perhaps self-aware definition of femininity.

But the question remains: are these different representations of femininity different enough to encourage consumers to read them against each other, to indeed use lingerie as a kind of performative masquerade? They are for *Vogue* writer Dodie Kazanjian, who ponders, tongue-in-cheek, why she is so eager to shop at the VS stores, even though what she most often buys there is not sexy lingerie but a white cotton nightgown, what she calls "affordable luxury." Kazanjian describes the various aspects of femininity represented: the vulnerable and ultraromantic, as in the "whisper light baby doll" the catalog sells; the *Playboy*-style pornographic, as in the satin teddies and thongs; the working woman, as in skirts, dresses, and sportswear. She concludes that this contradictory mix is what attracts her: "For too many of us, the secret goal is to be sexy and demure, ultrafeminine and madly desirable; we're caught between Queen Victoria and Brigitte Bardot" (226). For Kazanjian as consumer/spectator, identification with the images of femininity is a process of recognition of similarities and differences, between herself and the images, and between the images themselves. As Jackie Stacey describes in her study of female spectatorship and Hollywood cinema of the 1950s, identification is not simply a process of confirming static identities, "offering the spectator the illusory pleasure of unified subjectivity" (172). Rather, identifications "speak as much about partial recognitions and fragmented replications" and "involve the transformation and production of new identities" (172). In pointing to the different femininities represented by the high-necked nightgowns and black teddies, Kazanjian situates herself within an ambiguous kind of femininity that sides with neither the virgin nor the whore, but possibly both, at different times.

Furthermore, the catalog represents for Kazanjian and her husband a mutually consumed pornographic text: "The Victoria's Secret model appeals to me as much as she does to my husband, and often for the same reasons" (226). Hence, the ambiguities of pleasure: Does Kazanjian identify with the models because she wants to look like them, thus enhancing her pleasure in her body? Enhancing her husband's pleasure in her body? And/or does she desire them herself, in a manner not necessarily tied to what Radner calls the "linchpin of the male gaze"? Undoubtedly, Victoria's Secret fuels women's fantasies of looking like the models, and in that sense, it participates in the utopian world of advertising; as Roger Silverstone says, "Goods are imagined, dreamed about, in their coveting." However, as Silverstone goes on to argue, these fantasies are always informed by the actual uses to which the goods are put: "The focus of those dreams is both the ideal world that they come to signify and the real world that they will enhance with new meaning. Whereas the first can be, and is, protected within the world of goods, the second is entirely vulnerable to the erosion of everyday life" (125). Consumption is a productive process, in which the contradiction between the imagined and the real serves not just to make the consumer aspire hopelessly to the advertised image, but rather to work to make the product fit within her realities. This work potentially "erodes" the advertisers' intentions for the consumption of the lingerie as a means of transformation into the New Woman; the catalogs' distribution to and circulation within the home encourages women to use lingerie for their own pleasures. Of course, these pleasures could be recuperated in a fairly conventional way—as I will show by analyzing how John Gray's *Mars and Venus in the Bedroom* puts lingerie to use. But lingerie may also be used in a manner that completely overwhelms the producers' intentions, as an aid to sexual pleasure that evades all the associations of lingerie with conventional beauty, with heterosexual romance, with whiteness.

There are many texts to consider as an alternative articulation of lingerie, since it figures frequently in much women's erotica. We might consider just one story, Maria Helena Dolan's "Collision Course," reprinted in *Best Lesbian Erotica, 1997*, because it challenges almost every feminist criticism of lingerie as a patriarchal artifact. First, the context in which the lingerie appears. Gloria is an African American butch lesbian who has successfully made her way into corporate America; she has a huge, ritzy home in Atlanta and a reputation as one of the sexiest, most sought-after butches in town. Gloria's race is eroticized without being exoticized; stereotypes are confronted without being perpetuated:

Gloria is as dark as Octavia is light. Her well-oiled, cafe-au-lait colored skin glistens across defined muscles, hard-won from years of carpentry and sweat in the gym. Her dark eyes stare piercingly, a perfected look that has been known to turn women into pliant puddles while they clutch at their pissed-off dates.

Gloria's height commands attention, as does her ass. It's covered in fine black silk, daring a hand to run across fabled contours. This ass is an engineering marvel, high and firm and succulent. She often quips that, if she were a white girl, she wouldn't be able to sit, 'cuz white girls just don't have the right kind of support.

This white girl bears a respectable ass though, Gloria thinks. (150)

The "stringy-ass white girl" is Octavia, who comes from white trash Louisiana background, where "you didn't have shit, but at least you weren't black" (151). As a prostitute in New Orleans, she learned her trade from transvestite hookers, who "taught her about high femme and happily instructed about the effects of the tiniest nuances with great flourish and care" (152). In the descriptions of their backgrounds, race is identified as a shaping factor yet not one that overdetermines sexual desire or any other aspects of their lives. At the party where they first meet, it's lust at first sight. Octavia's stockings are the grist for Gloria's first seduction line; the conversation proceeds rapidly and the two women go to Gloria's house. Dancing to Marvin Gaye, they kiss and explore; Gloria begins to undress Octavia: "Freed to do its own bidding, this hand seeks the softness of Octavia's breast. First, the camisole strap is peeled away. Then, the push-up bra is pulled down, so the small mounds can ride out in the open. The hand covers a tit, exploring the miracle of woman flesh. Already, the nipple is hard" (155). The push-up bra could well be a Miracle Bra, or perhaps another one of the many marketed in a similar fashion, yet here it functions in the interest of a lesbian pleasure that is decidedly raw, unromantic, and not at all nostalgic for Victorian England. The language draws out the contradictions: the camisole and push-up bra pulled away, the tit exposed. The lingerie is domesticated—put to work in a context different from any represented in a lingerie catalog, yet still dependent on access to commodities that can then be used within a "private" sphere.

Of course, lingerie can be largely recuperated within a fairly traditional model of domesticity, in that manner contradicting the Victoria's Secret emphasis on the independent woman but also drawing on the conservative elements of the catalog that I have described, such as its reliance on a certain degree of private/public sphere distinctness. In John Gray's instructions to couples for better sex, he advises both men and women on the semiotics of lingerie, identifying different categories that indicate various stages of sexual desire. Black lace or garters indicate that "she wants sex . . . and what she wants is hot, lusty, and intense sex; not only does she want sex but she longs for it" (106). White silky satin, on the other hand, indicates that she would like "sensitive, gentle, and loving sex. It is as though she is a virgin and wants him to go slow and be tenderly affectionate with her" (106). Silky pink or lace indicates she is "ready to surrender to sex as a romantic expression of loving vulnerability and eventually wild abandon." A "black bra and panties" suggests that she "wants to be seductive, arousing, and more aggressive than usual. Although she begins strong, inside she wants him to dance with her but eventually end up on top and in control of his passions as she lets go and surrenders to his love" (107). A "short and loose nightgown with no panties" means "she may or may not be in the mood for an orgasm. Maybe she just wants to feel him moving inside her through intercourse and is happy and satisfied by feeling his orgasm inside her" (107). And old cotton flannels clearly mean "she's not in the mood!" (108). Actually, each of these items could be found in the pages of a Victoria's Secret catalog, indicating that the catalog's appeal to female pleasure and working women's autonomy could be fairly easily rearticulated into a more conservative notion of romantic love in a traditionally coupled relationship. Although Gray is definitely interested in women's pleasures and orgasms, he subsumes these interests to the broader health of a traditionally gendered marriage, one that thrives in a private sphere that is clearly marked off from public spheres, as I explain in the next chapter.

5

Behind and Beyond
the Bedroom Doors
From John Gray to Candida Royalle

It's 10 P.M. on a Sunday night at the Marriott Hotel in Indianapolis, the night before the seminar I'll attend: "Men Are from Mars, Women Are from Venus," an offshoot of the thriving industry of "relationship guru" John Gray. This city seems like the perfect place for Gray's offerings; in the early 1980s it passed a city ordinance written by Catharine MacKinnon and Andrea Dworkin that made pornography a violation of women's civil rights.[1] But even the most sexually prudish of cities can't keep national hotel chains from offering adult programming on cable; I choose what seems to be the most "transgressive" in terms of this place, a selection called *Hardcore*. Ironically, however, the movie turns out to be a sort of critique of hard-core porn; even though it still has a good deal of sex, the three featured couples all find their happiness in romance and reject the crass and nonmonogamous pornography industry. And, true to most cable programming, the sex is decidedly soft-core—with no shots of either male or female genitalia.[2]

Hardcore opens with a "typical" porn scene—a woman in a revealing red bodysuit and a naked, well-built man have sex on a stairwell, in a variety of positions employing the steps and the railing. But after several minutes, the scene is interrupted by a director who inquires whether the man needs a different woman in order to climax. The woman in red is obviously angry: "Can't we just get to the cum shot?" she says in an obvious slam of the predictability of the standard pornographic money shot, the male orgasm.

Tired of the emptiness of sex on stage, the porn star decides to hire a double to take her place so she can vacation. In a romantic mountain setting, she attends her best friend's wedding and herself falls in love with the best man, a sort of genteel cowboy. Scenes of kissing, romantic walks, and soft-core lovemaking on grassy hillsides are interspersed with the newlyweds' soulful campfire sex. Meanwhile, back on the porn set, the star's double finds herself in over her head with repugnant male costars. Finally, she agrees to do a kitchen sex scene but will do it only with her manager and only because, it seems, they have fallen in love. The pornographic set thus becomes a site of romantic coupling; furthermore, the star and her double merge in that both have found love and thus offer the audience the pleasures of pornography *and* the promise of a happier relationship.

The theme of the Mars and Venus seminar—although there's no explicit discussion of sex—is not all that different from *Hardcore*: a celebration of gendered differences in the pursuit of better relationships. Men—that is, Martians—define their sense of self through their ability to achieve results (the cum shot, the conquest) and to protect and provide (courtship and marriage). Women—that is, Venusians—achieve their sense of self through sharing their feelings and emotions; they need to be understood and reassured (particularly as a respite from the demands of the work world). In short, says Curt, the facilitator of the Indianapolis seminar, "Love blossoms when we respect and accept our differences. . . . As soon as we start to try to change each other, problems escalate. When we acknowledge that we're from different planets, love starts to flow." The porn star couldn't find fulfillment in her world of money, fame, and sex but only through realizing that what she needed was a cowboy to take care of her.

These two events represent the ironic intersection of the thriving sex-advice-for-couples industry and the couples' porn industry. Both kinds of texts take up in explicit detail the importance of sex to the health of a heterosexual relationship, often concentrating on women's pleasures; John Gray's book and video *Mars and Venus in the Bedroom* spend a great deal of time discussing the importance and the technology of clitoral stimulation. Pornography generally (and the somewhat nebulous subcategory of "couples' porn") for the last twenty-five years has been moving in a similar direction, as Linda Williams argues in *Hard Core*. But the intersection is also marked, at least for a segment of the porn industry, by a preoccupation with sex between couples as a means of achieving a more intimate and long-lasting relationship, and of infusing the benefits of sex into all aspects of coupled life. These companies thus build their profit margins on and help further produce the valorization of monogamy and, to varying degrees, marriage, that is part of the family values agenda discussed in chapter 1—a rather ironic role for the couples' porn industry to be playing.

In between the mainstream legitimacy of the John Gray books and the still somewhat questionable access of couples' hard-core video porn (see chapter 1), there is a growing genre of sex education videos for couples that are regularly advertised for order by mail in magazines including the *New York Times Book Review, Playboy, Details, GQ, American Woman,* and *Redbook* and available in many local video stores. This subgenre represents the merging of several discourses discussed thus far in this book. Like women's erotica and masturbation discourse, erotic education valorizes the clitoral orgasm and other forms of female pleasure; furthermore, like women's erotica, these videos show sex occurring within a "realistic" context, often using "real" people talking about and demonstrating their sex lives in their own homes. Erotic education often reproduces certain mainstream conceptions of everyday life—often a white, heterosexual, middle-class lifestyle. Like visual pornography, the imagery is explicit, with close-up attention to genitals and techniques of better sex (in this sense, much pornography is a sort of manual for the techniques of better sex). Yet even as it relies on pornographic conventions, erotic education seeks to ensure accessibility and legitimacy by distancing itself from some of the common stereotypes about porn and by rearticulating pornographic images within everyday contexts. Good sex means talking about good sex; pornographic images are often interrupted by sexologists who exhort viewers to "stop the tape and talk about what you've just seen." Fantasy and reality merge in the combined goal of achieving a more "intimate, enduring" relationship, a process that is facilitated by a sexologist/therapist. As such, erotic education for couples participates in the sex therapy/talk show discourse generated in part by "sexperts" like Dr. Ruth Westheimer, who became a national celebrity in the 1980s through her cable sex talk show, *Good Sex!*

Women's access to this subgenre of erotica/pornography would seem to be fairly unimpeded, particularly for texts as mainstream as Gray's *Mars and Venus in the Bedroom.* However, access depends on the woman's identification as part of a couple; unlike much women's literary erotica, which lends itself more to the private act of reading and individual pleasures and often, in terms of content, stresses the fleeting nature of different kinds of relationships, couples' porn articulates pleasure to the overall health of the relationship and thus suggests that one needs to be heterosexually "coupled" in order to identify with the content and to gain the full pleasures of sex. In fact, "couples' porn" in the industry has become a sort of shorthand for "women's porn," leaving the rest of porn still defined mainly as a male genre and suggesting that women watch porn only when they're with a male partner. Many of the industry and popular attempts to estimate the number of women who watch and/or rent porn use the category "women and couples." Although coupled sex is not necessarily a bad thing, access becomes more problematic when the formation of the relationship relies on clearly gendered, dichotomous roles, as it does with John Gray and, to varying degrees, the erotic education videos. Domestication in these texts suggests a reassertion of the home that relies on connections between traditionally gendered relationships, privacy, and the heterosexual, monogamous bedroom. There is, as the Mars and Venus motif indicates, something very reassuring about the clear lines of gender, in which sexual desire follows directly from an easily identifiable gendered identity, a cause-and-effect relationship that solidifies the bonds of heterosexual marriage and family.

Access, in these more problematic texts, is linked to the bedroom as the site of sex, as if the very invocation of this most cloistered site within the home could legitimate for discussion the seemingly "private" activities that occur there. The erotic education series often incorporate the word "bedroom" into their titles, such as *Mars and Venus in the Bedroom* and *Beyond the Bedroom Door*. Merely by invoking the bedroom, the videos, books, and many articles on sex in women's magazines acquire a certain sanitized voyeurism that both links the discussion to privacy and divulges the secrets that characterize what Americans do in their most "private" spaces; as Foucault wrote, it is part of society's propensity to "speak verbosely of its own silence" (*History of Sexuality,* 8). In its April 1996 issue, *Ladies' Home Journal* headlined an article titled "America Undercovers: What Even Nice Couples Are Doing in Bed"; the subtitle read, "A Special Report from Behind Bedroom Doors." *American Health*'s January 1997 survey of the sexual happiness of women between thirty-five and fifty-five was subtitled "The Eye-Opening Findings from Our Peek into the Bedrooms of Women in Their Prime" (79). References to the "bed" function metonymically to represent the legitimacy of the bedroom; as Laura Chester says in the introduction to her edited collection of erotica, *The Unmade Bed: Sensual Writing on Married Love*, "commitment is no longer the dirty word it used to be, and monogamy is clearly back in favor" (xvi).

It would seem that the bedroom as an invoked space of privacy, perhaps even more than the home, represents all that feminists have come to distrust about the purported division of private and public spheres. What gets elided in this valorization of the bedroom, in other words? What public sites and spaces shape the bedroom and then get erased in the desire to believe that sex does indeed occur in a space removed from broader social conditions? Lauren Berlant argues convincingly in "Live Sex Acts" that zones of privacy such as the bedroom are critical to the construction of a national heterosexual identity that simultaneously congratulates itself for protecting citizens' sexual privacy and ignores the fact that this notion of national identity is formed through the exclusion of homosexual identity. Berlant cites, for example, the infamous 1986 *Bowers v. Hardwick* case, in which the Supreme Court upheld a Georgia court's ruling that the act of homosexual sodomy, even when it occurs in the privacy of the bedroom, is not constitutionally protected under the Fourteenth Amendment. Says Berlant in analyzing this case and other examples,

> [I]nsofar as you think that the sex you have is an intimate, private thing, you are having straight sex, you are having sex authorized by national culture, and you are practicing national heterosexuality, which makes your sex act or acts dead, in the sense I have described, using a kind of metaphor about personhood that foregrounds a notion of identity that secures it as a sacred national fetish of a kind beyond monumentality or representation, protected by a zone of privacy. (26)

In Berlant's analysis, the only live sex is that which refuses to cower in this zone of privacy, that which performs its identity in a "non-infantilized political counterpublic" sphere (27). Most of the texts described in this chapter would not, for Berlant, qualify as live sex; although I agree with the general political thrust of her argument, it also falls into the same trap I described in the introduction: many prosexuality feminists assume that the only progressive sexual representation is that which occurs in a seemingly liberated, undifferentiated public sphere.

Much as this book argues that feminists cannot cede the site of the home to conservatives, this chapter argues that we cannot give up on the bedroom as a place where "live sex" can indeed be practiced. In part, this means acknowledging that even the most conservative attempts to contain desire are not always successful; slippery, sweating bodies have a way of evading institutions, even when that institution is invoked as powerfully as marriage is in the United States. Considering the bedroom as a potentially progressive site of sex also means acknowledging that even as texts participate to varying degrees in a national valorization of marriage and monogamy, they may also rearticulate that agenda through the very act of bringing together the erotic or the pornographic and the everyday. The Kensington Ladies' Erotica Society, for example, a group of white, upper-middle-class women in San Francisco, is firmly located within the confines of the heterosexual nuclear family; however, some stories in its two volumes eroticize practices—such as nursing babies—that could rival Robert Mapplethorpe's transgressions in the eyes of Jesse Helms precisely because of the conjuncture of the erotic and the everyday. The point, again, is not transgression for the sake of transgression but rather the expansion of access to materials and practices that have previously been denied to women because of work and roles deemed antithetical to sex. The erotic education videos especially represent the domestication of an otherwise taboo pornography in their reliance on the same visual conventions, even, in some series, using actual cuts from hard-core porn (without openly identifying them as such) in the context of discussions about better sex for couples. Before analyzing in more detail the conventions of erotic education for couples, I want first to consider the ways it has been shaped by two other subgenres, women's literary erotica for couples and hard-core video pornography for couples.

Revisioning Porn?

The pornography industry started targeting women as consumers as early as the 1970s, according to Linda Williams; the couples' market expanded considerably in the early 1980s with the advent of the home video recorder. Williams characterizes couples' porn as offering a "softer, cleaner, nicer version of the stock numbers and narratives of feature-length hard core. The improved qualities include higher production values, better lighting, fewer pimples on bottoms, better-looking male performers who now take off their shoes and socks, and female performers who leave on shoes and expensive-looking lingerie" (1989, 232). Couples' porn is also likely to "strike a more mature tone" and to "take more seriously the different nature of the woman's own desire and pleasure and accept the challenge of helping her to achieve them" (233). Couples' porn usually belongs to the category Williams calls "integrated" porn, in which the sexual numbers are situated in a kind of realistic context; "because this is the category most capable of admitting problems from the social world into narrative discourse for purposes of utopian resolution, it is also the category most capable of addressing the sexual problems of modern couples" (239).

Williams spends some time describing the evolution in the porn industry toward this emphasis on female pleasure and couples; however, she also remains skeptical about the extent to which the paradigm can be rearticulated, arguing that even in films that take as their explicit focus the question of women's desires, "the solicitation of difference is suspiciously in the interest of, and produced on the model of, the phallic 'norm'" (234). The most successful attempt at revisioning hard-core, argues Williams, is the work of Femme Productions, an adult film production company started in 1984 by Candida Royalle, a former mainstream porn star who wanted to produce "couples' erotica from a woman's point of view." Although the video productions of Femme still rely on some of the conventions of porn—such as the "time-honored rhetoric of hardcore's quest for secrets, taking viewers 'deep inside'" women's sexuality—Royalle and her cohorts have "turned this rhetoric around, posing their female selves as the different 'explorers' of human desires who 'know' that realm as well as the entrepreneurs" (Williams, *Hard Core*, 250). In the Femme videos, the penis is no longer "asserted as the standard and measure of all desire" (247), and sex becomes more of a question than an assertion. Says Williams, "What is really different . . . is the encouragement of more male-female conversations about sex, more give-and-take, more questioning of 'what's the sex all about'—and much less answering exclusively from the perspective of the phallus" (250).

It is not just the content of the Femme videos that is important for women; we can see through a brief analysis of its reception in the eight years following the publication of Williams's book that the very existence of a company that does not shy away from explicit content yet emphasizes its address to women has helped legitimate the whole idea of women watching porn. However, to return to my earlier arguments about the importance of the erotica/porn distinction, it is also clear from the reception of Royalle's work that its accessibility is produced partially by its asserted differences from porn. Royalle's work and persona have been widely reviewed in the mainstream media, from *the New York Times* to *Elle,* which in 1992 featured Royalle in an article called "Debbie Directs Dallas: Video Erotica Made by Women for Women."[3] Her videos are generally perceived to be "tasteful" but explicit; the reviews point to differences from standard porn in that, for example, they feature a wide variety of performers of different ages and body types and that they do not fetishize the male orgasm. The *Elle* article, for example, initially rehearses the arguments made by antiporn activists about the exploitation of women in porn. Norma Ramos, general counsel for Women Against Pornography, even accuses Royalle of making the same old porn: "That it is a woman, Candida Royalle, behind the camera doesn't matter to us. Her films do exactly what other pornographers do, which is reduce women to body parts. Pornography eroticizes women's inequality. It's prostitution on paper or celluloid" (Gould, 144). Yet the article goes on to describe in considerable detail how several of Royalle's videos are not pornographic, discrediting Ramos by emphasizing the differences between erotica and porn and yet valorizing the idea that women's erotica can still be very explicit. Royalle is quoted: "Women have wild fantasies. I've known women who complain that their men weren't raunchy enough in bed. I think a really raunchy fantasy depicted tastefully is where it's at" (148). *Screw* magazine video reviewer David Aaron Clark consolidates the distinctions between erotica and porn when he opines that men don't like Royalle's films because they "are not raunchy enough" (Gould, 148). At the same time, Femme's marketing as porn in adult video stores hasn't hampered its endorsement in more "legitimate" circles; Femme has received the approval of sexologists and marriage counselors; Femme's *Three Daughters*, which includes the story of a young woman's initiation into sex through masturbation, a romp with her girlfriend, and then an affair with an older man, was recommended by the Association of Sex Educators, Counselors and Therapists. Patricia Love and Jo Robinson, authors of *Hot Monogamy*, recommend Royalle's videos over pornographic videos that, they say, make both men and women feel inadequate. This legitimation of a genre in turn helps produce the public perception that women's desires should be specifically addressed and legitimately accessed, in a manner that exceeds the immediate texts of Femme.

Distribution is also crucial to mainstream accessibility and depends in part on already established conceptions of the porn market, which generally does not recognize the lesbian market. When she started Femme, Royalle had difficulty finding big-name distributors for her products, but by 1986 VCA, one of the biggest porn distributors, picked up three Femme videos. Femme is currently distributed through PHE Enterprises in a deal that Royalle is happy with (Nagle, 163). In contrast, the Femme counterpart in lesbian video porn, Fatale Video, which also started in the early 1980s, has had much more difficulty getting distributed. As Debi

Sundahl, Fatale's founder, told an interviewer, "Big distributors wouldn't touch us with a ten-foot pole." Sundahl describes the rejections: *Ms.* magazine wouldn't take Fatale's ads because they were too sexual, the adult porn industry wouldn't take its products because they were an "all-women product," and feminist bookstores wouldn't take its products because they were "overtly sexual" (Nagle, 163). Over the last decade, Fatale has done its own distribution, piecing together mail-order lists and relying heavily on the magazine *On Our Backs*.

We must also consider the fact that eight years after the publication of Williams's *Hard-Core*, there are still only a handful of women directors in the industry, and no company that has remotely rivaled Femme in terms of producing a public legitimation of women watching adult videos. Fortunately, the women who do influence the porn industry as either directors, writers, or actors are strong, articulate feminists, including Nina Hartley, Annie Sprinkle, Gloria Leonard, and Veronica Hart (Hart often works under the name Jane Hamilton). The relative dearth of women in producing/directing roles does not preclude the possibilities that women consumers might very well like hard-core that is produced and directed by men; rather, it points to the difficulties that women have entering the field and expanding the representations of pleasures, which, as can be seen with the Femme line, has effects that extend far beyond the immediate text. In other words, my argument here does not rest on the essentialist assumption that women producing and/or directing porn will necessarily produce something that more women will like and that men can't; rather, women who make porn will more likely increase the many conditions of access that contribute to the "environment" in which women feel comfortable watching porn. In this formulation of access, it matters not so much whether Royalle's porn attempts to "educate desire," to return to Andrew Ross's criticism as described in the introduction, but whether it will be produced, distributed, and received in a manner that contributes to women's access to a variety of sexually explicit materials.

Ladies' (Pleasures) First

At roughly the same time that the pornography industry was recognizing the home video market for couples, some women were writing their own versions of couples' porn, or, for them, erotica, a genre ignored by

Williams but one that did represent a significant revisioning of pornography.[4] In 1977 a group of upper-middle-class, middle-aged women from the San Francisco Bay Area began meeting once a month at each other's homes in the hills of Berkeley. They were prompted, writes their founder, Sabina Sedgwick (all of the women use pseudonyms), by these questions: "Do women and men agree about what is erotic? Are our experiences different from theirs? Do we really know what turns us on, or do we just go along, accepting and acting out what male writers proclaim to be erotic?" (Kensington Ladies, *Ladies' Own Erotica*, 1). Sharing gourmet meals and sexual fantasies, they called themselves the Kensington Ladies' Erotica Society. In 1984 Ten Speed Press of Berkeley published the first volume of their collected erotica under the title *Ladies' Home Erotica* (later changed to *Ladies' Own Erotica*). The book sold well—it went through ten editions, sold about seventy thousand copies (and remains in print), was translated into German and Japanese, and earned them nationwide media attention. In 1986 Ten Speed published a second volume, *Look Homeward Erotica: More Mischief by the Kensington Ladies' Erotica Society*, which has sold about thirty thousand copies.

Both volumes attempt to integrate the erotic with the everyday, to show how the daily lives of these women who have identified themselves mainly as wives and mothers for twenty-some years can also serve as the basis for a highly sexual identity. The Ladies extend the notion of integration—admitting problems from the outside world (although a pretty wealthy, white world) into the world of sex—in an explicit attempt to eroticize the entire home, moving from room to room in the interest of better couples' sex and, more broadly, better relationships. The Ladies let their "erotic imaginations and memories wander into the delivery room, the beauty salon, and other places where menfolk fear to tread" (*Look Homeward*, 66). They describe a woman's erotic experience with nursing, a woman's orgasm immediately following childbirth, and the sensual sensations of a shampoo and haircut.

The Ladies' erotica is in many ways a marriage sexual advice manual, albeit less didactic. Said the *San Francisco Chronicle* of the second volume, "Let wives and lovers substitute one of these volumes for the more clinical how-to books stuck in the back of the drawer, and men might find out a few things they want to know—and (dare I say it?) in a manner not nearly so dry." Sex in many of the stories occurs in this implied marital bedroom; "Marriage in the Morning," for example, describes how a husband seduces his reluctant and sleepy wife to have sex in the morning, with her private thoughts interspersed with his persistent caresses. But sex within marriage does not always occur in strictly monogamous terms: Emma Hawksley's "Anniversary Waltz I" describes a woman's fantasies about her friend's husband on their twentieth-eighth anniversary. "Tonight, we could celebrate his anniversary, and I could be her," and then she fantasizes in the bathtub what making love to him might be like.

The integration of fantasy and everyday life leads to an eroticization of practices that are regularly excluded from most pornography because they are assumed not to be erotic, such as pregnancy and nursing.[5] Take, for example, this description of nursing:

> Lightly she touched the damp fuzz covering the barely completed head and guided the questioning mouth toward her nipple. He caught and held. Sweet warmth began to creep up her back, across her shoulders, her throat, her breast and belly; she felt the tight weight, the aching engorgement, the prickling release, and she gave a little moan and turned over on her side, enveloping him in the warmth of her milky body. She inhaled her own sweet and rancid odors as the milk began to trickle from her unengaged breast and the tiny, fierce fists struck and kneaded the flesh around the other nipple, hastening the flow into the famished, new mouth. (Vaughan, 71–72)

In "Ergasm," a woman delivering her baby girl describes her labor as a sensual experience: "We were in perfect synchrony—horse and rider, lover and beloved, mother-to-be and daughter-to-be—both of us absolutely ready for the moment when, all at once, the warm, gelatinous home that had been hers alone for so long would collapse" (Pearson, 73). At that moment, the mother's "last wild cry filled the room and hers began" (73). In these stories, women are not victims of a sexually explicit world that objectifies them, as the Meese Commission would have it, nor are they chaste and moral, protecting their children from a pornographic world, as the Communications Decency Act posits. The home becomes a site of erotic mobility in which mothering itself acquires a sexual charge, distinct from the male partner. Although mothers still remain largely within a fairly isolated home, they refuse the roles traditionally assigned to them, eroticizing the very tasks that in other contexts are used to dichotomize mothering and sexuality. In fact, writing erotica becomes a sort of family affair. Rose Solomon describes how her erotic writing has become a subject of open discussion and occasional amusement in her family. Returning from one "particularly sapping television interview," she found her teenage children "writhing on the floor enacting a merciless parody: 'Ohhh, see how the erotic permeates every aspect of my life! Just inhale the freshness of my laundry as it tumbles from the dryer into my waiting arms! Ahhhh, here, feel the warmth! How sensual is each sock and towel. Oh, let me press them to my lips, to my breasts'" (217–18). Interestingly, teenage children who are normally oblivious to their mother's sexuality and to her workload recognize both in the same instance, and in a manner that does not force the mother, as the proverbial nag, to drive the point home. This articulation of mothering and sexuality is extremely rare in any erotica, as I argue in more detail in the next chapter.

Somehow, erotica must find a way to reference the everyday and yet avoid becoming overdetermined by it—validating a major part of these women's identities while also allowing opportunities for sexual mobility within these identities.[6] In "Constant Interruptus," Solomon describes writing erotica amidst her hectic everyday routine. Erotic sentences from her short story intermingle with the voices of sons, daughters, repairmen, and husband making various demands: arranging rides, picking up clothes from the dry cleaner, fixing dinner, and so forth. The erotic story describes an encounter with a stranger on a train; the man begins to kiss the woman's breasts and they seem headed for intercourse when the telephone of real life rings, and it's the writer's mother-in-law, apparently representing the ultimate in unerotic interruptions, for there the story ends. The train takes the woman away from the everyday routines that squelch desire; on the other hand, the story also acknowledges that these routines cannot be simply ignored in the writing of erotica.

The Ladies also reserve the right to take refuge in those traditional gender roles that securely defined them before their forays into erotica, and many of the stories reflect this harking back to the protection of masculinity. "Nice Girls Don't" describes Nell Port's memories of petting in high school in the back seat of her boyfriend's 1953 Mercury. "The rules were so beautifully clear for me then," she says. Port describes the ecstasy of prolonged foreplay, which finally, one night, produced her first orgasm—through fingering, as her "principles, at least, remained intact" (163). She says, longingly, "We loved each other like this on and off for over four years. Then came the sexual revolution of the 1960s, and, with it, no more cars parked on Mulholland or Outpost Drive" (163). But if there is a nostalgia for a 1950s model of domesticity, where girls were taught to save their virginity for the sanctity of marriage, "Nice Girls Don't" also integrates the importance of women reaching orgasm, which may happen more quickly through manual clitoral stimulation than through intercourse.

The Ladies use sexual desire to rearticulate gender relations within the home such that they seemingly *choose* those strong men and monogamous relationships rather than fall into them out of some kind of essential femininity; their paths lead not out of the house but through it, from the control gained through the preparation of meals to the control over one's sexual pleasure. Their notion of home does not escape the governmental models' emphasis on heterosexuality, monogamy, and children—in these aspects, the Ladies share some concerns with even the Meese Commission. It is precisely in the shared concerns, however, that the potential to intersect and redefine those models may exist—in the eroticization of nursing and childbirth, for example. These stories acknowledge that a woman's consumption of erotica necessarily occurs in relation to the other practices that define her life, and that reading erotica is itself a practice that must be given space and time amidst the other activities.

Sex therapist Lonnie Barbach pursued the idea of erotica as a kind of sexual advice text for couples with the publication in 1994 of *The Erotic Edge: Twenty-two Erotic Stories for Couples*; she argues in her introduction that by helping couples understand their biologically determined sexual differences, she will help their overall relationships. Her introduction reinforces all the stereotypical differences between male and female desire, such as the idea that women focus on foreplay and men on the immediate act of sex. In her introduction, entitled "Very Male and Very Female," Barbach urges her readers to cover up the names of the authors and predict their "sex," saying, "I think you'll be surprised to find how easy it is to identify the sex of the author" (13). She also exhorts her readers to use these stories in order to better understand their differences: "You can read them to each other during lovemaking as an innovative way to spice up your sex life . . . you may want to discuss afterward your reactions to the various tales. In this way, you may learn something about each other that may enable you to be a more conscious, considerate, or pleasing lover" (5). Barbach as critic thus serves as a rather extreme form of the aesthetic moral exemplar described in chapter 3; literature comes to embody natural sexual differences, which she then sets up as a means for the reader to be educated about the proper way of reading. She also sets in motion one of the primary components of couples' erotica/porn—the mandate to *talk* about differences in the interest of better sex.

By the early 1990s, then, we can see the ways some women's erotica and couples' porn, especially Royalle's adult videos, intersect with their emphasis on gendered differences and women's pleasures in the context of everyday life. In many ways, this development increases women's access to sexually explicit materials; we must also ask, however, whether the process of domesticating porn does sometimes lead to a greater prescriptiveness about the "appropriate" connections between sex and everyday life. As Williams notes, pornography has historically been one of the few genres that does not punish women for being promiscuous. What happens when promiscuity gets replaced by monogamy, albeit a monogamy that emphasizes the importance of female desire? Although it is not inevitable that this integration of "reality" with sexual numbers will lead to more prescriptive roles for women, that possibility does increase the more that pornography and erotica attempt to appeal to women as part of a (monogamous) heterosexual couple.

Erotic Education

Because erotic education videos articulate their sexually explicit content to the health of a relationship, they offer couples a legitimate way to access porn without calling it porn, an especially important consideration given the fact that visual material has enjoyed much less legitimation as sexually explicit material than has print (see chapter 1). Consumers are savvy about the overlap, of course; in a review of ten such videos, *Cosmopolitan* asked, "Are they simply hard-core porn in a socially acceptable wrapper? More like those dreary sex-ed classes you snoozed through in high school?" *Cosmo* writer Stephanie Gutmann actually gives one of the more ringing endorsements to Gray's *Mars and Venus in the Bedroom*, despite the fact that there is no sex at all, just Gray talking. But "talk" is one of the most important ways these videos distinguish themselves from porn, an essentially "talkless" genre. In erotic education, everyone talks, from the sexologists to the couples to the assumed viewing couple, who are frequently exhorted to use the video to enhance communication. As the publicity sheet for Royalle's *LOVERS: An Intimate Portrait* series announces, "LOVERS provides many opportunities for couples to open valuable conversations. . . . Once again, FEMME proves that education and erotic entertainment are not mutually exclusive." Interestingly, this claim about the educative effects of a set of texts that sometimes visually resemble pornography coincides with the antiporn claim that pornography by itself causes certain behavior—only in the case of erotic education, the behavior is assumed to be better sex for couples and not the debasement and even rape of women.

Erotic education videos feature couples who reveal their sexual problems and practices to a featured sexologist, who acts as a mediator and potential problem solver for the audience, in much the same way Nancy Friday has solicited women's fantasies through interviews for the last twenty-five years (see chapter 2). The genre also participates in what Mimi White has called the therapeutic and confessional discourses of television, in which communication is "understood as the injunction to participate in confessional discourse within the highly mediated channels of contemporary technology" (11). Dr. Ruth Westheimer's popular sex talk show on the Lifetime cable channel offers a paradigmatic example of the injunction to talk about sex in a format that both emphasizes the importance of sexual literacy and puts such talk in a moral framework that suggests sex is still a taboo subject. As White says, Dr. Ruth endorses consensual, monogamous sex and virginity until marriage: "Sexual pleasures and sexual techniques are thus circumscribed and confined in conventional social relationships. For all Dr. Ruth's image as the popular maven of sexual openness, the values that she purveys are relatively conventional" (39–40).

Similarly, erotic education encourages communication about sex in the interest of a stronger, monogamous, often explicitly stated marital relationship, with a sexologist moving the program along in a manner that reveals how sex can be used to achieve these goals. The erotic education video constructs a subject position for the couple to occupy—and often, this is in fact one subject position rather than two, indicating the extent to which the genre relies on the heterosexual unit. The couples may begin the video by telling their different stories, but by the end, their voices have merged in one unified endorsement of the importance of sex to their relationship. By telling their story, the couple come to recognize the "truth" about sex, in a process that is facilitated by the sexologist, who prods them along and reconciles potentially discordant statements or practices. As Foucault describes the relationship,

> The confession is a ritual of discourse in which the speaking subject is also the subject of the statement; it is also a ritual that unfolds within a power

relationship, for one does not confess without the presence (or virtual presence) of a partner who is not simply the interlocutor but the authority who requires the confession, prescribes and appreciates it, and intervenes in order to judge, punish, forgive, console, and reconcile. (*History*, 61)

Nearly all these videos start with a sexologist or other authority figure who is dressed very conventionally, foregrounding the professional nature of the ensuing program. A rather matronly Judith Seifer, a prominent sexologist, appears at the beginning of each of the forty *Behind the Bedroom Door* series; Seifer also helps narrate the Better Sex Video series, where she is joined by Drs. Della and Max Fitz-Gerald, both members of the American Board of Sexology. (The Better Sex series commanded 90 percent of the market as of 1993, according to a *Redbook* article cited in Robert Eberwein's study of sex education videos.) *Better Orgasms: Lovers' Guide Series* opens with Andrew Stanway, who is a sixtyish British fellow, sitting in a leather armchair in a book-lined drawing room. Even the usually audacious Candida Royalle introduces her *LOVERS* series looking more like a schoolmarm than a former porn star. Her hair is pulled tightly back into a bun, and she wears a white blouse that is buttoned up her neck. Royalle speaks in a calm, measured, occasionally didactic tone, ensuring her viewers that adult entertainment "can foster a mood of intimacy and bring you closer together." Addressing the perception that pornography represents a world of pure fantasy that distorts and inhibits its users' attempt to function in the "real" world, Royalle asserts that these "actual lovers" can teach couples lessons on "how to prevent boredom in the bedroom." Royalle ends her monologue with an offer for referrals for marital or sex therapy at 1-800-456-LOVE.

These videos intersect with the predominant message in popular women's magazines that the primary component of good sex is communication with your partner. The assumption is, obviously, that men aren't very good communicators and that they won't know what you like—or tell you what they like—unless you initiate a conversation. An article in *Ebony* called "Sex and Sisters: What Turns Women On" lists communication as one of the critical components of better sex:

Women love men who can communicate as well as demonstrate their feelings. Women want to know what men think, how they feel, what they need, not just through words but through actions that inspire passion. They want to hear how good they are making their man feel and exactly what he wants them to do. Sometimes, it can be difficult to express one's innermost feelings, especially when it comes to sex, but all couples should work to improve their communication skills. (Norment, 48)

In turn, good sex helps couples communicate better, in a tautology that ensures that the romantically defined couple find all their answers within the terms of the relationship. In *Redbook*'s article "The Secret of Couples Who Love Sex," Catherine Dennis reports that couples who have sex more often (four or more times a week) "share a special bond. They feel especially close. They communicate particularly well. And they adore their sex lives" (81–82).

Erotic education uses "real" people with regular bodies, standing in considerable contrast to the beautiful, sculptured bodies of most porn films. Pornography is not a homogeneous category, and, as Laura Kipnis notes in *Bound and Gagged*, there are subgenres appealing to different body types, such as fat porn. But it's fair to say that most porn uses beautiful people, which means the conventions: a preponderance of slender women with large breasts, long legs, and shapely buttocks, and men with muscled torsos and sizable penises. In contrast, erotic education focuses on the average body—neither extremely fat nor thin, for example—nothing that will impede the "average" viewers' ability to identify with the people, to find parts of their own bodies that compare favorably as well as unfavorably. Furthermore, the body is presented as fallible, unlike in hard-core porn, where men retain erections for long periods of time and women seem to have voracious appetites for sex in many orifices, all of which are lubricated and ready to go. In one volume of *Behind the Bedroom Door*, featuring Jim and Patti, Jim, thirty-eight, describes how he no longer always has orgasms and can't maintain erections for long periods of time, as he could when he was younger. Jim describes his feelings about this only after an extended session in which his wife, Patti, sucks his penis, with frequent cuts to his satisfied face, suggesting, when we learn that he doesn't always climax, that his pleasures are not dependent on orgasm. He then confirms this sentiment with a voice-over as he and Patti walk in the woods, saying that he has come to accept his body as it ages. Patti adds that she doesn't mind: "I know I give him pleasure even when he doesn't have an orgasm." The natural setting underscores the connection between sex and a kind of whole body pleasure: sex isn't about particular body parts, and orgasm isn't even necessary—very much in contrast to hard-core porn's historical emphasis on the visible proof of male ejaculation and its pursuit of the evidence of female orgasm. Dr. Seifer appears between the sex scene and the walk in the woods to normalize Jim's individual problem; many men don't have regular orgasms as they get older, she says reassuringly.

Sex is linked to whole bodies, health, and healing; couples talk through the process of self-empowerment. The *Ordinary Couples, Extraordinary Sex* series even provides viewers with a five-step program to follow, participating in the national obsession with self-help recovery programs like Alcoholics Anonymous. In *Ordinary Couples*, a thirty-something woman named Barbara describes how she didn't want to have sex after childbirth because she was too tired and had trouble getting wet. Then the video shows the couple in bed, with Dr. Scantling's voice-over describing what the couple is doing: applying lubricant and discussing why Barbara chooses, for her own comfort, to be on top of Donald. Barbara also describes how she overcame her concerns about her body after childbirth and after breast cancer surgery; in one scene she stands in front of a mirror and caresses her own body, examining each part and explaining how she came to love herself. Then Donald joins her and they explore each other's "ordinary" bodies, pointing out parts and flaws that they find particularly endearing.

In its emphasis on health articulated through monogamous relationships, erotic education implicitly contrasts itself to the stereotypes about pornography as a promiscuous underworld of AIDS and other sexually transmitted diseases. In *Hot Monogamy*, Love and Robinson endorse fidelity as an "intelligent choice" given the rise of AIDS and other sexually transmitted diseases, and then link the benefits of monogamy to all kinds of emotional and physical health: "People in supportive love relationships live longer and have fewer health problems" (14). Some of the connections between sex and health do seem to have at least minimal biological support: for example, "women who have regular sex have higher levels of estrogen, which helps prevent heart disease, preserves bone mass, minimizes hot flashes, and lowers the risk of depression." However, this medical support is then assumed to be relevant only for monogamous, heterosexual sex. Love asserts, for example, that "monogamous weekly intercourse promotes fertility and physiological well-being in women" (14). Why, one wonders, does not daily intercourse with different partners promote fertility and physiological well-being? Because these texts are so unremittingly heterosexual, gay sexual practices also get implicitly linked to AIDS and other diseases. In her introduction to *Hot Monogamy*, Love, for example, professes to have nothing against gays and lesbians; rather, she is simply "not . . . an expert in gay and lesbian sexuality" and thus has limited her book to examples of heterosexual couples (4). Most erotic education videos do not even acknowledge their own heterosexuality, assuming that the "couples'" market will share their assumptions that gays do not form couple relationships.

In its emphasis on real people with regular bodies, erotic education resembles amateur hard-core porn, in which "regular" people videotape themselves having sex and send in the tapes to companies like Home-Grown Video, which makes compilation videos for sale as hard-core porn. As with the Kensington Ladies, the bedroom as a site of sex is located in relation to other parts of the house—sometimes sex occurs in other rooms, sometimes the couples interact in other parts of the house after they've had sex. In this way, the bedroom is expanded; its benefits extend beyond the immediate marital bed into other aspects of everyday life. Barbara and Donald are shown in different parts of the house, outside jogging, and at times playing with their young daughter. Sex is normalized; it becomes just one component (albeit a very important one) of a fulfilled life. Rarely does sex cross the boundaries of the house, although Patti and Jim have sex in the woods. Thus, despite the fact that we are positioned as voyeurs of a private act, the couple seem to retain a sense of the legitimacy of the home and the bedroom. By contrast, Royalle's *Intimate Portraits* crosses the boundaries of public and private; in doing so, the video—combined with its distribution and circulation—represents one way of rearticulating the bedroom as a site of "live sex."

In the first volume of *Intimate Portraits*, we hear Jennifer and Steve tell their own stories; unlike other erotic education, there is no "expert" here mediating what the subjects say about sex, although Royalle has introduced the series as a tool for better communication. Although Jennifer and Steve are still "ordinary" people in a committed relationship, their everyday lives allow for a more expanded notion of how sexual practices and reality might coincide. Jennifer, who identifies herself as "an academic and a stripper," asserts that there is no contradiction between her public life as a stripper and her private, intimate relationship with Steve, with whom—she keeps asserting—she is totally in love. In one scene, Jennifer is at work, stripping at a male club, when Steve walks in. Jennifer is in the middle of spreading her legs directly in front of a customer, who is slipping a dollar bill into her g-string, but she still finds a moment to blow her lover a quick kiss as he stands, seemingly discomfited, in the doorway, becoming another one of her patrons. During sex at home later, Jennifer connects this public performance to the kind of sex she likes with Steve, describing how for her, all sex is a kind of performance for a man, or men, who she wants to seduce. Steve, however, says something different in a voice-over that begins as he enters the bar to watch her perform. Although he seems to feel comfortable with the fact that she is a stripper, he also claims that "She doesn't do these things at home," and, as they leave the bar, "We usually just go home and fall asleep," as if he needs to distinguish between her public and private sphere performances. Also Jennifer asserts that Steve loves to watch her perform, maybe even gets off on it, but Steve denies that, and we have his awkward entry into the bar juxtaposed with the gaze of the other male patrons complicating the question of how the public performance inflects their private relationship. Even though Steve apparently has some desire to distance their sex at home from the public site of the strip bar, the very relationship between the sites becomes a matter of discussion, and viewers, as voyeurs positioned differently by the different performances, are invited to compare their own reactions to public and private sphere sex acts. Because there is no therapist to intervene and mediate the dispute, the couple's confessions do not seem so normalized; although sex is brought into the context of everyday life, some tensions between the two remain. Furthermore, the text rearticulates governmental discourse that posits the home and adult entertainment as antithetical by putting home into a set of social relations that shows its potentially *positive* imbrication with the public presences of "pornography," insofar as Jennifer's stripping is connected with porn. The video, particularly with Royalle's introduction, repeats the governmental concern with love, mutuality, and consent within monogamous relationships, yet it shows that pornography is not a threat to these values but rather can actually facilitate their development.

Because of the constant threat of resemblance to porn, the experts in most erotic education videos often take care to explain how what's represented is different from porn. Again, the emphasis on communication resurfaces: sex must always be completely consensual, with each partner trusting the other to do only what he or she has agreed to in advance, addressing the stereotype that women are forced to perform in or to watch pornography. Before Jennifer and Steve's story, Royalle asserts that although the couple portrayed do engage in "some acts of domination and surrender," these acts are "mutually consenting," done with "love and respect . . . there is no actual force or degradation of women or men." In Jim and Patti's story, Patti spends a long time sucking Jim's penis, and he occasionally holds her head, seemingly pushing her mouth down. Dr. Seifer's voice-over assures viewers that Jim is sensitive to Patti's feelings: "He doesn't want to push his penis too far into her mouth," she says. "While Patti is comfortable with this position, it's not for all women. It takes a partner she trusts a lot." Patti explicitly contrasts what she has learned about sex since marrying Jim with the messages she received about sex as a child—either that sex was dirty, from her Catholic parents, or that it was scary, from a teenage friend who shared a porn magazine with her. In the story of Donald and Barbara, Donald at one point shaves Barbara's genital area; Dr. Scantling is quick to assure viewers that not all women will like this but that Barbara finds it very sensual. The emphasis on Barbara's consent counters conceptions that shaved female genitals in porn are meant to appeal to male viewers who fantasize about young girls or for whom hair is just too masculine.

The implications of open, communicative sex in the broader relationship are quite significant: sex can even transform gender roles, suggesting, again, that even sex that is articulated to monogamy and the bedroom can sometimes be used to rearticulate relationships outside the bedroom. In *Ordinary Couples*, another middle-aged, upper-class white couple, Larry and Hue, illustrate step four of the five-step program: "Break out of old patterns; create an oasis for tenderness that's interwoven in your busy days." In part, these patterns include traditional gender roles. Larry confesses to being a "proactive man who didn't listen to women," but then describes how allowing himself to feel passive in sex enabled him to become a better listener; he speaks of a more "blended relationship" that has resulted from this role switching. Straddling Larry and demonstrating her dominance in bed as he lies perfectly still, Hue says, "It's time for men to experience their nurturing roles. Women can be assertive and still feminine." Here, sexual practices effect changes in everyday life because the couple carry the lessons of the bedroom into their other forms of communication.

The tensions between sex and everyday life are also maintained through the endorsement of fantasy; most of these videos do encourage partners to engage in fantasy as a "healthy and natural" part of their sex lives. Fantasies are just a normal, everyday activity, and the Better Sex videos focusing on fantasy life emphasize this point by interspersing the sexologists' advice about fantasies with person-on-the-street interviews.

The format and setting suggest that camera people are roaming the streets of southern California, occasionally stopping people of various ages, races, and genders, and eliciting their confessions on subjects like "Do you fantasize when you masturbate?" "Should we act out our fantasies?" The people respond in various ways, but always in a manner that normalizes fantasy, encouraging viewers to think that everyone fantasizes, from a sixty-five-year-old grandmother to a twenty-year-old punk with a mohawk dressed in leather. The sexologist elaborates on the interviewees' answers; then the video turns to a fantasy that illustrates the topic. While the fantasy—which, as we learn later, is a cut from an adult video—plays, a voice-over of the unseen "fantasizer" describes what is going on and why he/she likes the scene. One woman describes her fantasy of having sex in the forest with her husband of many years; "he knows my body so well," she says. In another fantasy, a woman describes how her lover rubs ice cubes over various parts of her body; her words function as an instruction guide to what the image reveals: "He rubs my clit. He spreads my lips" (extreme close-up of genitals, with ice cube entering the vagina; switch to her straining face, eyes closed, head thrown back, panting). "Faster, faster, faster." At a point, the fantasies seem to become reality; the visual impact of an ice cube entering a vagina seems to deny that this is occurring purely in the realm of fantasy. Furthermore, the voice-over provides such a detailed, somewhat objective description of the acts occurring that it begins to seem more like an instruction guide than a fantasy. As such, fantasy is normalized—its mysteries explained in no uncertain terms—and brought into line with the reality of a couple trying to have better sex for the sake of their relationship. In a way, then, pornography is also normalized, in a manner that, paradoxically, corresponds with the antiporn argument that denies the realm of fantasy and claims that pornography *is* reality. Robin Morgan's oft-quoted phrase "Pornography is the theory, rape the practice" argues that men act on pornographic images, making them the literal reality of women victims and bypassing the realm of fantasy. The erotic education videos similarly suggest that men and women both will act on the fantasies they see enacted—in the interest of better relationships.

The videos often conclude with an attempt to reconcile the potentially embarrassing contradiction between the confession of sexual practices and problems—an intensely private act—and the public airing of these problems in the homes of potentially thousands of viewers. If pornography is to be domesticated, finally, through the viewing of these videos, yet at the same time remain interesting and erotic enough to maintain spectators' attention, then the video must somehow hold in tension the different subject positions a viewer has come to occupy: voyeur of private sexual acts, participant in the pursuit of better sex and relationships, and therapist who has heard the couples' problems revealed. We see these three positions merging in Patti's final statement in the *Behind the Bedroom Door* series: "Jim and I have never made love in front of a camera before," she says, acknowledging the voyeuristic nature of the video. "It's a sin that people are made to think that sex is dirty. Sex is a very natural function for all people," she says, alluding to her upbringing in a strict Catholic household, which is frequently referenced as a hindrance to her sexual expression early in her marriage. This statement mitigates against the viewer's potential to see Patti as a porn star and rather draws the viewer into a position of sympathy with Patti, who has throughout the video "confessed" her sexual inhibitions even as she has sex in a seemingly uninhibited fashion. And, finally, says Patti, in a statement that tries to unite all (Christian) spectators in the pursuit of better marriages: "Jim and I don't have much money, to buy toys or to go places. Our main enjoyment in life is our lovemaking. Sex is one of God's greatest gifts to mankind."

Just the Facts, Ma'am

The erotic education videos cannot be completely subsumed within a conservative agenda—even when they appeal to Christianity—both because their reliance on pornographic visuals continually suggests the relationship to porn and because the videos stress, to varying degrees, the way sex can rearticulate the bedroom into a less isolated site. Erotic education thus maintains a degree of fluidity and movement between public and private sites, suggesting that especially for women who don't have access, for various reasons, to other sexually explicit materials, the videos might enhance their sense of sexual mobility and increase the possibilities of pleasure within relationships. That sense of movement dissipates—although does not completely disappear—in the most conservative of this genre I am calling erotic education, the sex education book and video of the remarkably popular John Gray. Dr. Ruth and the sexologists act as friendly therapists eliciting the confessions of couples hungry for the truth of sex in a format that depends on a degree of interaction; John Gray, however, is the benevolent but authoritarian minister, a version of the southern evangelist, roaming the stage with magic marker in hand, diagramming female pleasure without ever actually soliciting audience confessions. The visual conventions of porn cannot come into contact with the site of the bedroom; if one is to bring sex into the open in relation to monogamy and marriage, it can be done only by talking about sex, and talking about it in a way that uses sex to reinforce gendered differences.

As such, Gray intersects with conservative notions of marriage that insist on a distinction between pornography and the marital bed. This precept is illustrated in a *Ladies' Home Journal* article on "How to Make Passion Last . . . and Other Advice from a Top Expert on Love and Sex." In this article, Barbara De Angelis, author of *The 100 Most-Asked Questions about Love, Sex, and Relationships*, opposes pornography to intimacy. A woman asks De Angelis what to do about the fact that her husband reads porn magazines: "It's ruining our sex life, because I feel angry and turned off to him. Should I just try to accept it?" De Angelis says no way: "Pornography destroys intimacy because, by definition, it introduces a third person into your relationship. Although some couples claim they enjoy sharing pornography, I strongly doubt that it enhances intimacy. What it does is create more eroticism, which many couples mistake for intimacy" (86). De Angelis argues that "adding fantasy to the relationship is a cover-up that distracts you from the real problem." At the same time, it seems, pornography has become the real problem for this couple: "his porn habit has shaken your self-esteem, undermined your sense of safety within the marriage and damaged the trust between the two of you. Tell your husband the magazines have to go. And if they don't, you will" (86). The *Ladies' Home Journal* also carries the popular feature "Can This Marriage Be Saved," which it calls "The most popular, the most enduring feature in the world."

Valorizing marriage in the 1990s, however, often involves a complicated maneuvering in which old values are recontextualized within contemporary notions of women's roles—a tenet Gray also illustrates. Most popular representations of marriage in the 1990s integrate aspects of feminism, simultaneously recalling a time when marriage was more stable and defining women's roles in marriage as more equal than they were in this "previous time." *Redbook*, a magazine that unabashedly celebrates the romantic couple, is one of the most indicative examples of this somewhat complex version of a backlash. At times it seems frankly nostalgic, as in a special section on marriage in September 1996 entitled "Why

Marriage Is Hot Again." The article declared, "Today, for the first time since the mid-1960's, smart women in their twenties—in some cases in their early twenties—are not only unafraid but eager to become brides." This assertion involved some maneuvering, including defying Census Bureau statistics, which, *Redbook* acknowledged, "continue to show a rise in marriage age among Americans overall." The magazine relied instead on "people who toil in the marriage field—from sociologists to wedding planners," who "tell a different story: among well-educated, career-minded women, becoming a wife at around age 25 has grown not only socially acceptable but enviable" (Brady, 122). The article endorses all the pressures on women to marry that Susan Faludi cites and debunks in *Backlash*, such as the fear of fertility complications by age thirty-five and the threat of never finding a husband if you wait until your mid-thirties. An accompanying article describes *Redbook*'s poll of 506 women under thirty-six, all married seven years or less, which asked "the new young wife" what she would and wouldn't do for her new husband. The poll is startling in its backlash tone; for example, in response to the question "If the opportunity arose, I'd think about cheating on him with" (then a list of celebrities including Antonio Banderas, Tom Cruise, Brad Pitt, Bill Clinton, and Mel Gibson), 64 percent said, "I would not cheat on my husband with anyone." (Mel Gibson was second with 21 percent.) Responding to another question, "I would tell my husband if . . . ," 52 percent of the young wives said they would tell their husband if they made eye contact with another man!

On the other hand, *Redbook* ran an article in October 1996 that provided quite a scathing critique of a book that would very much support the magazine's marriage special: *The Rules: Time-Tested Secrets for Capturing the Heart of Mr. Right*. Also a *New York Times* best-seller, this 1995 book is an unabashedly retrograde set of, well, rules for capturing the heart of Mr. Right and ensuring a marriage proposal. They include such gems as "Don't talk to a man first (and don't ask him to dance); Don't call him and rarely return his calls; Always end phone calls first; No more than casual kissing on the first date; Don't expect a man to change or try to change him; Don't live with a man (or leave your things in his apartment)." *The Rules*' authors, Ellen Fein and Sherrie Schneider, concede that women can still have their careers, but counter feminism (without specifically citing it) by describing their deep longing for romance: "We didn't want to give up our liberation, but neither did we want to come home to empty apartments. Who said we couldn't have it all?" (2). "Nineties women," say the writers, need to learn the "basics" of how to catch a husband, and basically that means forgetting what they've "been taught about male-female relations" and learning the set of rules that their grandmothers and mothers followed.

In a similar fashion, "Grayism" sets up rules for men and women of the 1990s to follow, both acknowledging, albeit reluctantly, the ways feminism has altered relationships and using those very changes in order to argue for the reassertion of a fairly traditional marriage. In terms of access, Gray's *Mars and Venus in the Bedroom* and his video *The Secrets of Great Sex* represent an important description of female anatomy and orgasm; his explicit emphasis on how to bring a woman to orgasm through oral sex is a significant departure from any previous Christian attempts to discuss marriage and sex, such as the 1976 book *The Act of Marriage*, coauthored by the Christian fundamentalists Tim and Beverly LaHaye.[7] Much like hard-core porn, Gray has responded to the feminists and sexologists who have valorized the distinctiveness of female pleasure. Yet, much as Williams argues that hard-core porn "remains suspiciously in the service of the phallic norm" even as it stresses female pleasure, so do Gray's texts use the very notion of different sexual pleasures to reinforce a patriarchal household.

Men Are from Mars

John Gray got the idea for his *Men Are from Mars* series from watching the movie *E.T.*; he told a *People* magazine reporter, "When E.T. came to this planet, people tried to figure out the needs he had in his world. That's what women should do with men—treat us like we're from another planet and respect our ways instead of trying to fix, change or improve us" (Small, 35). Gray, in his mid-forties, is sort of from another planet; he grew up in Houston, the son of a wealthy oil family. Beginning in the late 1960s, he spent nearly a decade with the Maharishi Mahesh Yogi; he told a *New York* reporter that his unlined complexion was due to "the reabsorption of nine years' worth of semen into his system" (Mead, 69). When he emerged from celibacy, he says he had sex almost daily with a variety of women for a year; he then married and began to build a business doing seminars on sex and relationships.

Gray still has a sex appeal for women; in its review of sex education videos, *Cosmopolitan* raves about his videotape *Secrets of Great Sex,* which consists solely of him onstage, fully clothed: "A big plus is that Gray is a pretty sexy dude himself" (Gutmann, 82). In 1995 Gray performed for three hours at none other than Carnegie Hall to a sold-out audience. He has the sex videotape, audiotapes, and a CD-ROM, in which "the reader interacts with a miniature shirtsleeved Gray" (Mead, 68). He also has a calendar with tear-off quotations, the John Gray cruise in the Mediterranean or Caribbean, and a line of Hallmark greeting cards (Mead, 68). *Men Are from Mars* was on the *New York Times* best-seller list for more than 120 consecutive weeks; the book has sold more than 100 million copies and has been translated into more than forty languages.[8] Spreading his word as well are about a hundred facilitators across the country, running seminars like the one I attended in Indianapolis.

John Gray discourse offers an ahistorical—indeed an otherworldly—explanation of gendered differences, one that conveniently bypasses any political, historical, cultural, or social realities. It is worth quoting the allegory that Gray uses to support his mini-industry. This passage appears on the first page of the book that participants of the day-long seminar receive:

One day long ago the Martians, looking through their telescopes, discovered the Venusians. Just glimpsing the Venusians awakened feelings they had never known. They fell in love and quickly invented space travel and flew to Venus.

The Venusians welcomed the Martians with open arms. They had intuitively known that this day would come. Their hearts opened wide to a love they had never felt before. The love between the Venusians and Martians was magical. They delighted in being together, doing things together and sharing together. Though from different worlds, they reveled in their differences. They spent months learning about each other, exploring and appreciating their different needs. . . .

For years they lived together in love and harmony. Then they decided to fly to Earth. In the beginning everything was wonderful and beautiful. But the effects of Earth's atmosphere took hold, and one morning everyone woke up with a peculiar kind of amnesia—selective amnesia!

Both the Martians and Venusians forgot that they were from different planets and were supposed to be different. In one morning, everything they had learned about their differences was erased from their memory. And since that day Martians and Venusians have been in conflict. (4)

One wonders what caused this "selective amnesia," if perhaps the "one morning" refers to the nearly twenty-five years of second-wave feminism that preceded the publication of *Men Are from Mars*. Indeed, Gray told a *People* magazine reporter that "All I'm trying to do is honor the instincts inside of people. With the feminist movement, we've forgotten men and women are different. Now we're realizing we can be different and equal." Gray has devised a powerful apparatus for simultaneously acknowledging and dissipating feminism's critique of gender inequities.

During the Indianapolis seminar, for example, the facilitator returns often to Gray's notion that men seek refuge in their "caves," which generally means they want to be left alone in front of the TV in order to escape the constantly chattering women.[9] These gendered differences need to be acknowledged if communication is ever to improve, says the discourse. However, Grayism exports these feminist critiques into his discourse, in which, during the seminar at least, the facilitator uses the terms "Martians" and "Venusians" in place of "men" and "women," and never mentions the concepts masculinity, femininity, feminism, gender, or sexism. Furthermore, the differences are not challenged but rather celebrated and upheld; accepting each other's sometimes biological, sometimes socialized, but always inevitable differences is critical to developing and maintaining a healthy and passionate relationship.

Unlike the erotic education videos, Grayism does not offer the opportunity of confession in the interest of helping the couple participate in the realization of truth; rather, Grayism relies on people's already formed associations and stereotypes about gender in order to elicit their affirmation, either through the raising of hands or applause. In Indianapolis, Curt's anecdotes about the differences between men and women, sometimes drawing on his own marriage, often elicited nods, murmurs of "yes, yes," and knowing chuckles. Curt often followed a string of advice with a comment like "Isn't that so, Venusians?" to which many of the women nodded or at least smiled. The audience members are offered what they already know to be true—husbands communicate with facts and information, women via "feelings"—and then told that this is the order of things, nothing need really change, it's just a matter of accepting and learning how to cope with these differences.

There are moments, however, when the coping advice verges on a deconstruction of difference. Martians are encouraged to listen to Venusians, for example, rather than following their instincts to immediately tell them what to do to fix their problems. Martians should strive for empathy; they should practice relational skills that are usually ascribed to the feminine world. Yet when asked by an audience member (OK, it was me) whether he was not advocating a lessening of some differences in the interest of better communication, Curt quickly reasserted the importance of difference. In fact, he said, with many women pursuing careers (where they have to sometimes act like Martians), it becomes even more critical for them to be clear-cut Venusians at home.

Sadly, many women in the audience seemed to think that John Gray holds the key to their relationship problems. In my small discussion group, three women in their fifties and another woman in her late twenties—all friends who jointly decided to pay $69 each for the day-long event—latched on to the valorization of dichotomous difference in order to explain why they all had the same problems with their husbands in the morning: none of the husbands wanted to talk; all the wives were eager to begin the day with conversation. As one of the women said, "It took thirty years for my husband to realize that what I really wanted was just for him to say a few words to me before he left for work." Recounted another woman of her first husband, who had died, "He said to me one morning, 'Do you know how disgusting it is to have to talk to you every single morning?'" The women agreed that they would have agonized less over this situation if they had simply understood that Martians just aren't as talkative as Venusians. The twenty-something woman, who had recently separated from her husband and wanted desperately to save her marriage, nodded as the older women recounted their stories, occasionally blinking back tears.[10]

Grayism works best when it can isolate relationships within the home and isolate sex within the bedroom. Yet it must acknowledge the ways outside influences (such as women's careers) shape marriage; cannily, it posits these intrusions as reinforcement for the reassertion of difference. For example, Gray's argument in his bedroom book is that men want sex and women want romance. Yet Gray also notes that this binary may be altered when women enter the traditionally male work world: "Having spent most of the day in a traditionally male job, she too wants a 'wife' to greet *her* when she gets home. She too wants the release that sex brings. Great sex fulfills her as much as it fulfills him" (5). Almost as if he fears acknowledging his own deconstruction, however, Gray spends much of his bedroom book asserting the sex/romance distinction, with women constantly posited as the more romantic, men as the more physical. Interestingly, because these roles are discussed precisely as roles, there is an unintended denaturalizing of gender, to the point that the advice Gray gives approaches that of performance. For example, under the heading "When Men Stop Initiating Sex," Gray advises women not to be too aggressive in their pursuit of sex, lest their partners become too passive. Gray ascribes this aggression to a woman's "masculine pursuing side" and says its expression forces a man to "move too far to his feminine receptive side. This imbalance slowly erodes the passion in a marriage" (114). Rather, a woman should "initiate sex in an indirect manner," thus "ensuring that her partner can find his masculine side that desires her and seeks to pursue her" (114). Gray's latest book, *Mars and Venus on a Date: A Guide for Navigating the Five Stages of Dating to Create a Loving and Lasting Relationship,* applies these roles to dating: "To create a relationship, a woman must be careful not to pursue a man but to be responsive to his pursuit. This kind of receptiveness and responsiveness is expressed through flirting" (195–96). Flirting is like shopping, Gray explains, and pursuing is like going on a job interview. Gray's instructions about how to enact these roles are so explicit as to be almost an exercise in the art of performance—how does a woman flirt? Gray provides a list of twelve ways, including "bat her eyelids," "brush up against him," "be playfully argumentative in a discussion or even challenge his point of view," and "revel in his brilliance."

Gray's *Mars and Venus in the Bedroom* adapts the best-selling formula of *Men Are from Mars, Women Are from Venus* to the bedroom, relying heavily on various notions of gendered differences, such as the concept that men get aroused quickly and women need to be "romanced" into wanting sex. However, this assertion of difference works in the interest of women when it comes to the actual techniques of sex. Gray insists that men acquire a thorough knowledge of female anatomy, including drawings and specific descriptions; he tells men they should get used to the idea of "camping out 'down south.' Sometimes it's good to grab a pillow and plan to camp out down south for a full fifteen minutes," he says. "You should just resign yourself to the fact that you are not going anywhere for quite a while. In this relaxed position, you can experiment with some of these suggestions" (169). Gray then describes in great detail a variety of moves men should try, using both fingers and tongue, encouraging them to listen carefully to their partners to gauge the success of their efforts. Here's a sampling:

The added advantage of licking is that the sensation for her is super smooth and lubricated. To provide another sensation, he can delicately suck the clitoris into his mouth and then flick it with his tongue or sometimes just suck it into his mouth and gently massage it back and forth. . . . Sometimes while licking or sucking her clitoris, he can gently insert one or two fingers in her vagina and slowly move in and out. . . . Reaching her in this way, he can stimulate another point that some sex researchers call the G-spot, located about two inches in and toward her front rather than her back. (172)

Gray also devotes considerable space to describing how a woman can stimulate a penis, both manually and orally (although there are no helpful drawings in this section). However, Gray never wanders from the assertion that women need much more attention: "Don't forget that, as a general rule, a woman needs about ten times more foreplay than a man. . . . A man should remember that it is not what he does but how long he takes to do it that ensures her fulfillment" (149). And he urges women to revel in this much-deserved pleasure, to claim a "feeling of entitlement" rather than to assume that she must continue in the traditional role of giver: "Many times, when a woman is particularly good at giving to others, she has a difficult time receiving. In sex, she may be so busy thinking about her partner's need or so concerned for him that she doesn't give herself permission to focus on her own needs" (133).

This mild form of deconstruction reaches perhaps its most overt in Gray's video *Secrets of Great Sex*, in which he roams a stage for an hour in a suitcoat, holding a magic marker with which he occasionally diagrams desire, in the form of charts and a drawing of a female body. Gray begins with a chart that divides men's and women's needs for pleasurable sex; the woman's list is long, including romance, time, and tenderness. The man's list contains only one item—to fulfill the woman. Thus, after initially erecting a set of clear gendered differences from which women's sexual desires seemingly flow naturally, Gray decontructs the differences by bringing male desire into line with female desire. And Gray takes the deconstruction one step farther; why does a man want most to bring a woman to orgasm? Because then he can say, "I did that," and with this, Gray struts proudly about the stage, derisively imitating a macho man who has just given his woman the orgasm of her life.

The emphasis on women's selfish pleasures thus shows desire exceeding the boundaries of the traditional gendered roles that Grayism elsewhere upholds; however, the emphasis on women's desire does not redefine any other aspect of coupled life. In fact, Gray is often quoted as an expert in matters of the home and family in women's magazines in a manner that reasserts a kind of traditional family values. In a 1996 article in *Working Mother* entitled "Moms Are from Venus, Sons Are from Mars," Gray's theory is used as the starting point for explaining why mothers need to accept the essential difference of "boy talk" from "girl talk." Among the tips for mothers seeking better communication with sons: "Make requests using five words or less," and "Accept boy/guy talk" (Graham, 48–49). This article indicates that Grayism's deconstruction of gender occurring around female sexual pleasure does not reconfigure gender relations outside the bedroom; rather, the excesses of bodily pleasure that disrupt bedroom relations dissipate and keep the bedroom isolated from the rest of the house. In Gray's formula for a successful relationship, men take out the trash, women do the dishes, men order at restaurants, women say they like the movie even when they don't, and so forth. Furthermore, keeping sex in the bedroom means that certain issues surrounding sexuality's imbrication in daily life are never addressed— such as the question of children and sexuality. And certainly the excesses of bodily pleasure do not extend beyond the walls of the house: Grayism acknowledges public sphere influences on the home only in order to reassert the importance of the home's isolation. For example, because women are spending so much time at their careers, they no longer have time to develop relationships with other women; but, says Gray, this actually provides a wonderful opportunity for men to step in and fill this void. Men may no longer be needed as the providers and protectors to the degree that they were before women could be economically independent, but they can recoup that role, in a slightly different fashion, by becoming better listeners. Although this advice does encourage men to be less "typically" masculine, it also serves to isolate the couple from the rest of the world: women don't need other women friends—indeed, these friends could upset the dynamic of interdependence between husband and wife (191). This degree of interdependence extends to sex as well, again indicating the ways the emphasis on female pleasure is dissipated in the interest of a more cohesive coupled unit. Gray says women can fantasize, but only about their husbands (102); women can masturbate, but only in preparation for sex with their husbands. Says Gray, "She never has to feel as if she can't get the sexual fulfillment she is looking for. This is why it's good for her to masturbate when he's around instead of just when she is alone" (103). With this advice, Gray both endorses masturbation as a means of women's pleasure and incorporates it into the procreative economy, thus depoliticizing it as a means of autonomous female pleasure distinct from intercourse. And he distances his advice from any reliance on pornography or erotica by suggesting that the only fantasy material a woman needs is right there beside her, even if he's snoring. Who needs pornography/erotica when you have the real thing—a notion that brings us back to my opening anecdote about the intersection of *Hardcore* and *Gray*.

Hardcore's emphasis on marriage and romance is not representative of all hard-core porn; however, its intersection with *Gray* does indicate one of the dangers of celebrating a kind of couples' porn that begins to prescribe roles for women that fit within national conceptions of monogamy and marriage. Domestication here becomes a process in which the private sphere does indeed become largely private; the texts function to increase some women's access to pleasurable activities—which I am not dismissing—but in a manner that is mitigated by its reliance on the terms of a traditionally gendered relationship. It is not surprising, then, that access to texts like *Mars and Venus in the Bedroom* is as easy as a trip to the table of the *New York Times* best-sellers at Barnes and Noble. Yet neither should the possibilities of couples' porn be dismissed; as Femme Productions' videos show, it is possible to maintain a sense of movement between public and private spheres even when locating sex in the bedroom. I refer here both to the content of the videos and to their heterogeneous circulation—in adult video stores, feminist mail-order catalogs like Good Vibrations, and sex therapist conventions. It is *possible* that domestication will encourage a movement between public and private spheres, even the bedroom, in the interest of practicing "live sex."

6

Eroticizing the Television

In the spring of 1997 cable operators across the country announced their participation in a new advertising campaign: the "Make Every TV Set a Cable TV Set" campaign. Based on a "whole-house concept," operators are aiming to wire up every set in the home by offering free installation of additional cable outlets after an initial onetime installation fee of ten dollars. The operators are banking that cable viewing will follow the patterns of television watching: a 1995 study found that in homes with two or more sets, prime-time viewing was increased by 33 percent (Forkan, 26).

By 1997 about a dozen cable networks had reached 70 percent penetration of U.S. households with TVs, a threshold percentage in the industry because of the implications for attracting advertisers and one that indicates the degree to which cable has gradually eroded the broadcast network monopoly (*Economics of TV Programming*, 193). Furthermore, some cable channels have targeted women as an audience equal in importance to men—especially upscale working women, who attract advertisers not only because they remain the primary household consumers, in the tradition of women historically targeted by radio and TV, but also because they have considerable money to spend on their own pleasures. The Lifetime channel started operating in 1984 with a mix of programming that appealed mainly to women and in 1995 explicitly announced itself to viewers as "Television for Women." In 1996 the American Movie Channel announced that it was starting a new channel specifically for women, the Romance Classics channel. Says the company's ad in the industry journal *Cablevision*: "For Years Men Have Enjoyed Monday Night Football. Now It's Her Turn ... give an underserved audience something to cheer about."

Numerous media critics have noted the ways leisure technologies often function as part of and help reproduce the already established social organization of domestic space, in which women work and men relax. Yet it would seem that within the troubled history of women's access to new technologies, cable is becoming a more women-friendly medium, assuming a place within the intersections of women's work and domestic leisure time and thus holding considerable potential as a source of pleasure for women—including erotic pleasure.[1]

Premium channels like HBO, Cinemax, and Showtime regularly feature "adult programming"—another category claiming distinctiveness from pornography, especially pornography's threat to children—in the late-night hours, and much of this programming features women protagonists exploring their sexual fantasies and desires. Even Playboy, with its long history of catering to a male audience, has tried to attract women through its cable channel. In fact, the focus on women as sexual agents, especially on the premium channels, usually overwhelms any attention given to men, and in this sense we can see that adult cable programming shares many of the conventions of women's print erotica. As with women's erotica, adult cable programming expands the conventions of traditional pornography, retaining the emphasis on sex but integrating it into a sometimes complex set of other details about different kinds of everyday life. The upwardly mobile professional woman trying to fit romance into her busy schedule, the bored suburban housewife neglected by her successful husband, the twenty-something woman struggling to figure out her sexuality, the femme fatale of the erotic thriller, and the hardnosed female detective who needs a good dose of passionate sex are just some of the women who populate these erotic shows. Television has historically represented the potential to blur public and private spheres, to, as Lynn Spigel writes, "giv[e] the private citizen the chance to travel imaginatively into the outside world while remaining in the comforts of the home" (182). The question remains, however: what kind of relationship between public and private spheres does cable programming represent? To what degree does it contribute to a definition of women's sexual agency that is situated as a product of their mobility between public and private spheres? If agency, drawing again on Larry Grossberg, is "a matter of the structured mobility by which people are given access to particular kinds of places, and to the paths that allow one to move to and from such places" (102), how does adult cable programming expand those paths? How does it limit them by ignoring the structuring variables that determine access?

It is difficult to answer these questions quickly because cable offers conflicting representations of the relationship between erotic mobility and everyday life; I examine the different kinds of programs in detail in this chapter. However, it is possible to assert that much adult cable programming defines mobility in terms of white, straight, upwardly mobile women; unlike print, it has generally not represented women of color and lesbians as equal participants in the struggle for access to sexual mobility. This is no doubt due to the cable companies' desire to appeal to the most affluent, somewhat homogeneous consumer base; indeed, some advertisers may be more interested in cable than in traditional television precisely because of the built-in ability to "divide the audience into people who can afford to pay a monthly fee and people who cannot," as Jackie Byars and Eileen R. Meehan note in their analysis of cable, particularly the Lifetime channel for women. The average monthly bill for basic cable service rose 7.8 percent in 1996 to $26.95, an estimate that does not include fees for pay-per-view channels like Playboy (Colman, "Cable Rates," 47). Cable adult programming unself-consciously ties erotic mobility to class and race mobility, indicating serious limitations in the degree to which the kind of agency posited does indeed represent a kind of *structured* mobility.

Cable's representation of sexual mobility is also hampered by the far stricter regulations on sexually explicit content on television than in print, as I describe in chapter 1. Due to these regulatory standards, adult cable programming must be less explicit than either women's erotica or hard-core porn, which also means that it offers much less in the way of explicit description of female pleasure than does most erotic literature or, for that matter, hard-core porn. The clitoris does not reign supreme on cable, unlike most of the other texts discussed in this book. Especially on the premium channels, cunnilingus is only suggested, and even that suggestion is quite rare compared to the frequent images of simulated intercourse. There are no explicit images of women's genitals, although the premium channels will show a flash of pubic hair from a medium-long shot, and the Playboy channel quite often shows the female genital area (an image that is not *essentially* in the interest of female pleasure, particularly in the context of Playboy programming). Women's breasts get the most attention, followed perhaps by women's legs, backs, and buttocks; men's bodies are much less prominent, but when they are shown, the focus is on muscled torsos and nicely shaped buttocks. One never sees an erect penis and hardly ever a flaccid one, even on the exclusively adult channels, an absence that greatly distances soft-core from hard-core porn. We must therefore question the terms of access to information and pleasures, not because explicit sex is the only component of women's erotica but because the lack of clitoral emphasis within a context of women's pleasures leaves many of the programs implicitly endorsing a kind of conventional Hollywood intercourse, with the woman inevitably simulating orgasm, issuing the requisite moans and groans as proof of climax, shortly after the man enters her (or, rather, pretends to enter her, since the intercourse is simulated). Thus the need to clearly distinguish itself from pornography takes on a different form in cable than it does in print; the history of harsher legal standards for visual pornography, especially on television, shapes a textual content that is much less explicit in its description and representation of female pleasure than is most erotic literature. There is thus a contradiction between the narrative focus on female pleasure and the visual focus on the (conventionally attractive) female body, often to the exclusion of the male body. A 1997 episode of *Red Shoe Diaries*, for example, showed a woman swimming naked, the camera remaining at a respectful distance but nevertheless panning over her entire body, including pubic hair. However, when her male lover joined her, he was wearing a bathing suit that barely but adequately covered his genital area.

This chapter positions women's access to cable within two histories: women and television and women and visual pornography, both within the framework of domesticity. I first sketch a brief history of women and television, asking how adult cable fits within this trajectory. Then I examine the history of the Playboy Entertainment Group, asking how successful it has been at transforming its everyday porn for men into everyday porn for couples via cable. Then I will analyze the various kinds of adult programs available on premium cable, focusing on the representations of mobility between public and private spheres. Throughout this analysis, I consider the question of cable's relationship to the home: what potential is represented by the increasing concentration of technologies of pornography within the so-called private sphere? My analysis suggests that the greater the investment that cable programming has in the history of conventional pornography, the less likely it is to offer women access on their own—albeit diverse—terms. Another factor is the manner in which technologies like cable interact with other technologies of pornography that are themselves rooted in the traditional conventions of porn aimed at men. This argument suggests that the premium channels, which are definitely less invested in the conventions of pornography than the Playboy channel, have more potential in terms of marking out cable television as an area of domesticated erotic access for women.

Television and the Home

At the end of her study of television's integration into the home in the post–World War II years, Lynn Spigel argues that many of the discursive conventions shaping the reception of television in the 1950s remain relevant in the 1990s, even as they are articulated differently according to changing historical conditions. For example, TV was lauded in its early days for its ability to transform the home into a theater, a concept that has been deployed even more intensely with the development of new technologies like cable, satellites, video technology, and computers. The increasing interactivity of communication technologies promises to transform the home into a self-sufficient cocoon, offering all the entertainment one could possibly imagine without the "inconvenience" of stepping outside one's front door. Much as advertisements for television in the 1950s spoke of the medium's ability to bridge public and private spheres, advertisements for new communication technologies promise to "bring the outside world into the home," creating a kind of home theater that "replicates experiences in social settings" (Spigel, 182–83). Technologies promise, once again, to bring the family together around the viewing of television, yet also suggest the potential for the television to divide families; as Spigel says, in the 1950s TV "came to be associated with social differences and segregation among family members" (69). Similarly, as indicated by the "Make Every TV Set a Cable Set" campaign, new technologies offer possibilities of differentiated private spaces, of a home divided along areas of interest. With cable, this segmentation has been enhanced through narrowcasting—the proliferation of channels appealing to specific interest groups, which was partially enabled by Reaganist deregulation. The cable television experience suggests images of isolated viewing: teenagers watching MTV in their bedrooms, young children watching Nickelodeon in the playroom, Dad watching ESPN in his study, Mom watching Lifetime in the kitchen . . . and Mom and Dad in their bedroom watching the Playboy channel after the kids are in bed for the night (presumably, although there's always the computer to worry about).

In some ways, adult cable programming's appeal to women represents a continuation of the historical positioning of women and television within family and household relations, especially the programming that articulates sex to romance. Early radio daytime programming appealed to women as the primary household consumers through serial dramas and talk shows, switching over in the evening hours to family shows like situation comedies and variety shows. Television maintained these generic practices, targeting women in the home with soap operas and talk shows, programs that purportedly offered enough repetition and fragmentation to allow women to accomplish their daily chores and still follow the narrative. Indeed, as Byars and Meehan argue, soap operas and talk shows still dominate network programming "during the heart of the house worker's day, when the (presumably male) primary wage earner and older children are expected to be away from the house" (16). The formula of soaps has remained basically the same, emphasizing "personal relations, familial ties, and emotional crises, which are generally worked out in domestic space or in a domesticated work place," and relying on the same stock characters—"powerful matriarchs, scheming vixens, clever businesswomen, and sincere beauties ... along with their male counterparts—powerful patriarchs, scheming gigolos, clever businessmen, and sincere hunks" (16). Soaps have not remained completely static. They are more sexually explicit than ever, for example, and they are more likely to discuss social issues than before (16). Talk shows have integrated the melodramatic aspects of soaps, "focusing mainly on sexual relations, familial ties, and emotional crises" (Byars and Meehan, 17). Although talk shows may still have a somewhat dubious reputation, soaps have increasingly gained respectability in the industry, indicating a new consideration for the possibilities of melodrama, even on prime-time programming. As Byars and Meehan note, elements of melodrama can be found in traditionally male genres, such as *Hill Street Blues* and *NYPD Blue,* and in talk shows like *Current Affair* and *Hard Copy;* "this embrace of melodrama suggests a rise in the industrial status of women's television and female audiences" (18).

Of course, one reason that networks and cable programmers have been motivated to appeal more to women during prime-time hours is that they have increasingly come to represent both the main household consumer and the (sometimes) upwardly mobile career woman. In 1976 the A. C. Nielsen company added a new category to its demographic measurements of the television audience: working women. Advertisers began trying to reach particularly upscale working women. "Marketing studies not only demonstrated that women in dual income households retained some control over their own wages, but also that they continued to fulfill the traditional female role as domestic purchasing agent for the household" (Byars and Meehan, 20). In 1977 Nielsen began measuring cable viewing, which, even more than TV, attracts upscale viewers: "having paid the toll to get cable, subscribers organized much of their leisure time around the consumption of its channels. So, although these channels had relatively small audiences, those viewers were of high quality" (Byars and Meehan, 21). The boom in the purchase and use of videocassette recorders in the 1980s suggested that working women were taping programs for later viewing; cable and the VCR have worked together since the mid-1980s to offer busy women multiple possibilities for viewing pleasures when their schedules allow.

All these factors made possible the creation of Lifetime, which began operating in 1984 with a mix of programming that appealed mainly to women—shows on children, decorating, and celebrities. Lifetime's basic movie formula "revolves around a strong, competent woman who overcomes adversity. Generally, the films involve a social issue believed to be of particular concern to women, such as domestic violence, sexual harassment, adoption, AIDS or rape" (Byars and Meehan, 26). However, the appeal to special interest groups—such as "women"—remains fairly broad because cable channels are worried about defining the audience so specifically that they will not reach the requisite number of viewers that constitute a broad advertising or subscription base (Byars and Meehan, 34).[2] Lifetime, for example, offers prime-time programming that appeals to men as well as women, featuring "hybrid" programs that blend traditional elements of men's and women's genres, shows like *L.A. Law, Cagney and Lacey,* and *thirtysomething.* The success of hybrid programming indicates that men's and women's tastes are not so clearly divided: men like elements of melodrama and romance, women like elements of action films.

Similarly, adult cable programming rarely appeals specifically to women in the manner that women's print erotica markets itself, indicating that the cable channels hope to convince both men and women that the erotic programming speaks to their desires. This financial imperative helps explain why a considerable percentage of adult cable programming appeals to the heterosexual couple, sometimes but not always in the context of romance and occasionally of marriage. As Byars and Meehan argue, even economically independent women remain emotionally invested in romance: "In Lifetime's enactment, feminine television offers viewers a complex, contradictory vision: women act in the public domain, work in the 'real' world, and earn their independence—but ultimately rely on heterosexual relationships to round out their lives" (35–36). But this is a much more egalitarian appeal to the coupled viewing experience than the one Spigel describes in the 1950s as it relates to sexuality. Representations of TV in that decade often showed women trying to control their husbands' viewing, especially when the viewed objects were beautiful women. This kind of surveillance, in turn, became a way of allowing men to engage in their voyeuristic activities without leaving the watchful gaze of their wives. As Spigel says, "television's blurring of private and public space became a powerful tool in the hands of housewives who could use the technology to invert the sexist hierarchies at the heart of the separation of the spheres. . . . women policed men's access to the public sphere and confined them to the home through the clever manipulation of television technology" (122). In contrast, erotic programming of the 1990s does not position the woman as police but rather as a generally equal participant in the screen's offered pleasures. Romance has been redefined, much as I argued in chapter 3 in relation to the prototypical Black Lace protagonist.

In fact, much adult cable programming isn't really concerned with romance, indicating that the more focused attention on women's sexual pleasures has potential for an even greater redefinition of the conventions of feminine television narratives than does the hybrid programming of Lifetime. This attention to sexual pleasure is heightened by the fact that the premium cable channels do not rely on advertisers for income but rather on subscription fees. No commercials for Lysol disinfectant, douches, or Miller beer interrupt the erotic experience. Women viewers are not positioned as product consumers within the home; this opens a bigger space, perhaps, for the consumption of sexually explicit materials in a manner somewhat removed from the immediacy of household routines.

In general, adult cable programming's availability in the home at a reasonable price and its representation of women as sexual agents work to undermine the governmental discourse described in chapter 1 that positions women as victims of sexually explicit materials; cable shows how women within their homes can find sexual pleasure through a technology that antiporn activists would say could only harm them. However, governmental regulation still has some impact on the viewing experience; I described in chapter 1, for example, how local cable franchises can decide, based on their perception of community standards, whether or not to offer adult channels like Playboy and Spice. The scrambling provision also described in chapter 1 represents a serious obstacle to adult channel access. And even the premium channels are subject to a series of ratings systems that foreground their illicit nature. Politicians are fond of complaining about "sex and violence" on television; although virtually *none* of the erotic cable programs are violent, they are certainly sexy and thus have been subject to the new ratings system agreed on by Washington, cable, and the networks in 1997. Cinemax, Showtime, and HBO, for example, now offer three different ratings codes for nearly all programs: the Motion Picture Association of America system (for movies released in theaters); their own ten-point content advisory system (offering specific information about whether the content includes nudity, adult language, sex, and/or violence), and the new general industry ratings agreed on by the Clinton administration and network executives (Cooper, "Everybody," 30). Although these ratings systems may not actually deter many viewers from tuning in, especially women who already subscribe to the premium channels, they do act as part of the national discourse on the family and sex that positions sexually explicit materials as antithetical to domestic harmony.

I want next to consider another history that has shaped the formation of adult cable programming, especially its greater visual reliance on the female body than the male. *Playboy* has perhaps been the most influential male pornographic magazine in the United States; it succeeded, beginning in 1954, in its mission to bring pornography for men into the mainstream, to naturalize it and make it part of men's everyday lives. In the last decade, it has tried to some degree to become part of women's everyday lives, especially through its cable channel and, to some degree, through its erotic education videos for couples. However, Playboy has not fully succeeded in making its cable channel part of women's everyday routines, mainly because it remains invested in the conventions of male porn that it helped establish. Playboy's potential for giving women equal access to porn in the private sphere is also hampered by the fact that its profits rely on the interactivity of technologies within the home, and most of those technologies are still reliant on the conventions of *Playboy* magazine. My history of Playboy illustrates that there is nothing *essentially* liberatory for women about the increasing concentration of technologies of porn within the home.

From the Girl Next Door to the Girl on the Couch

When the first *Playboy* appeared in 1954, it was marketed as a clean, healthy alternative to underground porn—a kind of everyday porn for white men. In order to understand how Playboy as a company has arrived at the end of the twentieth century, we can divide its history into roughly four historical phases: (1) in the 1950s and early 1960s, Playboy was mainly a magazine featuring the girl next door, establishing the concept of men's everyday porn via the expression of healthy sexuality within a consumerist lifestyle; (2) in the 1960s and early 1970s, Playboy expanded into public places, such as clubs, resorts, and gambling casinos, corresponding with the more general expansion of sex into public that I described in chapter 1; (3) In the late 1970s and for much of the next two decades, Playboy struggled to stay in the black, gradually divesting itself of public sphere ventures and trying to establish itself in video and cable; (4) since 1995 Playboy has enjoyed renewed profitability due to relative success at rearticulating its connection to the domestic sphere, with the home as an interactive site of erotic pleasure for both men and women.

Hefner's vision of female bodies as he conceived it in Chicago in 1953 filled a gap in the marketplace; *Playboy* was not the dirty, illicit sex magazine for men common at the time that showed women as prostitutes and suggested sex was dirty, nor was it in the genre of the artsy photography magazine that represented the female nude as a lovely nymphet in a garden. The magazine, using Marilyn Monroe as its first centerfold, showed sex as open and natural; Monroe was at this time acquiring a star image as the dumb blonde completely without artifice. As Richard Dyer argues, Monroe's connection with the naturalness of sex perfectly represented *Playboy*'s philosophy of legitimating pornography consumption for the well-heeled business and family man:

> much of what it did in its pages seems an attempt to integrate its sexual freedom into suburban and white-collar life—itself pretty well taken as the norm in fifties' iconography. Playboy's greatest success was to get itself sold in the most ordinary newsagents and drugstores, taking a sex magazine out of the beneath-the-counter, adult-bookshop category. (39)

This integration of the erotic with the everyday occurred in many of the same ways that I have thus far discussed in relation to the integration of women's erotica into everyday routines, although there are significant differences, having mainly to do with the appeal to upwardly mobile men. But as with women's erotica, sex was represented as healthy; *Playboy*'s models were supposed to represent the girl next door (albeit the girl with the stunning figure), a strategy Hefner seized upon in 1955 after a woman who worked in the Playboy subscription department attracted his attention and soon was featured as the July playmate. The story accompanying the image of the centerfold, Janet Pilgrim (actually her name was Charlene Drain), included this comment: "potential Playmates are all around you: the new secretary at your office, the doe-eyed beauty who sat opposite you at lunch yesterday, the girl who sells you shirts and ties at your favorite store" (qtd. in Miller, 50). These were nice girls, who would pose nude only this once, and who fit nicely with the image of the aesthetically discerning male reader. It's a strategy *Playboy* has pursued through the years, only gradually growing more explicit in its representations of the female body but always distancing itself from the more graphic *Penthouse* and *Hustler*.[3] In the 1975 annual report, Hefner restated the original *Playboy* philosophy: of the thirty-seven competitors on the market, he said, "none approaches *Playboy* in covering the full scope of interests of the contemporary male. Generally, they focus on only one of those interests—sex—often exceeding the bounds of the most liberal of contemporary tastes. In these matters, our standards will be our own and will not be dictated by competitive pressures" (qtd. in Miller, 192).

From the late 1950s, *Playboy* has situated sex within other contexts, commenting frequently on politics and the arts. The magazine quickly acquired a reputation for thorough and sometimes insightful political analysis (hence the oft-cited rationale, "I only buy it for the articles").[4] *Playboy* also heightened its legitimacy through its literary pretensions; in fact, the list of famous authors published in the magazine in the late 1950s alone included Vladimir Nabokov, James Baldwin, John Steinbeck, Kenneth Tynan, Nelson Algren, and Jack Kerouac. We might say that *Playboy* was engaged in the definition of a certain aesthetic, with Hugh Hefner as the moral exemplar overseeing the definition of this philosophy through the various features of the magazine. As Hefner described the *Playboy* philosophy in his introductory editorial to the first issue, "We like our apartment. We enjoy mixing up cocktails and an hors d'oevre or two, putting a little mood music on the phonograph and inviting in a female acquaintance for a quiet discussion of Picasso, Nietzsche, jazz, sex" (qtd. in Miller, 39).

In 1960 the first Playboy club opened, and the (in)famous bunny cocktail waitress was born. The Chicago club was an immediate success; by 1961 it had 106,000 members and in its first year sold more food and drink than any other restaurant or club in town (Miller, 82). Clubs soon opened across the country; with these ventures, Playboy began its public expansion—congruent with the spirit of the decade and the early 1970s—

in which sex began assuming a more unabashed public presence.[5] Playboy also began investing in real estate and opening several resorts; by the early 1970s Playboy owned eighteen clubs in the United States, gambling casinos in Britain, and five hotels. It also had divisions specializing in books, records, and other products, as its bunny logo became a highly profitable marketing device. The company was building an empire—taking over the world. Executive vice president Bob Preuss decribed his vision in 1972:

> A man gets up in his Playboy townhouse, calls a Playboy limousine to get him to the airport, where he gets a Playboy chartered plane, flies to New York, takes a Playboy limousine to a Playboy hotel in midtown Manhattan, changes into his Playboy suit, takes a Playboy ferry to a Playboy convention center on Randall's Island for his business meeting, that night goes to a Playboy restaurant and then to a Playboy theater where he sees a Playboy movie. That's the Playboy Environment and while we don't have all those things yet, we have many of them and we're exploring the rest. (qtd. in Miller, 236)

With this more public presence came more protest as well. In Baltimore, for example, "indignant housewives mounted a picket and temporarily stopped a Playboy Club from opening" (Miller, 92). And Gloria Steinem, on undercover assignment for *Show* magazine, was hired to be a bunny and then wrote a scathing exposé of her four-week stint. The bunnies were objects of constant harassment, forced to wear outfits that were too tight—except around the bust, which often had to be padded; they worked long hours and had to give the club half of their tips (Miller, 97). As second-wave feminism gained momentum in the early 1970s, protests against *Playboy* escalated, even as Hefner proclaimed that the magazine had helped women by "liberating" their sexuality. Of course, there were numerous ways feminists could counter this argument, most obviously by pointing to the conventional standards of female beauty represented in the magazine and the exclusion of male bodies; they gained extra ammunition in 1970 when a secretary at the Playboy Building secretly copied a Hefner memo that described why he didn't want to publish an article on the women's movement that the magazine had specifically commissioned from a freelance writer. The damning memo revealed that Hefner wanted an article that thoroughly lambasted feminism by linking all participants in the movement to the most radical fringes and then distorting the goals of radical feminism: "What I'm interested in is the highly irrational, emotional, kookie trend that feminism has taken. These chicks are our natural enemy. It is time to do battle with them and I think we can do it in a devastating way" (qtd. in Miller, 181). Appearing on the Dick Cavett show to defend himself, Hefner found himself face to face with a more articulate Susan Brownmiller who, when asked to define sexual equality, said, "When Hugh Hefner comes out here with a cotton tail attached to his rear end, then we'll have equality" (qtd. in Miller, 181).

After twenty years as publisher of the profitable magazine, Hefner was one of the country's wealthiest men, worth $157 million when the company went public in 1971. Yet due to a variety of factors, including feminism and the growing antiporn movement, heightened competition, recession, and an FBI drug investigation that turned up nothing but hurt the company's reputation, Playboy started to struggle; the decline began in the mid-1970s and lasted, to varying degrees, for almost two decades. The move out into the public sphere had to be reexamined. Playboy's five resort hotels were losing money. The clubs, hurt by the deterioration of many downtown areas, began to go into the red as well; there was a clear discordance between the magazine's image of its suburban, upwardly mobile reader and the men who now frequented downtown Playboy clubs, largely blue-collar workers. In the mid-1970s Playboy closed eight clubs, its Jamaican resort, and its movie theater, and withdrew from the record business (Miller, 278). Of its more public enterprises, only its London casinos profited; in fact, the gaming operations basically kept Playboy Enterprises in the black throughout much of the late 1970s (Miller, 307). It came as a severe blow to the company when it was convicted of violating Britain's Gaming Act in 1981 and lost its license to run the casinos, which that fiscal year alone had brought in revenues of $110 million, compared to $6 million for magazine publishing (Miller, 330). Shortly thereafter, its license for its Atlantic City, New Jersey, casino was also withdrawn. Struggling to compensate for these losses, the company sold two more of its faltering resorts and its book division, announcing that it would concentrate on its flagship magazine—and "its new venture in cable television" (qtd. in Miller, 343), a venture that, for the first time in Playboy's history, would require it to consider women as viable consumers.

Interestingly, Playboy's move from public sphere entertainment for men to domestic technologies aimed at women as well as men within the home coincided roughly with the announcement that Hugh Hefner's daughter, Christie, would, at age twenty-nine, become the new president of Playboy Enterprises. Already a board member and vice president at the company for several years, Christie assumed her new position in 1982 amidst a chorus of skepticism from feminists, which she answered with a defense of Playboy's hiring and promotion of women and its support of abortion and the Equal Rights Amendment. Hefner's role raises interesting questions about the claims I have been making that women as producers of porn will be more likely to increase women's access as consumers. In part, this would indeed seem to be the case at Playboy; however, the fact that production at such a diverse company involves many people in positions that have been historically determined by the success of the magazine suggests that one woman or even a handful of women cannot by themselves completely alter the trajectory of such a powerful institution as Playboy. Nor, would it seem, do they want to, given where the lion's share of the profits in pornography still lie.

Nevertheless, Christie Hefner's insistence that the company move steadily into new technologies has offered Playboy a convenient way to rearticulate its historical appeal to men: market cable and video as a way of improving the sex life of couples. Cable offers the shared viewing experience in the privacy of the home that the clubs, resorts, and casinos never did. Cable thus required Playboy to develop an alternative conception of sexuality to exist side by side with its swinging single male conception—the at least temporarily monogamous couple. Early in its venture into cable, the company reported that focus groups on its cable channel showed that "Playboy's programming has helped them improve their relationships by providing guidance and information about the delicate balance between the sexes, and that our programs have made their mates more loving" (qtd. in Miller, 351). In 1984 Playboy posted a profit, after two years of losses, and its cable and video operations were starting to take off; the Playboy channel signed up 500,000 subscribers in its first six months. But it took more than a decade for Playboy's venture into a variety of new technologies, including video, satellite, and the Internet, to really pay off. As late as 1995 *Forbes* was criticizing Christie Hefner for her failure to revive the company, pointing to lackluster earnings in nearly all divisions except the magazine, which is still run by Hugh, and strongly suggesting that the company replace Christie. But by early 1997 analysts were acknowledging the comeback. *Business Week* reported that analysts are starting to look favorably upon the company after a twenty-year drought, largely because of its expanding cable and satellite divisions. In the last quarter of 1996 the number of cable-TV homes with Playboy available as a pay-per-view channel increased by 200,000 to 11.2 million ("Why Playboy Is Hot Again," 122). In late 1995 Playboy launched a second adult channel—AdulTVision—which shows more hard-core stuff; in 1995 pay-per-view revenue increased 33 percent and direct-to-home satellite grew 64 percent (O'Leary, 28).[6]

In short, Playboy has tried to transplant its public sphere aspirations into private sphere technologies, while still offering the viewer the simulated experience of the swinging Playboy lifestyle. The last U.S. Playboy club (located in Lansing, Michigan) closed in 1988. However, you can still experience the Playboy environment by visiting Hugh Hefner's Los Angeles mansion on the Web: "Put on your pajamas, have a glass of champagne, and explore the beautifully landscaped grounds surrounding Hugh Hefner's Mansion West." The first page of Playboy's Web site shows a sort of galaxy of sites circulating around the Playboy rabbit head; each of the sites in this cyberporn space represents one of the company's ventures—cable TV programming, products, magazine, video catalog, and so on—to which a consumer can be immediately transported, *sans* limousine. Playboy went online in 1994; in 1996 it was receiving approximately 800,000 hits a day (Donaton, "Hopping," 15).[7] This interactivity is obvious on the Playboy cable channel. One night in July 1996, the channel advertised a video called *Playboy's Girls of the Internet*.[8] Then viewers were invited to call 1-900-933-8900 and listen in on an intimate conversation with a playmate for $2.25 a minute. The *Erotic Escapades* video, in which the "girls next door reveal their wildest pastimes," was offered free when you subscribe to the magazine for one year at $29.97. On the *Night Calls* show, hosts Juli Ashton and Doria urged callers to fax in their responses to their sexy young guest in red: "The more faxes you send, the more clothing she'll take off." Spectators are offered the liberation of their sexuality through the purchase of products and images disseminated through various media forms; the interactivity of technologies, each of which invites the viewer to take some action, makes accessing Playboy an increasingly participatory process within domestic space.

But are women as well invited to participate? Especially in the last five years, the company has been trying to convince women that the Playboy discourse is indeed women-friendly. The *New York Times* in 1994 described the magazine's new $500,000 advertising campaign: "Open up your mind. Playboy is about honesty and freedom and the desire to understand, not undermine, the opposite sex."[9] Playboy recently made an interactive compact disc that contains interviews with twenty-three women explaining why they support the magazine. The women include Christie Hefner, Playboy vice president of public relations Cindy Rako-witz, author Betty Friedan, comedian Nora Dunn, author (of a book against censorship) Marcia Pally, and centerfold model Dian Parkinson.[10] Playboy's emphasis on cable and couples suggests, logically, that the company considers watching television the erotic practice most likely to be shared—in contrast to reading a magazine. And the company claims it's succeeding in attracting women: Playboy entertainment group president Tony Lynn told *Brandweek* in 1996 that "on any given night, 30 percent of [cable] viewers are women; 60 to 65 percent of the audience are couples. We're older, more educated, higher income viewers. Other more X-rated services have a more narrow reach. Typically they're male, younger, lower educated" (qtd. in O'Leary, 29). Lynn here tries to blend women into the mix that has historically characterized Playboy's marketing appeal—more sophisticated and higher-income, an image that women, apparently, help to bolster. The fact that Playboy tries to hold on to its visual appeal to the male viewer and simultaneously direct some programs at couples produces a sort of schizophrenic programming mix that offers a real challenge for women. How does a female viewer disarticulate these multimedia appeals in order to find pleasure in those moments that are indeed directed at women?

Consider, for example, perhaps the most experimental, gender- and sexuality-bending show on Playboy cable—the call-in talk show *Night Calls*. The hosts—notwithstanding the fact that they are beautiful, busty, and blonde—unabashedly proclaim their diverse tastes, for women and men, in different positions, in various locations, public and private, and regularly urge their callers to inhabit similar positions. They are relentless spokeswomen for female pleasure, however it may be packaged. In one show on masturbation, for example, Juli and Doria urge a rare female caller to climax on the air, breaking their supposed rules against an actual on-air orgasm. "Come on, Marie, pretend my mouth is down there licking your pussy," says Doria. "You're just dripping all over my face."

However, the conclusion to this hot lesbian ménage-à-trois recovers Playboy's reigning heterosexuality, as Juli asks Marie, "Is your husband going to fuck you now?" and Marie replies, "I hope so!" In fact, most of the callers are men who comment on the hosts' bodies and then go on to tell their own stories on the topic at hand, the hosts often prompting them to provide a bit more erotic detail. The camera roves over the hosts' bodies as well as the bodies of other, occasional female guests, many of whom submit willingly to the caresses and spankings of Juli and Doria. During one of these exchanges, a woman called in and confessed that "Last week was the first time I masturbated to [a fantasy about] women." As the hosts encouraged her to admire their guest's nipples, Juli asked the caller, "Do your breasts look like this?" And the woman replied, "No, but I wish they did. My husband wishes they did."

These frequent narrative appeals to men's tastes and desires combine powerfully with the visual images of beautiful women to make it difficult to claim that Playboy programming makes a serious attempt to become an everyday text for women in the same way that it has historically appealed to men's desires for a certain kind of reconciliation between sex and everyday life. To illustrate this, I want to consider the "flow" of one evening's programming; I am drawing here on Raymond Williams's concept that television is not a collection of discrete texts but rather a flow that includes different kinds of programming, advertisements, promotional trailers, and various other interruptions. For the woman viewer, we might say that Playboy's programming represents a constant series of interruptions, consisting of moments when she is clearly being addressed and longer periods of time when the obvious addressee is the male consumer.

Beginning at 10 P.M. on June 30, 1997, the channel features a 90-minute Playboy original movie called *Damien's Seed*, in itself a mass of contradictions about female pleasure and sexual agency. The plot centers around a group of women calling themselves Daughters of the Dark; known in town as a lesbian coven, these women are awaiting the return after thirty-three years of a man they believe to be their leader, Damien. They lure an unsuspecting detective whom they have identified as Damien to their nightly ritual, drug him, tie him down, and "force" him to have sex with them in order to impregnate themselves with his "seed." The detective, Barry, can only vaguely remember the sex in the morning; in the meantime, he has "actual" affairs with a young woman who offers to help him crack the case and an older woman. In both of these scenes, the sex is fairly good for cable fare—Barry appears to enjoy (simulated) oral sex, and immediately goes down on both women before the lovemaking switches to the conventional simulated intercourse. However, the movie demonizes the aggressive lesbian sexuality of the Daughters of the Dark, even as it exploits their potential as male fantasy; interestingly, it is a sort of a reversal of the female rape fantasy as Barry apparently enjoys the sex even though it occurs "against his will." Other characters in the film even doubt Barry's suspicions that he has been raped, and eventually he begins to fear that the women have become pregnant.

The narrative counterposes to these "rape" orgies the sex scenes between Barry and more sexually "normal" women, in which female pleasure is clearly an important component. In another twist, the film resists romance: the Daughters of the Dark are sent to jail, of course, and the young assistant does end up romantically involved with a local boy; however, Barry's offer of romance with the older woman is at least temporarily rejected, and both drive off alone. Unlike much premium cable fare aimed at couples, then, *Damien's Seed* refuses romantic closure, and it posits the male protagonist as more interested in romance than the female characters. In contrast to the premium channels, Playboy usually offers an alternative to sex within romance and marriage, although it also has a feature program, *Private Liaisons*, that focuses on couples and foregrounds the female narrative voice.[11]

Following *Damien's Seed*, the channel airs an advertisement for an upcoming feature, *Playboys' Twins and Sisters, Too*, which culminates with the line, "Guaranteed to change the shape of your jeans," leaving little doubt as to the gender of the addressed viewer. Next there is a short interview with *Night Calls* host Juli Ashton, who describes her multiple sexual pleasures—lesbian, straight, and bi, vaginal, clitoral, and anal, and decidedly nonmonogamous. Here is that somewhat rare Playboy moment when almost any viewer could be addressed. Says Ashton at one moment, "I love women—their taste, their smell." Then, "I love being fucked in the ass with a hard cock." Ashton is followed by an ad for a volunteer group that makes meals for homebound people with AIDS; the narrator of the ad is a man, speaking about a friend of his who died of AIDS. The announcement indicates Playboy's recognition that all its viewers should be concerned with practicing safer sex; it is also a discordant moment, indicating the channel's homophobia precisely because this is perhaps the only time the channel acknowledges gay men.

A seductively dressed woman next introduces the Playboy home shopping program; here the address is to both men and women. Women can buy an emerald bustier set for thirty-six dollars (one size only); men are offered a black satin pouch thong for fourteen dollars (comes only in large—"If you're all man and not afraid to show it"). As Allan Northcott argues, Playboy's strategy is "to position itself as against the repression of sexual pleasures, and then to commodify those pleasures as they come to be represented in Playboy's own discursive conventions" (2).

In the next program, *Fabulous Forties*, forty-six-year-old marketing executive Patricia Marquis describes why she agreed to participate in Playboy's *Fabulous Forties* video series. The program represents the manner in which Playboy has tried to update and expand the concept of the girl next door: Marquis is African American and older than the original "girls," but the emphasis is still on her "everyday" status. The implication is that even "you"—the ordinary albeit beautiful everyday female viewer—can star in a Playboy video or cable program. This suggestion is reinforced in another Playboy feature, *Naughty Amateur Home Videos*, featuring sexy videos of "ordinary" couples. Not only can everyday women become playmates, but everyday people can make pornography in their homes and distribute it for showing on the Playboy channel.[12] Part of the appeal lies in the model's seeming innocence; Marquis does a somewhat shy, partial strip routine for the camera, removing her bra and fondling a string of pearls around her neck, inserting them in her mouth at one point. Then her twenty-something daughter enters; the partially naked mother and daughter engage in a series of poses, directed alternately at the camera and at each other. Thus, while on the one hand it would seem that the women are appealing to the male viewer using poses and routines associated with the male space of the strip bar, they are also addressing each other, seemingly finding pleasure in each other's bodies and, furthermore, cementing their relationship as mother and daughter as they tell each other at the end how much they love each other and exchange kisses on the cheek.

Thus far in the evening's viewing, the address has been broad enough to include viewers with somewhat different sexual preferences, although the body made most vulnerable to scrutiny has clearly been the female body. However, the final program in this three-hour segment, a music-video show, positions women as objects rather than spectators, leaving little room for a negotiation between those positions. The male host of the videos is a large, imposing man who cavorts on a boat with three women—two very busty blondes and one slender Asian woman. The women follow his orders, giggling as he guides them through a "pussy taste test" in which the Asian woman is blindfolded, tastes the pussy of each of the other women, and then correctly guesses whose pussy belongs to whom. The host punctuates this event with rude comments about the women's bodies, such as "Well, she couldn't tell which was which based on their breast size—since they're both D cups." He also affirms that this act is not intended for female pleasure: "That's enough now," he says to the Asian woman after only a brief moment during which she licks one woman's genitals. The host introduces music videos that are generally abusive to women, such as Body Count's *Strippers*, which includes the lyrics "I want my dick sucked," "I want to bang you in the ass right now," and "You push your silicon breasts together." Then, rapper Ice T makes a guest appearance; he describes how much he likes to watch women and criticizes the recent spate of anti-stalking legislation. "If I want to stalk a woman for a few weeks, it's just because I want to see what she's like," he comments.

Despite its attempt to articulate the relatively new technology of cable programming to women's pleasures, Playboy still seems highly invested in, even nostalgic for, the 1950s, a time when the magazine could posit itself as a pioneer in the enterprise to liberate (male) sexuality. Interestingly, Playboy and its founder have been able to relive some of these early, headier experiences with its expansion into former communist countries; in 1996 it began publishing a Russian edition of *Playboy* magazine, complete with Russian playmates. And the company is even entering the casino industry again, with a joint venture in Greece. As Hefner said, when asked about the definition of the Playboy bunny in the 1990s, "in some areas of the world, it's part of the '50s just beginning to happen" (O'Leary, 30).

Premium cable programming shares some of Playboy's visual conventions, both because of the general history of soft-core pornography and its focus on the female body and because when these soft-core standards are applied to television (as opposed to the magazine), there is an even greater need to avoid explicit imagery. Women's breasts are the most frequently eroticized site, which means that even when the narrative emphasizes women's sexual agency, they are rendered more vulnerable visually than men because the penis cannot really be represented on cable. Although this eroticization of the breast and the emphasis on simulated intercourse does not necessarily detract from women's pleasures, it often has the effect, especially on the Playboy channel, of detracting from women's sexual agency—as in the "pussy-eating contest" described above. Furthermore, unlike the premium cable channels, Playboy is generally not concerned with representing any kind of female agency that is the product of movement between private and public spheres, in part because it is generally not concerned with representing women in the contexts of their everyday lives. This is not to say that texts by themselves produce agency; as this entire book has argued, agency is a matter of a larger negotiation between public and private sites, and texts are just one component of that negotiation. Precisely because texts are shaped by a set of relations that determine women's mobility between public and private sites, we can use the premium channels' representation of mobility as one indicator of the increasing legitimacy of women's sexual pleasures within everyday routines. Furthermore, we can see how cable programming is itself conditioned by the overall genre of domesticated porn and by women's television practices. I next consider four subsets of premium erotic cable, defined by their reliance on the figures of the New Woman, the suburban housewife, the femme fatale, and the cyborg. By combining these subgenres, we can draw a rough map of erotic cable's representaton of the relationship between public and private sites.

The New (Cable) Woman

In the classic formula, the romance served to consolidate women's place in the home; as I argued in chapter 3, in these postmodern times, "romance itself has become *the obstacle* which the desirable love relationship must overcome" (Pearce and Stacey, 37). Overcoming—which often means redefining—the obstacle of romance entails making it fit into other components of everyday life, such as careers and sexual pleasure, producing as well a redefinition of home. The New Woman selfishly pursues her own desires, and this pursuit is enhanced by her financial mobility; men may in fact represent part of the impediment to overall fulfillment even as they are necessary for sexual pleasure and some degree of emotional companionship. In fact, in the long-running Showtime erotic series *Red Shoe Diaries*, it is the male narrator who is most concerned with establishing the importance of romance as he struggles over the years/episodes to understand why his fiancée felt the need to take a lover and then commit suicide when she had his unconditional love. Because the series seems aimed at couples, its emphasis on the male quest for romance and the female quest for independence within romance indicates a shifting in the terms of the heterosexual couple; it is now the man who more desperately needs the reassurance of a secure relationship.

    Red Shoe Diaries is based on the film of the same name produced and directed in 1990 by Zalman King ($9^1/_2$ *Weeks, Wild Orchids*). The original *Red Shoe Diaries* describes the conflicted love relationship of a yuppie couple, Jake and Alex (a woman); the film opens with the revelation of Alex's suicide, and much of what unfolds occurs through Jake's reading of Alex's diaries. Here, he discovers his fiancée's affair with a construction worker/shoe salesman (he sold her the red shoes); what began as a casual tryst quickly escalates into a situaton Alex could not control as the construction worker, Tom, refuses to take no for an answer. Unable to choose between her successful fiancé and the working-class shoe salesman, Alex kills herself. Anguished, Jake places an ad in the local newspaper: "Women. Do you keep a diary? Have you been betrayed? Have you betrayed another? Man, 35, wounded and alone, recovering from the loss of once-in-a-lifetime love. Looking for reasons why. Willing to pay top dollar for your experiences. Please send diary to Red Shoes. . . . All submissions are strictly confidential." Thus positioned within the legitimacy of a private, written fantasy, each of the thirty-minute cable episodes plays out the diary entry of a woman who is responding to the ad.[13] Each episode begins with this scenario: Jake, still seemingly shell-shocked, wanders into the post office with his loyal dog, Stella, pulls a letter out of his box, reads the first few lines—which set up the woman's problem—and offers an ambivalent commentary. The narrative then switches to the woman's voice and the situation is enacted, with the problem seemingly resolved; at the end, Jake comments on the original dilemma, offering his judgment, or sometimes just expressing his bemusement, to the loyal Stella on how the woman responded.

Like almost all of the women's erotica discussed in this book, each of these episodes begins by establishing the identity of a woman who has a problem that is somehow connected to sexual desire. In *Red Shoe,* these problems are often articulated through the perspective of career women who are now discovering that they have sacrificed love and/or sexual relationships for their jobs. In "Safer Sex," a career woman struggles with the loneliness that has resulted from her single-minded pursuit of success; in "You Have the Right to Remain Silent," a female cop suffers from unreturned lust for a man who works out at her gym; and in "Double Dare," an advertising executive confronts the boredom of marital monogamy by playing erotic disrobing games with the man in the skyscraper directly opposite her office.[14] These sexual problems are not divorced from other aspects of everyday life, although they are seen in many ways to supersede other issues and even offer ways of resolving them—the quest, again, for the truth of overall identity through the resolution of sexual identity. In fact, these vignettes all present the woman resolving her problem as she enacts—or has enacted for her—her sexual fantasy, at which point the fantasy ceases to be a fantasy and becomes part of "everyday life." We see here, again, the reconciliation of fantasy and everyday life; if the erotic vignettes are meant to represent fantasy material for the viewing audience, then they are also meant to show how fantasies can actually correspond to things that could really happen to "you," the viewer. Enacting the fantasy produces a resolution of some significant problem or lack in the woman's life, and this quest for resolution is connected to the woman's mobility. These stories can be read as attempts to define sexual agency as a product of a woman's movement between different sites. Sexual desire is not isolated but rather posited as a product of other factors, related to different sites—although, again, the emphasis on sexual agency does, to varying degrees, often present sex as the answer to other problems. In "You Have the Right to Remain Silent," the cop's sexual agency is foregrounded as a product of her overall mobility. She assumes the male role of predator/voyeur from the start, when she walks through the gym surveying male bodies: "I love looking at men's bodies: biceps, torsos, hamstrings, abs." The camera pans over these male parts from the point of view of the woman. "Like 98 percent of the faithful, I'm here to check out and to be checked out." Miffed that the sexiest man at the gym, Nick Willet, will not return her gaze, she surreptitiously breaks his taillight, then follows him in her police car, pulls him over, handcuffs and blindfolds him, and takes him to a deserted art gallery, where she sits him in a swivel chair and interrogates him about his lack of interest in her. Mobility is connected to sexual desire as it gets practiced in many sites other than (although sometimes including) the home. The advertising executive, for example, after engaging in her erotic games with the mysterious businessman across from her window, returns home each night and finds that this play actually enhances her marital sex.

In the introduction I argued that we should read texts not for their deep meanings but rather as a set of instructions for readers to follow; the texts themselves, in relation to other sites, thus become places where issues of access are partially determined. For the *Red Shoe Diaries* series, these instructions are mainly relevant for white, straight, upwardly mobile women. In "Safer Sex," for example, the wealthy white protagonist is presented as deserving of our sympathy at the start because of a series of unfortunate incidents: "the Dow fell 60 points," it's pouring down rain as she stands on the curb, and she can't get a taxi to stop for her. And, of course, "her heart has been broken one too many times." The conflict has been how to find time for the emotional commitment of a relationship, which is temporarily resolved when she meets a stranger (he offers to share his taxi with her) who wants the same kind of relationship that she does—casual sex twice a week. "For the first time in my adult life," she says, "I found someone who wanted the same thing as me—Tuesdays and Thursdays. The perfect solution for the single working woman. No commitments. No lies. No expectations. No names. Anonymous. Monogamous. The safest sex going." Ironically, the sex that the couple have is not safe sex in the physical sense of the word: they have intercourse on the first meeting without using a condom or even bringing up issues of AIDS or other sexually transmitted diseases. In fact, they both agree not to ask each other's name or anything about their backgrounds. "Safer Sex" is unaware of how class and race privilege shape sexual practices; yuppies seemingly don't have to worry about contracting HIV or the material consequences of scheduling sex in the middle of a working day. The episode assumes either that actually representing the use of a condom would de-eroticize the content or, naively, that for most of its viewing audience, practices of safer sex may not be an issue.

In each of these episodes, the women either from the start or eventually take the lead in defining the terms of the relationship; even in "Safer Sex," in which the mysterious man disappears after his identity becomes known to his lover, he ends up returning and seeking her out to pursue a more conventional relationship. Thus, although romance is definitely filtered through the ambitions of career women, most episodes end with the valorization of the (sometimes married) couple. "You Have the Right to Remain Silent" ends with Nick Willet professing that "We're going to be like normal people," with the implication that normality means marriage (he wants to meet her grandmother, he says). "Double Dare" ends with the woman declining an offer by her erotic games partner to have sex in the back of his car; rather, she professes fidelity to her husband and returns home to have sex with him.[15] The women's erotic mobility facilitates their acquisition of a partner/husband who does not completely dissipate their independence; however, sexual pleasure is ultimately legitimated via heterosexual romance.

It's worth considering as a contrast to *Red Shoe Diaries* another Showtime series, *Women: Stories of Passion*. Advertised as an erotic anthology "directed and written by women," this series is one of the few on cable that specifically markets itself as women's erotica, with women writers and directors. It thus illustrates one of the arguments I have made throughout this book about the importance of women gaining control of the means of production of sexually explicit materials; although women will not necessarily create something more accessible to women than men do, the chances are greater that women-directed and -written texts will circulate in a manner that increases access to sexual pleasure—especially in relation to information about sex. This does seem to be the case with *Women: Stories of Passion*, especially in terms of its representation of the body, both male and female. In contrast to *Red Shoe* and to most adult cable programs, *Women* regularly shows as much of the male body as the female; furthermore, women are often presented in the role of teachers, instructing men on how to give women greater sexual pleasure. For example, in "The Bitter and the Sweet," written by Elisa Rothstein, a forty-something single woman named Ellie finds out that she has inadvertently encouraged the sexual attraction of her best friend's eighteen-year-old son, Tim. Although she initially resists his attempts to make love to her, she eventually concedes to his sensitive love letters and proposes one night of passion. Initially Tim makes groping, awkward love to Ellie. Then she says, "Now we'll do it my way." In the ensuing scene, Ellie licks Tim's nipples, caresses his body, and teaches him how to slowly savor her body. "The way to get a woman to open to you is to make her believe that you could wait forever to be inside her," she says. After a tender night together, Tim purports to have fallen in love, but Ellie sets him straight, saying she wants never again to feel the pain of losing someone. She tells Tim that her lesbian lover of seven years recently died of breast cancer. The story thus represents several important differences from the *Red Shoe Diaries* series, or, for that matter, much of adult cable: it focuses on the non-monogamous, bisexual desires of an independent older woman who initiates a young man into the art of pleasuring women and then goes on her way, pursuing her career as a successful photographer. "We have to go back to real life," she tells Tim. The interlude is thus represented as a fantasy; indeed, the entire episode begins with Ellie on an airplane, next to a woman who, recalling Nancy Friday, is writing a book about women's sexual fantasies and records Ellie's words. However, unlike the fantasies elicited by Friday, Ellie's fantasy really happened, indicating once again the need to reconcile fantasy and reality. Ellie possessed the agency to make her fantasy come true; furthermore, she enhances other women's real sexual lives by instructing a young man how to better pleasure women.

Sex in the Suburbs

The *Red Shoe Diaries* episodes often conclude at the precise moment of romantic closure, offering the impression of monogamous or marital bliss without delving into the "realities" of married life and sex. In contrast, some erotic dramas take up the problematic of sex in the suburbs: bored housewives become prostitutes, take young lovers, and murder their wealthy husbands who no longer have time to give them the sexual attention they need. Unlike the New Woman, these protagonists have not been liberated from suburban domesticity; they are still reliant on their husbands for money (although money is never a problem) and they still define themselves largely through their identity as wives (although rarely mothers, which I'll discuss in a moment). It would seem at first glance that these women inhabit the world of Betty Friedan's work *The Feminine Mystique*, the 1960s feminist classic that argued that the (suburban) home confined women to an endless routine of housework and child care. Yet while Friedan posited capitalism as the cause of the housewife's containment, the adult cable drama posits the lack of satisfying sex as the problem. Clearly, then, answers to sexual mobility remain within the terms of capitalism that Friedan was right to point to as constraints on sexual freedom—although her argument itself remained largely applicable to white middle-class women.

In the cable suburbs, the space of the home is reconfigured as one of female sexual pleasure through the protagonist's actions and in spite of her unsuspecting and often passive husband. For example, in "The Pick Up," a 1997 episode in the Showtime erotic series *Love Street*, a restless suburban housewife named Allison seduces a young man named Eric who works at the ranch where she bought a horse. They engage in several days of lusty sex (again, conventionally portrayed); Allison stabs her wealthy husband when he returns from his business trip and then frames her lover for the murder. The spacious suburban home is first presented as a site of Allison's unhappiness; her husband pecks her on the cheek and is out the door before they can even have their morning coffee. Yet almost from the start, we get inklings that Allison has a plan for gaining control of the home. At the ranch, for example, an older employee warns Eric not to get involved with Allison because she seems dangerous. And in the midst of their passionate affair, Allison turns angrily on Eric at a moment when he seems to question her devotion: "Who do you think I am? Some bored housewife with nothing better to do?" Allison's erotic mobility becomes the route to her financial freedom. The final shots alternate between a frame of the young lover in the back of the police car and the triumphant—and now very wealthy—housewife smiling at him from the doorway of her spacious home.

In Showtime's *Secret Games 3*, another bored housewife, Diana, with a too-busy husband decides to join a high-class bordello and there becomes fascinated with a dangerous male client, Terrell Baxter. Again, the posh home is defined as a site of Diana's loneliness and sexual frustration; one of the opening scenes shows her in the bathtub and suggests that she is masturbating and fantasizing. As her friend Gwen tells her upon introducing her to the bordello, "My guess is that masturbation just doesn't take up the slack." Diana needs to be persuaded, however. "I'm not some bored, disillusioned, frustrated housewife," she tells Gwen. But of course she is, and it is through "prostitution" that she reawakens sexually. This time, however, the home and the marriage are saved when Terrell becomes murderously obsessive and Diana's husband recognizes, just in time, the effects of his neglect. But there is a lesson to be paid, and Gwen, the naughtier housewife, must pay it. Terrell stabs her in the doorway to Diana's house and she is left there to die as the police arrive just in time to save Diana and her husband in the kitchen from the wacked-out Terrell. The program thus serves as a sort of backhanded valorization of illicit sex: it can revitalize your marriage but it can also get out of control; ultimately, the suburban housewife can find satisfaction in her home, if only her husband recognizes her sexual needs.

A more serious examination of sex and marriage, Showtime's *Married People, Single Sex 2* (July 1997), purports to a kind of documentary status, in which the stories of three married couples are interwoven with black-and-white interviews obviously conducted after the scenes from their lives have been filmed. Each couple represent a different kind of marital problem: in couple 1, David is bored with his anxious-to-please-and-get-pregnant wife and thus has an affair with Karen, the wife in couple 2; Karen wants to be dominated, to feel the passion of sex again, and considers her gentle husband a "wimp." In couple 3, John has had an affair; his wife, Carol, forgives him but cannot take him back in bed. He hires a prostitute through an escort service, his wife finds out, and the acrimonious cycle continues. Interestingly, although each of the characters is intended to represent a certain position on marriage and sex, these positions are not always congruent with traditionally gendered roles, and the show comments insightfully on the difficulties of maintaining sexual passion within marriage given the obstacles represented by children, careers, and different expectations about relationships. For example, the narrative gives some credence to Karen's restlessness and doesn't punish her for having an affair with David, who likes rough sex and even, at one point, hires a dominatrix to have sex with him while Karen is tied up and forced to watch. The characters sometimes verge on stereotypes—for example, Carol is rather prudish and sexually uptight, devoted to her children and trying to fill up her extra time with tennis lessons, quilt making, and other typical activities of the suburban housewife. Yet when she confronts her husband with proof of his philandering and he calls her an "ice queen," her cry that "I can't be a slut *and* a mom" seems not cliché but rather grounded in the obvious realities of her everyday life.

In fact, *Married People* is one of the extremely rare attempts to show not only how the demands of mothering can limit sexuality but also how sexual desire does not disappear when children are born. Eroticized suburban housewives like Diana and Allison don't usually have kids; the absence reveals just how hard it is for writers and directors of domesticated porn to imagine making sex part of an everyday routine that includes children. This absence extends to almost all domesticated porn, with the exception of the Kensington Ladies' Erotica, a few of the erotic education videos, and several films by Candida Royalle. In Royalle's *Three Daughters*, for example, a mother and father are shown rediscovering time for lovemaking as their three daughters, growing up, are exploring their own sexual desires. As Linda Williams argues, the representation of sexual mothers is so important because traditionally only men have been given the freedom to explore sexual desire in nonprocreative contexts. Using Jessica Benjamin's theories of socialization through identification, Williams says that

> [O]ne part of a real-world solution to the representation of desire thus concerns the social construction of mothers as sexual subjects. Since mothers actually *are* sexual subjects (though hardly ever in movies), such a solution is not beyond the pale; it means that the time-honored notion of the father as belonging exclusively to the outside world of freedom and the mother as belonging exclusively to the inside world of safety and holding needs to be changed—both in the real world and in our representations. (*Hard Core*, 259)

Williams hints here of the implications of this theory for material movement and mobility, although she relies heavily on Benjamin's notion of the inner, subjective spaces in which a transformation needs to occur. The transformation is thus a largely psychological one, connected to a heightened sense of self-esteem gained by seeing one's mother and in turn oneself as a healthy sexual person. Agency is defined in terms of interior spaces: "the recognition of one's own sexual subjectivity and outward agency comes, then, from the desire for access to one's own interior" (Williams, 262). My formulation of agency pushes this concept one step further; rather than assuming that physical mobility *follows* interior recognition, we can logically posit that material movement between the private space of the home and the public sites of sexual excitement and freedom will provide the basis for increased agency. For example, in *Married Couples*, Carol's movement outside her home—even just to take tennis lessons—prompts a brief sexual awakening, as she and her tennis coach kiss and he begins pursuing her. The show also represents the material restrictions to this affair, however; Carol must return home to care for her children, and her home has become a highly de-eroticized site since her husband's infidelities caused her to withdraw sexually. In contrast, John has the freedom to hire women from the escort service, who come to his office; his sexual pleasures are not limited to the space of the home or the terms of his marriage. *Married Couples* thus suggests both what limits mothers' sexual agency and what is necessary to facilitate its development: an equal relationship with a partner who shares the child care and housework, which in turn would enhance the woman's movement outside the home.

The Erotic Thriller

Recall that a powerful structuring device in the debates around women and pornography has been the representation of women as victims of the sex industry. Such a position suggests that all women—both participants in the industry and consumers of its products—are victims, either of the actual material conditions of porn's production or of false consciousness if they find some pleasure in these "oppressive" texts. It would seem at first glance that one subgenre of cable programming, the erotic thriller, does considerable work toward rearticulating this image of the sex worker as victim: women either working directly in the sex industry or who are associated with it are presented not as victims but rather as empowered agents, explicitly challenging myths produced in conservative discourses. However, it becomes quite quickly apparent that this agency is a matter not of *structured* mobility between public and private sites but rather of a public sphere agency awarded only to sexually dangerous women who move freely in public and thus represent a threat to the sanctity of the domestic sphere.

These thrillers follow in the tradition of *Fatal Attraction* (1988) and *Basic Instinct* (1992), both of which focused on sexually transgressive and (therefore) murderously dangerous women, versions of the femme fatale. Given the popularity of these films, we are perhaps not surprised by the fact that Showtime's 1997 original movie *Showgirl Murders* is not about showgirls who are murdered but rather about showgirls who murder. Jessica is a beautiful young stripper who seduces a bar owner as she transforms the struggling club into a booming business through her seductive strip routines. The bar owner's wife is portrayed as a pathetic alcoholic who desperately wants her marriage to work. After a conventional sex scene on the pool table—with Jessica climaxing as the bar owner enters her—she convinces him to kill his nagging wife in order to gain complete control of him and his business. Next, Jessica kills the bar owner and sets the place on fire in order to pocket the insurance money; then she kills her partner in crime, a no-good gang member whom she knocks off in the deserts of Mexico. Woman's sexuality is dangerous, conniving, and ultimately fatal, free to roam the illicit places of strip bars and Mexico and inimical to domesticity.

The erotic thriller plays on the voyeuristic pleasures of watching the sex industry but offers none of the self-reflexive awareness of hard-core porn, which, as I argued in chapter 1, often self-consciously references its own status as pornography in an attempt to demystify it. In contrast, the thriller's eroticism is based on the need to simultaneously capitalize on the illicitness of pornography and the sex industry and distance itself by offering an alternative image of female sexuality contained within a heterosexual relationship. The erotic thriller does little to represent female agency because it relies on that old dichotomy of the good girl/bad girl that has worked so powerfully to define the domestic sphere as one of female procreation rather than pleasure. The bad woman is enabled by her seduction skills and moves freely throughout the sex/crime world, contaminating domestic scenes (as in *Fatal Attraction*); the good woman is temporarily attracted to this dark world—like the viewer who finds herself momentarily drawn into the fantasy of participating in illicit sex but who ultimately wants to be returned to the comfortable securities of domestic life.

The Cyborg

In my discussion of the vibrator and computer sex in chapter 2, I argued that the introduction of new technologies into women's sex lives represents the potential expansion of the categories of fantasy and reality, providing their users with new practices of pleasure that are not directly linked to conceptions of the natural body. Women using machines for pleasure become cyborgs of a sort; as Anne Balsamo argues,

> Cyborgs are hybrid entities that are neither wholly technological nor completely organic, which means that the cyborg has the potential not only to disrupt persistent dualisms that set the natural body in opposition to the technologically recrafted body, but also to refashion our thinking about the theoretical construction of the body as both a material entity and a discursive process. (11)

This premise is further illustrated in the subgenre of erotic cable that shows women dabbling in virtual sex or encountering aliens from outer space. More than any of the texts discussed thus far, these programs blur the lines between fantasy and reality, even as they foreground the importance of this question in terms of women's desires. As such, they do have the potential, as Balsamo argues, to both retain the material specificity of the female body and its various pleasures and also reveal how those pleasures can multiply through fantasy's momentary reconstruction of the body. Not surprisingly, then, the pleasures represented in techno-erotica are more expansive than the norm of heterosexual desire. More surprisingly, these sometimes otherworldly desires are still situated within the terms of women's everyday lives.

Consider the 1997 Cinemax feature *Alien Abduction: Intimate Secrets*. Five twenty-something women, all longtime friends, sit around in a sauna and begin to recount their sexual fantasies, which begin with the real and gradually become otherworldly. The first woman describes a vacation she took with her lover on which she received an erotic massage; the second describes her fantasy of having sex with a cop. The next three women's fantasies, however, become more complicated and less "real": they revolve around a night the three friends' car broke down, due, it seems, to an intervention by outer space aliens. Splitting off into different directions to seek help, the three unsuspecting women have bizarre sexual experiences—but all these experiences have in some way to do with fantasies they had before their alien encounter. For example, an alien man takes one woman to a western saloon called Sweet Dreams; there she watches a showgirl ravished by several men. Recounting their experiences later, in the sauna, each woman realizes for the first time that her friend also had an otherworldly experience. Oddly, their fantasies/experiences begin to interweave—bits and pieces of one woman's fantasy are represented in another's. The fantasies narratively comment on each other, and thus they facilitate a discussion about what constitutes "correct" sexual desire. For example, after several disparaging comments about the lesbian sex that occurs in one fantasy, the friends, all of whom have at least one "incorrect" experience in their fantasies, conclude that lesbian desire is just one of many acceptable forms of sexuality, both in reality and in fantasy. The "collision of reality and fantasy"—as one woman puts it—that was wrought as the women came into contact with "alien" sexuality facilitates an empathetic acceptance of all kinds of sexual practices within everyday life, suggesting that no sexual practice is "alien." Thus, sexual agency is achieved through temporarily leaving one's body via a kind of technology, then returning "home" with a new awareness of bodily pleasures.

Of course, none of these texts by themselves determines sexual agency; they are more accurately seen as partial indicators of broader conditions of women's mobility. If we consider them for a moment as a whole, we can say that erotic cable as a technology that bridges public and private spheres does indeed represent at least some women moving between these spheres quite freely, experiencing sexual pleasure in the home, the office, the strip bar, the tennis court, and so forth. As such, erotic cable significantly revises the conventions of women's television, relying quite little on the romantic melodrama and very heavily on the empowered, desiring woman. Furthermore, unlike Playboy's programming, premium channels present a more "realistic" representation of women and their desires; even, occasionally, revealing the sexualized male body. In addition, premium cable channels do not depend on the kind of technological interactivity that ties the Playboy channel so firmly to its past; in fact, premium cable more often shows women gaining control of various forms of erotica, from print to computers. However, erotic cable is not the utopic answer to women's access to sexually explicit materials. The lack of representation of mothers, women of color, and lesbians indicates that sexual mobility is seen as belonging more fully to relatively young, relatively wealthy, relatively straight white women—precisely the women most likely to be able to make every TV set in the home a cable TV set.

Conclusion
Revisiting Transgression

In the introduction I opposed the concepts of domestication and transgression, using the opposition to advance a theory of agency in relation to women, pornography, and everyday life. Domestication, I said, drawing on Roger Silverstone, involves "the capacity of a social group to appropriate technological artifacts and delivery systems into a culture—its own spaces and times, its own aesthetic and its own functioning—to control them, and to render them more or less 'invisible' within the daily routines of daily life" (98). Pornography is domesticated when it becomes integrated into the routines of everyday life—not exactly rendered invisible, but managed by women who have achieved a degree of agency through a structured movement between sites of access and sites of consumption. This notion of agency was contrasted to the valorization of transgression that occurs in much prosexuality analysis of pornography, which relies on the premise that agency is defined in terms of the subject's ability to evade confinement to any place, able to freely transgress boundaries of public and private. As a means of considering the political implications of this book, I want in conclusion to consider the ways the process of domestication may sometimes constitute transgression. By transgression, however, I mean something quite different from the valorization of individuals' subversive abilities to appropriate texts; rather, I want to recall the Latin roots of the word: "trans," meaning "across," and "gradi," meaning "to step." Transgression means, literally, "to go beyond the bounds or limits prescribed by (a law, command, etc.)." This "going beyond" requires that we recognize the material factors that restrict movement before we can devise the means for the reconfiguration that will free one to "go beyond" the boundaries established by governmental regulation and other factors inhibiting women's access to sexually explicit materials. Material transgression is thus necessary for the domestication of pornography—it indicates the ability of women to literally enter into the means of production of erotica, to step across the threshold of an adult video store, to access an online sex chat room on the Internet. These are physical, material acts that depend on the ability to cross boundaries.

This book has subsumed a wide variety of texts under the theoretical framework of domestication; the danger here is that I have domesticated the texts for the purposes of advancing my own argument against the transgressive tendencies of other feminist positions on pornography. However, I have tried to maintain a sense of the differences among these texts, to indicate ways a genre is not cohesive but rather characterized by dissimilarity. Drawing on Foucault, I have theorized genre as a regulated dispersion, in which the objects that together constitute the genre of domesticated porn exist not as a coherent unity but in a field regulated at a number of dispersed sites. By examining texts ranging from the *Herotica* series to lingerie catalogs to vibrator debates to erotic education videos and by linking these texts to other sites, such as governmental regulation, publishing, retail stores, and various conceptions of home and everyday life, I have tried to capture a sense of what it would mean for women to acquire the ability to move freely between these sites. By addressing these different kinds of texts, I have also tried to avoid homogenizing "everyday life," recognizing that for women in small midwestern towns, access to John Gray may indeed be an important component of expanded sexual pleasure. At the same time, the fact that John Gray's books regularly become best-sellers while there are almost no women of color on adult cable programming is an indication of how access is unevenly distributed according to broader patterns of race and class privilege in this country. That is precisely why the expansion of erotica by writers who identify their volumes as linked to race and ethnicity is so important, and why it is critical not to dismiss these anthologies on the assumption that they are essentialist or that they are sold in a Barnes and Noble or that they benefit from the conservative regulation of visual pornography. Women's erotica addressed to different races, ethnicities, and sexualities constitutes transgression when it facilitates a material movement between the physical sites of access and consumption.

In distancing this project from claims about transgression in the introduction, I was also distancing myself as a critic from the urge to make judgments about desire based on the readings of texts, to say that certain kinds of texts constitute more transgressive fantasy material than others.

Yet in describing how various kinds of texts are produced by and help produce dominant conceptions of female sexuality, I have made many judgments—not about individual tastes and desires but about the conditions that make some texts more accessible and legitimately consumed than others. Thus, at the same time as I argued that Victoria's Secret's wide circulation makes lingerie a readily accessible sexual accessory for many women, I also analyzed the ways the company profits by its articulation to conservative discourses that ultimately will not increase women's mobility in any structural way. To inquire into what is accessible for women within the space of the home is also to inquire into what is not available, and what is necessary to make more materials available to more, different groups of women. My concern has been not so much with women as subversive readers of pornographic texts, which can occur under many conditions, but rather with the conditions necessary for women to become material transgressors.

In discussing these conditions, I have constructed a sort of cause and effect relationship between production, textual content, circulation, and consumption. Roughly, I have argued that as women have gained control of the means of production of erotic texts, they have emphasized the reconciliation of fantasy and reality within everyday contexts. The contexts defined here have been relatively broad when one considers the entire genre of domesticated porn—including texts set within the particular circumstances of women of color, lesbians, upper-class white women, and so forth. Although access to this production has occurred most intensely in the publishing of literary erotica, it has also begun to happen in the visual technologies and on the Internet. In turn, the production of texts by women, marketed in a way that sets them off from pornography, has facilitated their circulation in a number of mainstream venues, such as large bookstores, general video stores, cable programming, mail-order catalogs, and, in some locations, women-friendly sex stores. This mainstream circulation and the laudatory reviews of domesticated porn in women's popular magazines is due in part to the fact that the texts are not perceived as pornographic—and thus do not fall within the category of texts demonized in governmental and other family values discourse as antithetical to family values. Many women will thus find these texts more palatable for consumption within their everyday routines—contributing to varying degrees of redefinition of sexual mobility within the home.

Following this argument, we can conclude that the expansion of each of these steps will generally lead to an expansion of access for more, different groups of women. For example, visual technologies of pornography are generally less diverse and democratic than are print technologies, in part because fewer women, and especially fewer women of color, have been able to produce visual erotica than have been able to write erotica. We can also surmise that as access expands, the connection between these different stages of production, content, circulation, and consumption will become more complicated, less reliant on a steady, causal progression. In some ways, this is already beginning to happen. Susie Bright's *Best American Erotica* anthologies do not define themselves in terms of identity groups, but the content still suggests an investment in the way women and gay men have redefined "erotica" by writing identity erotica. And the widespread circulation of the *BAE* anthologies still relies on their definition as erotica rather than pornography. Producers of visual porn for women, such as Candida Royalle, have obviously had an effect on the general pornography industry, such that some men directing and writing scripts for pornographic features have integrated some of the elements of women's porn; in turn, these videos have gained a wider distribution, including in mainstream video stores. Adult cable programming also illustrates some of the ways erotica for women now circulates widely without being called women's erotica.

Domesticated porn is still characterized by a recognition of how sexual desire is always imbricated within daily routines, and by a circulation that brings it fairly easily into those routines. The ongoing conservative discourse challenging pornography's legitimacy within the home is one reason the category of domesticated porn is still incredibly important for many women. The challenge is to expand the representations of both sexual practices and everyday lives yet to retain, or, in some cases, achieve widespread access for women in different socioeconomic, age, race, and ethnicity categories. However, in this pursuit we cannot lose sight of the fact that such an expansion will not involve doing away with some of the (less transgressive) texts as women's desires "evolve" into some uniform standard of radical sexual practice. Nor should that be the goal of a feminist, cultural studies politics of pornography.

Ultimately, women's ability to transgress boundaries in the interest of producing and consuming more pornography that can be domesticated for use within the home depends on conditions that extend far beyond the parameters of this book. Fortunately, then, this book is produced not in a vacuum but in a context of cultural studies scholarship and grass-roots activism that addresses many of the conditions of women's every-day lives; by connecting pornography to these other issues, we will begin to understand the complexities of access and to formulate an effective politics of pornography.

Notes

NOTES TO THE INTRODUCTION

1. In characterizing the pornography industry as largely male, I am not agreeing with the antipornography position that any woman who finds pleasure in pornography is a victim of false consciousness. Rather, my focus is on the connections between production, access, and consumption: how can women as producers of texts increase women's access as consumers, thus jointly marking out more women-friendly spaces of access?

2. Information on how many women are watching porn is hard to come by; many articles and reports on pornography rely on a 1987 *Redbook* survey, which found that almost half of the women polled watched porn. The *Advocate*, a leading gay magazine, reported in a 1996 issue that 54 percent of its lesbian readers had watched an X-rated video in the previous twelve months. The 1993 Sex in America survey found that 11 percent of women interviewed had rented porn. These surveys all raise questions of definition: What qualifies as an X-rated video? Under what conditions is the video consumed? Is it difficult to obtain? If women watch porn, does that mean they feel comfortable renting it, or do they rely on their male partners to go to the video store?

3. See, to cite just a few examples, Linda Williams, *Hard-Core: Power, Pleasure, and the "Frenzy of the Visible"*; Drucilla Cornell, *Transformations: Recollective Imagination and Sexual Difference*, especially chapter 4; Wendy Brown, *States of Injury: Power and Freedom in Late Modernity*, especially chapter 3; and Gayle Rubin, "Misguided, Dangerous, and Wrong: An Analysis of Anti-Pornography Politics."

4. Of course, some antiporn feminists do not even acknowledge that there are different kinds of pornography. Susan Kappeler writes in *The Pornography of Representation* that even when women control the structure of pornographic representation, "the model of this subject is the male gender, the objectification it operates is modeled on the objectification of women" (50).

5. In *Sex Exposed: Sexuality and the Pornography Debates*, Linda Williams discusses the different kinds of pornography addressed to gay men, lesbians, sadomasochistic practitioners, and bisexuals. Gillian Rodgerson discusses the growth in production of lesbian erotic materials, including the literature of the

Sheba Collective and some lesbian-produced videos. Also in *Sex Exposed,* Loretta Loach's "Bad Girls: Women Who Use Pornography" discusses the increasing consumption by women of pornography within household routines. I do not mean to discount the other essays in *Sex Exposed* or in the other two volumes—*Bad Girls and Dirty Pictures: The Challenge to Reclaim Feminism* (Pluto Press, 1993) and *Dirty Looks: Women, Pornography and Power* (British Film Institute, 1993). Nor do I mean to argue that every essay on pornography needs to somehow take up the issue of the home as a site of consumption. However, these three volumes are representative of the tendency to generally elide this issue.

NOTES TO CHAPTER I

1. See "Are Music and Movies Killing America's Soul?" Time, 12 June 1995, 25–30, for an account of Dole's attack and a response by entertainment industry executives.

2. Quayle's attack on *Murphy Brown* occurred during a speech at the Commonwealth Club of California about the failures of family and of welfare reform. Said Quayle, "A welfare check is not a husband" and "Marriage is probably the best anti-poverty program of all" (*New York Times*, 20 May 1992).

3. The core of the 1868 *Hicklin* case was, as Edward de Grazia describes it, to base the test for obscenity on "whether the material in question had a 'tendency' to 'deprave and corrupt those whose minds are open to such immoral influences,'" a test which, according to de Grazia, "subordinated the freedom of writers, publishers, and readers to the imagined effects books might have upon impressionable young girls." Adds de Grazia, "Hicklin thereafter became the legal standard by which the freedom of authors and publishers in the United States was measured" (xi).

4. Because obscenity law dictates that the definitions of obscenity vary according to community standards, the public presences of pornography vary widely across the country.

5. In the 1986 decision of *City of Renton v. Playtime Theatres, Inc.*, the Supreme Court upheld the zoning ordinance regulating adult theaters of Renton, a suburb of Seattle, which had enacted an ordinance that prohibited any adult motion picture theater from locating within one thousand feet of any residential zone, family dwelling, church, or park, or within one mile of any school. See Rohan, 34–47, 34–48, for a summary of all the federal and state cases regarding zoning and adult entertainment, most of which have upheld zoning ordinances. The cities and counties that have enacted zoning ordinances include, to name just a few, Boston; Minneapolis; Houston; Phoenix; Biloxi; Michigan; and Jackson County, Missouri.

6. Raymond Williams first used this term to describe how different forms of broadcasting reconfigured relations between public and private spheres. See *Television: Technology and Cultural Form,* 20.

7. The Meese Commission attempted to prove that (1) pornography had become more violent and more widespread since 1970, when the U.S. Commission on Obscenity and Pornography issued a very different, much more tolerant report on pornography, finding no causal links to antisocial behavior; and (2) because of this increasing spread and violence, porn was responsible for certain antisocial behavior, specifically, sexual violence against women and children. As numerous critics of the commission have noted, the evidence presented for both these claims was at least ambiguous and often flatly contradictory. For a convincing counterargument to the notion that pornography causes violence, see Marcia Pally, *Sex and Sensibility*. She notes that even the social scientists who were called on to testify before the commission, including Edward Donnerstein, refuted the use of their studies by the commission. Donnerstein writes elsewhere that "there has actually been a decline in violent images within mainstream publications such as *Playboy* and that comparisons of X-rated materials with other depictions suggest there is in fact more violence in the nonpornographic fare" (xx).

8. Quotes from the Meese Commission come from the reprinting of the report introduced by Michael McManus.

9. See Janet Wasko, *Hollywood in the Information Age* for a good overview of cable television's growth. As Wasko notes, the number of cable users is always higher than the statistics reveal, due to the fact that some homes receive the service via unauthorized means, such as pirating (85).

10. Cox Cable of Gainesville, Florida, discontinued adult programming on its Escapade channel after denunciation of the service in 1981 by the Evangelical Coalition of Gainesville. In 1982 Roy City, Utah, passed an ordinance prohibiting dissemination over cable of "indecent" programming in an attempt to eliminate the R-rated films available via HBO and Showtime. However, a federal district judge ruled that the ordinance was unconstitutional (Trauth and Huffman, 2).

11. The commission recommends this change in the U.S. code partially to clear up confusion about the 1984 Cable Communications Policy Act's potential to regulate pornography. One provision of the act criminalizes the transmission of obscene material over cable, but other provisions prevent the cable operator from exercising any editorial control over any public, educational, or governmental use of channel capacity (McManus, 92). The 1992 Cable Act granted cable operators discretion to ban indecent programming from public, educational, or governmental and leased access channels.

12. Playboy estimates it could lose $1 million a quarter, out of its yearly $21.2 million from cable programming; Spice says it could lose between $1 million and $2 million for the remainder of 1997, out of about $15 million a year in adult cable revenue.

13. The CDA also made it a crime to display indecent material in a manner available to a person under eighteen. Many critics noted that the law was so broadly defined as to have been almost impossible to enforce.

14. The report was later discredited, both because of the unreliable tactics by which the head researcher, Marty Rimm, obtained information from adult bulletin board owners, and because it sensationalized the threat of online porn. Actually, said the small print, the 917,410 sexually explicit images and texts examined in the study represent only about 3 percent of all the messages on the Usenet newsgroups. The analysis of the content of these images, however, appears to be fairly accurate.

15. The biggest video chain in town, Blockbuster, carries no adult videos. With three stores in Champaign-Urbana, Blockbuster dominates the market here, as it does throughout the country; in 1992 it had $1.6 billion in revenues and owned over 2,100 franchises (Wasko, 154). Blockbuster has a policy of not carrying X-rated or NC-17 films; it announced in 1991 that it would destroy any films in stock with even an NC-17 rating (Wasko, 155).

16. Edward Cavazos and Gavino Morin describe two other federal laws that could be used to regulate cybersex: 18 USC 1465, which "prohibits interstate transportation of obscene material for sale or distribution," could apply to users who dial up out-of-state bulletin board services. Also 47 USC 223, which was enacted to deal with 1-900 adult services, could also be used for cybersex since it "prohibits obscene communications through the telephone lines." Cavazos and Morin warn that this code could be used to regulate chat rooms; in fact, this already happened in California in 1994. A systems operater engaged in hot chat with an undercover law enforcement agent who said he was a minor. The operator was arrested and charged with attempted child molestation and attempted use of a minor for an illicit purpose (104).

17. Digitized visual images can be downloaded from a bulletin board service or an online service that specializes in pornography. It is also possible to send them through electronic mail or through a message base, although that is apparently a less frequent method of transmission (Cavazos and Morin, 95).

NOTES TO CHAPTER 2

1. Not surprisingly, the percentage of women feeling guilty declines with the frequency of masturbation; but still, 14 percent of women who masturbate once a week or more have some guilty feelings about it.

2. Reubens was convicted and fined and required to use his own money to make, weirdly, an antidrug film. The hysteria about his activity was likely connected to his TV character, which defied gender and sexuality stereotypes.

3. In *Sex for Women Who Want to Have Fun and Loving Relationships with Equals*, sex therapist Carmen Kerr similarly stresses the importance of everyday routines. Her "three steps to orgasm" include (1) "Take time to be by yourself: Traditionally, women don't consider it proper to take time to be alone with themselves. Work schedules, study schedules, and motherhood schedules gobble up all of our available hours" (120); (2) "Use your masturbating as a first step in liber-

ating your children and yourself. Arrange care: leave the kids with a neighbor, hire a teenager, ask your husband or housemates to help. After all, it's only an hour" (124); and (3) "Setting up your place." "The point of all this is to start taking control of your environment. Women are not accustomed to actively creating their own settings, particularly sexual ones. So indulge your territory with your personality and sensuality" (125).

4. Other feminists were cautious about overemphasizing the clitoral orgasm, lest it become too fetishized as the single instrument of pleasure rather than one aspect of a woman's total sensuality. Germaine Greer wrote in *The Female Eunuch*, for example, "The banishment of the fantasy of the vaginal orgasm is ultimately a service, but the substitution of the clitoral spasm for genuine gratification may turn out to be a disaster for sexuality. Masters and Johnson's conclusions have produced some unlooked for side-effects, like veritable clitoromania" (33). Furthermore, she said, "If we localize female response in the clitoris we impose upon women the same limitation of sex which has stunted the male's response" (34).

5. Hysteria was not discredited until 1952, when the American Psychiatric Association dismissed it as a valid diagnosis (Blank, 3). The use of massage was apparently one of the milder treatments for hysteria, which often included beatings and humiliations (Ehrenreich and English, 125).

6. Joani Blank, the Good Vibrations founder, has been collecting antique vibrators at garage sales for more than twenty years. They are displayed at Good Vibrations stores in Berkeley and San Francisco; they are also featured on the company's home page, which can be accessed at http://www.goodvibes.com.

7. Statistics on vibrator usage seem unreliable. The frequently cited *Redbook* survey of 100,000 women in 1975 reported that one out of every five women used a sex toy during intercourse and that 20 percent of these women said the toy was a vibrator. Yet the 1993 *Sex in America* survey of 3,500 people by the University of Chicago showed relatively little interest in vibrator usage. Only 3 percent of women between eighteen and forty-four said they found the use of a dildo/vibrator "very appealing"; 13 percent said they found it "somewhat appealing"; 23 percent said they found it "not appealing"; and 61 percent said they found it "not at all appealing." Men in the same age group reported only slightly higher interest: in the same categories, the percentages were 5, 18, 27, and 50, respectively. However, these results were surely skewed by the wording of the question, which combined vibrators and dildos in one category; dildos are a less domesticated sex toy. The 1990 Kinsey report quoted an unnamed study that found that 26 percent of the women interviewed (who were between eighteen and thirty-five years of age) had used a vibrator for sexual stimulation at least once (Reinisch, 96).

8. In 1992 Blank sold the store to her employees and it now operates as a cooperative business. Workers are taught the advantages and disadvantages of each product sold; the co-op holds monthly educational seminars that all customer service staff must attend and requires that each employee read the monthly financial

statements, offering courses as well in finance. The store works as part of a broader community: it conducts outreach presentations at schools and other institutions, makes donations to HIV education programs, and networks with sex therapists and educators. The idea is to spread as much information about sex as possible; customers can pick up free brochures about products, sexual activities, and sexual resources, and an online sex education course is a possibility now being considered. Of course, Good Vibrations also likely recognizes that the more women know about different sexual practices, the more they will want to use sex toys and explicit materials to heighten their experiences. The co-op doesn't escape a capitalist economy but at least challenges the assumption that the scarcer the commodity, the higher its exchange value. Thus far, the philosophy has worked; in 1994 Good Vibrations opened its second store, in Berkeley; in fiscal 1996 it had $4 million in net sales and projected $5 million in the next fiscal year.

9. In fact, in striking down the Communications Decency Act, the Supreme Court ruled that speech on the Internet be accorded the same First Amendment rights as books and newspapers.

NOTES TO CHAPTER 3

1. John Frow argues that cultural studies has frequently defined itself in part through a "renunciation of the aesthetic concerns of literary or cinematic or art-historical studies" (1).

2. One can get a sense of the explosion of identity erotica through a search of the book list of the major distributor Baker and Taylor. In the summer of 1996, a search using the key word "erotica" produced 143 book titles, which includes books currently carried by the distributor and published in years dating back to 1969. Between 1969 and 1983 there are twenty-eight titles, most of them indicating the aesthetic and universal status of the work: Peter Webb's *Erotica Arts* (1976), Anaïs Nin's *Delta of Venus* (1977), *100 Years of Erotica: A Photographic Portfolio* (1973), and *The Browser's Guide to Erotica* (1981). The first "identity erotica" is the Kensington Ladies' first volume, which appeared in June 1984, followed four months later by Barbach's *Pleasures*; in 1986 the Kensington Ladies published their second volume, *Look Homeward Erotica,* and Barbach edited another collection for women, *Erotic Interludes: Tales Told by Women.* Titles from the 1980s are still dominated by non-identity erotica; in the late 1980s and early 1990s, however, one begins to see more specifically targeted collections. To name just a few: *Gay Video: A Guide to Erotica* (1986), the first *Herotica* collection (1988), the Sheba Collective's two volumes of lesbian erotica, *Serious Pleasure: Lesbian Erotic Stories and Poetry* (1991), and, shortly thereafter, *More Serious Pleasure,* the second *Herotica* collection (1992), and Michele Slung's *Slow Hand: Women Writing Erotica* (1992). Some collections in the last five years have also focused on ethnic and racial groups: *Erotique Noire: Black Erotica* (1992), *Pleasure in the Word: Erotic Writings by Latin American Women* (1993); *On a Bed*

of Rice: An Asian-American Erotic Feast (1995), and in 1996, *Speaking in Whispers: Lesbian African-American Erotica*. Publishers are now even willing to have their name associated with the genre in the title: in 1996 Penguin published *The Penguin Book of Erotic Stories by Women*.

3. E-mail correspondence, 14 March 1997.

4. In fact, as George Yudice argues in "For a Practical Aesthetics," the conservative Right has itself redefined the notion of aesthetics, appropriating the language of artists and activists who combine art and social practice. For example, Jesse Helms proposed in 1989 to ban public funding for "'obscene and indecent' art and for any work that 'denigrates or reviles a person, group, or class of citizens on the basis of race, creed, sex, handicap, age, or national origin'" (qtd. in Yudice, 210). The dismissal of aesthetics offers no way to counter the attacks by conservatives on progressive artists funded by the National Endowment for the Arts.

5. However, the introductions to each section in the *Erotica* collection warn readers not to read Califia and Wordsworth, for example, as erotic in the same ways. Editor Margaret Reynolds's introductions to each section reveal her own judgments about various authors. For example, in her preface to the section entitled "Danger," where an excerpt from Califia's *Macho Sluts* is included, Reynolds characterizes sadomasochism as a "power-based relation" in which the "woman is always the 'bottom,' man always the 'top.' . . . Loving is something done to her, suffering is what she does" (132). She advises the reader, "The extracts in this section must be read with caution," lest the reader think that the dominant/submissive roles that figure in the stories are meant to be really erotic: "What it does is show how convincingly and how persistently those elements have been forced into women's lives" (132).

6. In the case of *Story of O*, the author's anonymity worked to enhance the text's literary value; as Foucault says, "And if a text should be discovered in a state of anonymity—whether as a consequence of an accident or the author's explicit wish—the game becomes one of rediscovering the author" ("Author," 109). In 1994 Réage revealed her identity to John de St. Jorre in an article in the *New Yorker*; she is Dominique Aury, a journalist, editor, translator, and writer who wrote the book as a love letter to French intellectual Jean Paulhan.

7. Russell Leong, in his foreword to *On a Bed of Rice*, says that the volume's writings counter stereotypes of the Asian male as a dangerous Kung Fu artist and the female as sexually submissive and desirable. Again, well-known writers— Frank Chin, Shawn Wong, John Yau, S. P. Somtow—serve to cast literary legitimacy on lesser-known writers, redefining the notion of literary/canonical to include the sexually explicit as it relates to race. In *Under the Pomegranate Tree*, editor Ray Gonzalez describes how the selections "show how far Latino men have progressed from the stereotypes of the 'macho' rapist, adulterer, and cool 'Latino lover'" (xv).

8. This quote and all the following quotes, except those specifically attributed

to the introductions of the series, come from a personal interview with Bright conducted on March 25, 1996.

9. In *Herotica 4*'s "Pornophobia," two lesbian lovers return from an antiporn rally; however, it turns out one lover has actually been using her vibrator to masturbate to the images in *Playboy, Penthouse,* and *Hustler* that the antiporn group was using as propaganda. When her partner discovers this transgression, she is appalled. In the ensuing discussion, the porn user dispels the myth that porn is a "tool of patriarchal oppression that objectifies women"; rather, she says, objectification is implicit in any act of looking and lusting, even, or perhaps especially, in their loving relationship (231).

10. Barnes and Noble's sales rose 42 percent in the fiscal year ended January 31, 1996; the number of stores it operates rose 34 percent, to 358. It plans to open ninety more stores in 1996 (Milliot, "Superstore," 10). Barnes and Noble also operates 590 B. Dalton bookstores, most of them in shopping malls (Milliot, "Superstore," 16). Borders' sales in fiscal 1996 rose 65 percent and the company added forty-one superstores, a 33 percent jump from the previous year. Barnes and Noble, Borders, and the two other major book superstore chains, Crown Books and Books-a-Million, together account for nearly a quarter of all retail bookstore sales (Milliot, "Superstore," 16).

11. For example, at the same time that Barnes and Noble was opening three new stores in the New York City metropolitan area, *Publishers Weekly* reported the anticipated closure of A Room of Our Own, a gay and lesbian bookstore in the Park Slope section of Brooklyn ("Room of Our Own," 26).

12. We may also address the question of who reads erotica by looking at who reviews erotica. Women's erotica in the last decade has been reviewed in a wide variety of mainstream publications, indicating that women readers cross interest groups. Reviews have appeared in *USA Today*, the *New York Times Book Review*, *Playboy, Publishers Weekly, Elle,* the *Nation, Mademoiselle, Ms., Vogue, People,* and even the *Yale Review.* These reviews often weave together the mix of characteristics described in this chapter: the literary value, the emphasis on women's pleasure, and the differences from pornography.

13. Sharp's quotes in this section and the information on Black Lace come from a personal telephone interview conducted on April 3, 1997.

14. Black Lace writers employ one very easy strategy for negotiating the relationship between present-day realities and women's fantasies: about half of the hundred novels are situated in the past, from Victorian England to ancient Egypt. As I discuss in chapter 4 in relation to Victorian themes, this dislocation of contemporary desire onto a fictionalized past speaks of a nostalgia for times when sexual identities were purportedly not so complicated; furthermore, it conveniently sidesteps the issues of racism and imperialism that are often interwoven in the erotic representations.

NOTES TO CHAPTER 4

1. Indeed, the catalog has become more careful about pornographic suggestions in recent years. When current chief executive officer Cynthia Fedus took over the catalog in 1988, she did away with the shots of "scantily clad males and females grappling, ogling, or embracing each other that were common under her male predecessor" (Machan, "Sharing," 132–33).

2. Even before it was sold as a six-store and catalog operation to the Limited in 1982, VS took pains to represent itself in this manner. Its founder, Roy Raymond, conceived of Victoria's Secret in 1977 as a way to create a more comfortable place for men to shop for lingerie for their wives. Shopping for a gift for his wife in the lingerie department of I. Magnin and feeling rather awkward amidst the finery, he reasoned that other men must share his desire to buy sexy gifts for their lovers and wives in more intimate places, so he borrowed $80,000 and opened the first Victoria's Secret store in a Palo Alto, California, mall. He told a *Vogue* reporter that the original stores were "designed to make men feel comfortable, so we used dusty rose and dark wood.... Private, fanciful, a little bit sexy." Soon thereafter he began the mail-order component of the business. He chose the Victorian theme in part because of his own predilection for Victorian decor and architecture and in part because it represented an ideal of intimate togetherness.

3. In contrast, Victoria's Secret had only $7 million in sales when Wexner bought it from its founder in 1982. Since then, Victoria's Secret sales and profits have steadily increased while business at the Limited's women's retail stores has stagnated. In the fall of 1995, the Limited, attempting to lure stockholders to invest in its more profitable lingerie operations, spun off Victoria's Secret as a separate unit, retaining 83 percent ownership and offering the rest for public ownership through a stock offering. The resultant holding company, Intimate Brands, also includes Bath and Body Works and Cacique, another lingerie chain.

4. The financial information on Frederick's comes from its annual report and from *Women's Wear Daily*, 25 January 1994.

5. Victoria's Secret has even claimed not to track demographic information on customers' genders. In a January 8, 1996, article in *Brandweek,* company spokesperson Jonathan Baskin responded to a lawsuit brought by a woman who claimed that the catalog unfairly discriminates among male and female customers. Denize Katzman claimed in U.S. District Court that the winter 1996 catalog offered women a $10 discount on purchases of $75 or more and said that a male colleague received the same catalog with a $25 discount offer. Responded Baskin: "To allege discriminatory business practices against women is absurd. We don't even keep track of customers by gender or name."

6. The material location of nearly six hundred VS lingerie stores in shopping malls throughout the country further indicates the public side of what the catalog attempts to represent as private and intimate.

7. The content of Victorian pornographic novels often assumed certain things about its audience: that it had read the best-known literary novelists of the day, for example, such as Dickens and Thackeray, because the pornography often made allusions to these works. Class distinctions were marked in the flagellation pornography by frequent references to "the higher gentry and nobility" and to "common experiences at a public school" (Marcus, 253).

8. Victoria's Secret has gone to great lengths with its suppliers in order to give consumers the illusion that products are exclusively VS labels. A *New York Times* business section article in 1993 profiling Victoria's Secret president and chief executive officer Grace Nichols describes how when Nichols took over the company in the early 1980s, one of her missions—ultimately successful—was to persuade suppliers like Vanity Fair to let them "cut Vanity Fair labels out of Victoria's Secret bras, sew in Victoria's Secret labels, and sell the garments" as such in order to present an image of exclusivity.

9. Traditional Victorian erotica is frequently racist, eroticizing British imperialism and slaveholding. In the first volume of *Eroticon*, the protagonist describes his exploits as a sea captain; on one trip he purchases some Turkish and African slave women for his "harem." Here is one exemplary passage: "I marched the one I had just been fucking with to one side and picked out ten others, among which number was one black, a young African about fifteen years of age, who still retained her virginal rose, and who was, on the whole, the most voluptuously formed female I had ever seen and apparently better fitted for enjoying the pleasure of love than any female in my possession" (154). Girls and women in these stories are regularly raped, then, in the midst of the sex, begin to enjoy their ravishment, and by the end, desire the "instrument" all the more, turning into virtual nymphomaniacs in the rest of the story. The Black Lace novels set in Victorian England go to considerable lengths to transform the emphasis on male pleasure; *The Seductress*, for example, focuses almost exclusively on Lady Longmore's delights.

10. The *Forbes* article on Victoria's Secret reports that sportswear and evening wear constitute about 60 percent of the catalog's sales. Victoria's Secret now devotes entire issues to apparel with little emphasis on lingerie; these issues include specially designed "country" and "city" catalogs, with appropriate attire, as well as a special swimsuit edition.

NOTES TO CHAPTER 5

1. In 1986 the U.S. Supreme Court ruled the ordinance unconstitutional.

2. The video was probably "softened" for the hotel market; many video companies produce several versions of varying levels of explicitness; the most hardcore are sold to adult video stores.

3. An indicator of Royalle's cultural purchase and recognition as a women's erotica spokesperson: she now charges $250 for an interview.

4. In fact, Williams deals exclusively with visual pornography, both film and

video, and does not consider its relation to other technologies such as print and computer in terms of women's access.

5. Although some porn videos do focus on pregnancy and nursing, they do so in a fetishistic manner that abstracts them from the conditions of everyday life.

6. The Ladies seem to fear that bringing the erotic and the everyday too close together might make their work more transgressive than they'd feel comfortable with. Thus, they engage in several tactics of distancing their erotic selves from their everyday selves: the writers wear masks in their public media appearances and write under pseudonyms. At the end of the *Look Homeward* volume, each writer describes herself and her journey since the group began; often the writers refer to their writing persona and their everyday persona as if they were two distinct identities. For example, Sabina Sedgwick, the group's founder, writes about "Sabina" in the third person, enacting a sort of conversation between Sabina and herself about the differences between erotica and pornography. The "real" woman interrogates Sabina, making her defend the writing as distinctly different from pornography. Rose Solomon adopts a similar strategy in her confessional piece: she says about her erotic self, "My husband is secretly in love with her. He never complains when she takes off and travels, and he tacitly encourages her writing. Recently he gave her a word processor (and me a food processor). I think he would prefer me to be more like her; she never asks him to take out the garbage, and she is always eager to jump into bed" (218).

7. The LaHayes endorse manual stimulation of the clitoris but never mention oral sex.

8. Mainstream media have been almost uniformly derisive of Gray's success. *Newsweek*, for example, sarcastically quotes his publicist at HarperCollins, who says, "we get letters from people who are almost functionally illiterate" testifying to the power of Gray's books to change their lives. Even *People* refers to Gray's "retrograde insights."

9. The seminar was run by a company called SkillPath seminars, which hires independent contractors like Curt to lead a number of different self-improvement workshops on topics like relationships, computers, businesses, and stress management. Gray's company asserts that he has personally trained each of the facilitators.

10. The audience was not completely without moments of skepticism. Several women interrupted the facilitator's phony participatory gestures ("Isn't that so, Venusians?") to ask somewhat probing questions. "If a man goes in his cave to watch TV, how does that help solve the problem?" said one woman. "Is he actually thinking in there?"

NOTES TO CHAPTER 6

1. Studies in the 1980s on technologies and consumption in the domestic sphere indicated, for example, that although women certainly watch television,

they do so in a more distracted and interrupted manner than men often do, either in between household chores or mediated by a sense of guilt at not completing the work (see Hobson). Other studies have shown that men usually develop higher levels of competency over the VCR, video games, and home computers; these studies argue not that women are essentially unable to master these technologies but rather that technologies are constructed in gender-specific ways, often consolidating already existing power relations in the household. For example, in her work on women and video recorders, Ann Gray shows that the women in her study did not know how to use the different features of their VCRs, relying instead on male partners or children, but that they could operate other complicated machinery, such as sewing machines. The issue was not, thus, technical complexity but rather the VCR's incorporation into a principally masculine leisure domain. In general, researchers have found that "new technologies have tended to reproduce traditional work patterns across gender" and that "old ideas have largely become encoded in new technologies" (Morley, 229).

2. As Byars and Meehan argue, cable subscription's ability to sort the audience "into bona fide consumers and mere viewers was enhanced during Reaganist deregulation, as cable operators doubled and even tripled the cost of basic subscription while lowering the prices for extra services on pay channels. Such a divison of the audience, in conjunction with economic downturns and Reaganism, piqued advertisers' interest in cable, perhaps especially in the new category of upscale working women" (23).

3. *Penthouse* became *Playboy*'s first significant competition in the early 1970s, defining itself as more in line with the "sexual revolution" and showing pubic hair, for the first time in U.S. magazine history. In the controversial "pubic wars" that ensued, *Playboy* agonized over whether to follow suit; eventually it did, at first timidly, then with abandon, even showing playmates with their legs spread. But after *Playboy* ran a cover image of a young woman with her hand in her underwear, a move that met with widespread disapproval from both subscribers and advertisers, the magazine pulled back, conceding that *Penthouse* had won the war.

4. In 1962, for example, *Playboy* ran two extensive articles on civil rights, compared to only one significant treatment in *Life*. Nat Hentoff analyzed the black nationalist movement and Alex Haley interviewed Miles Davis; in 1963 Haley interviewed Malcolm X, and *Playboy* ran the largely unexpurgated piece, which turned out to be the seeds of Haley's *Autobiography of Malcolm X* (Weyr, 138). The *Playboy* interview was and perhaps still is its most respected journalistic feature.

5. Ironically, during the same period that Playboy was expanding its public presences, Hugh Hefner was becoming more and more of a recluse in his Chicago mansion. Insisting that all work and entertainment be brought to him, he basically did not leave the mansion for most of the sixties. He said, "What I've created is a private world that permits me to live my life without a lot of

wasted time and motion that consume a large part of most people's lives" (qtd. in Miller, 111).

6. Playboy lost no time moving in on markets that had recently opened their doors to capitalism; in this decade, it has acquired foreign licenses for its magazine in Czechoslovakia, Hungary, Taiwan, Poland, and Russia, and has also expanded elsewhere in Europe and Asia, including China, where its products sell well even though the magazine is still prohibited there.

7. The charge into new electronic media has been led since 1995 by Eileen Kent, vice president at the publishing group in charge of new media strategy. Kent started as a temporary secretary at the age of thirty-two and rose through the ranks, to editorial assistant, contracts administrator, and director of editorial services (Donaton, "Hopping," 15).

8. In 1995 Playboy launched a search for women who wanted to appear in a pictorial feature called "Girls of the Net"—women eighteen and older were asked to e-mail their height, weight, measurements, and favorite Internet sites and to scan into the system pictures of themselves in a bikini or less.

9. Some women are not convinced. Feminists over the years have acknowledged the company's fair treatment of women on the payrolls but not in the pictorials. In 1993 the Women's Equity Mutual Fund, for example, recommended that its investors not buy Playboy because of its representation of women. Yet fund comanager Amy Domini conceded that other factors made it a difficult decision: Hefner as chair, four women among its fourteen top officers, and a generous flex-time program (*Fortune*, 29 November 1993, 30).

10. Dunn makes the rather good point that fashion magazines like *Vogue* are as guilty of objectifying women as is *Playboy*, and Pally asks rhetorically, "Is it the goal of feminism not to have women ever thought of as sexual beings?" (qtd. in Donaton, "Playboy," 20).

11. Clearly, spectators are meant to see this series as an indicator of Playboy's commitment to female pleasure and a valorization of women's fantasies. In many of the vignettes, a woman is introduced by name and profession; she describes a particular fantasy, which then occurs, interspersed with cuts back to her description and "analysis" of the "liaison." The women's fantasies seem almost like a set of instructions for their male lovers to follow, conflating reality and fantasy in a manner that recalls many other women's erotic texts I have described. The *Private Liaisons* series intersperses these first-person accounts with two other kinds of videos. In one type, the stereotypical male voyeur occupies a rooftop position in order to videotape a couple making love—sometimes a heterosexual couple, sometimes a lesbian couple. The other type is the staged home video, in which male lovers videotape their female lovers in domestic environments. Their voice-overs comment on the woman's body, giving her instructions on how to disrobe, indicating that men control the technology and women occupy the traditional role, as an everyday kind of playmate. However, the videos do testify to the fact that pornography can not only be consumed within the home, it can

—and should be—*made* in the home as a kind of aid to better sexual relations.

12. This feature of the Playboy genre is part of the wider growth in homemade hard-core videos; the camcorders bought for high school graduation now serve in some homes as tools for amateur porn, a growing subgenre in the hard-core industry. Homegrown Video of San Diego, for example, pays amateurs twenty dollars for every minute of video it uses; the company has produced about five hundred compilations of amateur porn (Schlosser, 48).

13. The framework of the series—women writing diary entries—draws on the legitimation provided by women writing erotica described in chapter 3. Interestingly, in a 1997 episode, three women friends send Jake a *video* containing their erotic story. Most episodes still rely on the written letter, however.

14. My examples for *Red Shoe Diaries* come mainly from three episodes that were circulated on video after airing on cable in 1992; the series continues to rely on many of the same conventions.

15. There are occasional *Red Shoe* episodes that step outside romantic closure; "Dime a Dance" (July 1997), for example, portrays three friends' affairs with the same sexy musician, describing how each one seduced him without knowing of the others' escapades. In the end, the musician disappears mysteriously, leaving the three friends to wonder if he was just a fantasy and concluding on the nonromantic, sexually affirming chorus that the important element was the great—albeit fleeting—sex that they enjoyed. Says the narrator Jake in closing, "I don't know what to make of that one, Stella."

Works Cited

Adler, Jerry. "The Guru from Mars: John Gray Creates Passion at Carnegie Hall." *Newsweek,* 2 October 1995, 96.

Alleyn, Fredrica. *The Bracelet.* London: Black Lace, 1996.

Allison, Dorothy. *Skin: Talking about Sex, Class, and Literature.* Ithaca, NY: Firebrand, 1994.

Balsamo, Anne. *Technologies of the Gendered Body: Reading Cyborg Women.* Durham: Duke University Press, 1996.

Barbach, Lonnie. *The Erotic Edge: Twenty-Two Erotic Stories for Couples.* New York: Plume, 1994.

———. *For Yourself: The Fulfillment of Female Sexuality.* New York: Doubleday, 1975.

———. *Pleasures: Women Write Erotica.* New York: Doubleday, 1984.

Bastone, William. "The Porn Broker: State's Anti-Sleaze Drive Adds to Porno King's Coffers." *Village Voice,* 18 July 1995, 13.

Bell, Diane, and Renate Klein, eds. *Radically Speaking: Feminism Reclaimed.* North Melbourne: Spinifex, 1996.

Bell, Roseann P., Reginald Martin, and Miriam DeCosta-Willis, eds. *Erotique Noire/Black Erotica.* New York: Doubleday, 1992.

Bennett, Tony. "Being 'in the True' of Cultural Studies." *Southern Review* 26, 2 (July 1993): 217–39.

———. *Outside Literature.* London: Routledge, 1990.

Bennett, William. "America at Risk: Can We Survive without Moral Values?" *USA Today,* 11 November 1994, A14–16.

Berg, Rona. "High Heel Hell." Photographs by Helmut Newton. *Vogue,* February 1995, 214, 216, 220.

Berlant, Lauren. "Live Sex Acts (Parental Advisory: Explicit Material)." *Feminist Studies* 21, 2 (summer 1995): 379–404.

Bérubé, Michael. *Marginal Forces/Cultural Centers: Tolson, Pynchon and the Politics of the Canon.* Ithaca: Cornell University Press, 1992.

Birk, Gayle A. "Love Object." In Bright, *Herotica,* 54–57.

Blackwell, Erin. "Real Pleasure." In Sheiner, 69–81.

Blank, Joani. *Good Vibrations: The Complete Guide to Vibrators.* 3d ed. San Francisco: Down There Press, 1989.

Booth, Richard, and Marshall Jung. *Romancing the Net: A "Tell-All" Guide to Love Online*. Rocklin, CA: Prima, 1996.

Boston Women's Health Collective. *Our Bodies, Ourselves*. 1st ed. New York: Simon and Schuster, 1971.

Boudoir, The: A Journal of Voluptuous Victorian Reading. New York: Blue Moon Books, 1996.

Brady, Lois Smith. "Why Marriage Is Hot Again." *Redbook,* September 1996, 122–25, 146.

Bright, Susie, ed. *The Best American Erotica, 1996*. New York: Simon and Schuster, 1996.

———. *Herotica: A Collection of Women's Erotic Fiction*. San Francisco: Down There Press, 1988.

———. *Herotica 3: A Collection of Women's Erotic Fiction*. New York: Plume, 1994.

Bright, Susie, and Joani Blank, eds. *Herotica 2: A Collection of Women's Erotic Fiction*. New York: Plume, 1992.

Broder, John M. "Clinton Readies New Approach on Internet Indecency." *New York Times Cybertimes,* 27 June 1997. Available online @http://www.nytimes.com/library/ cyber/week/072797.

Brown, Wendy. *States of Injury: Power and Freedom in Late Modernity*. Princeton: Princeton University Press, 1995.

Butler, Judith. *Bodies That Matter: On the Discursive Limits of Sex*. New York: Routledge, 1993.

———. *Gender Trouble: Feminism and the Subversion of Identity*. New York: Routledge, 1990.

Byars, Jackie, and Eileen R. Meehan. "Once in a Lifetime: Constructing 'The Working Woman' through Cable Narrowcasting." *Camera Obscura* 33–34 (January 1995): 12–41.

"Cablecastings." *Broadcasting,* 11 November 1985, 10.

Carter, T. Barton, Marc A. Franklin, and Jay B. Wright. *The First Amendment and the Fifth Estate: Regulation of Electronic Mass Media*. 2d ed. Westbury, NY: Foundation Press, 1989.

Cavazos, Edward A., and Gavino Morin. *Cyberspace and the Law: Your Rights and Duties in the On-Line World*. Cambridge: MIT Press, 1994.

Chalker, Rebecca. "Sexual Pleasure Unscripted." *Ms.,* November–December 1995, 49–52.

Champagne, John. "'Stop Reading Films!': Film Studies, Close Analysis, and Gay Pornography." *Cinema Journal* 36, 4 (summer 1997): 76–97.

Cherny, Lynn, and Elizabeth Reba Weise, eds. *Wired Women: Gender and New Realities in Cyberspace*. Seattle: Seal Press, 1996.

Chester, Laura, ed. *Deep Down: The New Sensual Writing by Women*. Boston: Faber and Faber, 1989.

————. *The Unmade Bed: Sensual Writing on Married Love.* New York: Harper-Collins, 1992.

Colman, Price. "Cable Rates Jumped 7.8 Percent in '96." *Broadcasting & Cable,* 20 January 1997, 47–48.

————. "It's Scramble Time for Adult Channels." *Broadcasting & Cable,* 12 May 1997, 44–45.

Comfort, Alex. *The Joy of Sex: A Gourmet Guide to Love Making.* New York: Simon and Schuster, 1972.

————. *More Joy of Sex: A Lovemaking Companion to The Joy of Sex.* New York: Simon and Schuster, 1974.

Commons, Giselle. "Healing." In Barbach, *Pleasures: Women Write Erotica,* 13–18.

Cooper, Jim. "Caught in the Web." *Cablevision,* 11 December 1995, 32.

————. "Is Everybody Happy?" *Cablevision,* 27 January 1997, 30.

Cornell, Drucilla. *Transformations: Recollective Imagination and Sexual Difference.* New York: Routledge, 1993.

Coyle, Karen. "How Hard Can It Be?" In Cherny and Weise, 42–55.

Davidson, Joy. "You Always Have Orgasms . . . Then Suddenly You Don't." *Cosmopolitan,* December 1996, 90, 92.

Davidson, Sara. "The Politically Incorrect Orgasm." *Mirabella,* January–February 1997, 84–92.

Davis, Lennard J. "Text Sex." *Nation,* 29 March 1993, 418–20.

De Angelis, Barbara. "How to Make Passion Last . . . and Other Advice from a Top Expert on Love and Sex." *Ladies' Home Journal,* January 1997, 80, 84, 86.

De Certeau, Michel. *The Practice of Everyday Life.* Translated by Steven Rendall. Berkeley: University of California Press, 1984.

De Grazia, Edward. *Girls Lean Back Everywhere: The Law of Obscenity and the Assault on Genius.* New York: Random House, 1992.

Denfeld, Rene. *The New Victorians: A Young Woman's Challenge to the Old Feminist Order.* New York: Warner, 1995.

Dennis, Catherine. "The Secret of Couples Who Love Sex." *Redbook,* March 1997, 80–83.

De St. Jorre, John. "The Unmasking of O." *New Yorker,* 1 August 1994, 42–50.

Dodson, Betty. *Sex for One: The Joy of Selfloving.* New York: Crown, 1996.

Dolan, Maria Helena. "Collision Course." In Taormino, 150–58.

Donaton, Scott. "Hopping into New Media." *Advertising Age,* 19 June 1995, 15, 18.

————. "Playboy Makes Interactive Sales Pitch." *Advertising Age,* March 1994, 20.

Duff, Christina. "Women Are Buying More Lingerie, Even as New Clothes Leave Them Cold." *Wall Street Journal,* 26 March 1995, A3–4.

Duggan, Lisa, Nan D. Hunter, and Carole S. Vance. "False Promises: Feminist Antipornography Legislation." In Ellis et al., 72–88.

Dworkin, Andrea. "Dworkin on Dworkin." In Bell and Klein, 203–17.

———. *Woman Hating.* New York: Dutton, 1974.

Dyer, Richard. *Heavenly Bodies.* London: BFI, 1982.

Eberwein, Robert. "'One Finger on the Pause Button': Sex Instruction Videos." *Jump Cut* 41 (1997): 36–41.

Echols, Alice. *Daring to Be Bad: Radical Feminism in America, 1967–1975.* Minneapolis: University of Minnesota Press, 1989.

Economics of TV Programming and Syndication, 1996. Carmel, CA: Paul Kagan Associates, 1996.

Edwards, Marie, and Eleanor Hoover. "The Challenge of Being Single." *Cosmopolitan,* January 1975, 46, 50.

Ehrenreich, Barbara, and Deirdre English. *For Her Own Good: 150 Years of the Experts' Advice to Women.* New York: Anchor Press/Doubleday, 1978.

Ellis, Kate, Nan D. Hunter, Beth Jaker, Barbara O'Dair, and Abby Tallmer, eds. *Caught Looking: Feminism, Pornography, and Censorship.* New York: Caught Looking, 1986.

Eroticon. New York: Carroll and Graf, 1991.

Eroticon II. New York: Carroll and Graf, 1992.

Ewing, Elizabeth. *Dress and Undress: A History of Women's Underwear.* New York: Drama Book Specialists, 1978.

Faludi, Susan. *Backlash: The Undeclared War against American Women.* New York: Doubleday, 1991.

Fein, Ellen, and Sherrie Schneider. *The Rules: Time-Tested Secrets for Capturing the Heart of Mr. Right.* New York: Time Warner, 1995.

Fernandez Olmos, Margarite, and Lizabeth Paravisini-Gebert, eds. *Pleasure in the Word: Erotic Writing by Latin American Women.* New York: Plume, 1993.

Fisher, Seymour. *The Female Orgasm: Psychology, Physiology, Fantasy.* New York: Basic Books, 1973.

Forkan, Jim. "Wiring the Whole Home." *Cablevision,* 3 March 1997, 26.

Foucault, Michel. *The Archeology of Knowledge and the Discourse on Language.* New York: Pantheon, 1992.

———. *Discipline and Punish: The Birth of the Prison.* Translated by Alan Sheridan. New York: Vintage Books, 1979.

———. *The History of Sexuality.* Vol. 1, *An Introduction.* Translated by Robert Hurley. New York: Vintage Books, 1978.

———. "What Is an Author?" In *The Foucault Reader,* edited by Paul Rabinow. New York: Pantheon, 1984.

Friday, Nancy. *My Mother/My Self.* New York: Delacorte, 1977.

———. "What Your Sexual Fantasies Really Mean." *Cosmopolitan,* February 1973, 112, 114, 118.

———. *Women on Top: How Real Life Has Changed Women's Sexual Fantasies.* New York: Simon and Schuster, 1991.

———, ed. *Forbidden Flowers: More Women's Sexual Fantasies.* New York: Simon and Schuster, 1975.

———. *My Secret Garden: Women's Sexual Fantasies.* New York: Simon and Schuster, 1973.

Frow, John. *Cultural Studies and Cultural Value.* Oxford: Clarendon, 1995.

Frow, John, and Meaghan Morris, eds. *Australian Cultural Studies: A Reader.* Urbana: University of Illinois Press, 1993.

Gibson, Pamela Church, and Roma Gibson, eds. *Dirty Looks: Women, Pornography, Power.* London: BFI, 1993.

Golden, Tim. "Sixteen Indicted on Charges of Internet Pornography." *New York Times,* 7 July 1996, A10.

Gonzalez, Ray, ed. *Under the Pomegranate Tree: The Best New Latino Erotica.* New York: Simon and Schuster, 1996.

Goodwin, Jan. "America Undercovers." *Ladies' Home Journal,* April 1996, 98, 99, 100–103.

Gottwald, Laura, and Janusz Gottwald, eds. *Frederick's of Hollywood, 1947–1973: Twenty-Six Years of Mail Order Seduction.* New York: Drake, 1973.

Gould, Jodie. "Debbie Directs Dallas: Video Erotica Made by Women for Women." *Elle,* April 1992, 144, 148, 150.

Graham, Janis. "Moms Are from Venus, Sons Are from Mars." *Working Mother,* March 1996, 46–49.

Graham, Lamar. "A Love Map to His Body." *Redbook,* May 1995, 88–91.

Gray, Ann. "Behind Closed Doors: Women and Video." In *Boxed In: Women on and in Television,* edited by H. Baehr and G. Dyer. London: Routledge, 1987.

Gray, Jerry. "House Passes Bar to U.S. Sanction of Gay Marriage." *New York Times,* 13 July 1996, A1, A7.

Gray, John. *Mars and Venus in the Bedroom: A Guide to Lasting Romance and Passion.* New York: HarperCollins, 1995.

———. *Mars and Venus on a Date: A Guide for Navigating the Five Stages of Dating to Create a Loving and Lasting Relationship.* New York: HarperCollins, 1997.

———. *Men Are from Mars, Women Are from Venus: A Practical Guide for Improving Communication and Lasting Intimacy.* New York: HarperCollins, 1993.

Greer, Germaine. *The Female Eunuch.* New York: McGraw-Hill, 1970.

Griffin, Gabriele. "Safe and Sexy? Lesbian Erotica in the Age of AIDS." In Pearce and Stacey, 143–57.

Gross, Amy. "Marriage *without* Children." *Cosmopolitan,* May 1975, 190–93.

Grossberg, Lawrence. "Identity and Cultural Studies: Is That All There Is?" In *Questions of Cultural Identity*, edited by Stuart Hall and Paul Du Gay, 87–107. London: Sage, 1996.

Guillory, John. *Cultural Capital: The Problem of Literary Canon Formation.* Chicago: University of Chicago Press, 1993.

Gutmann, Stephanie. "What a Video Can Teach You about Sex." *Cosmopolitan,* July 1996, 80, 82.

Hales, Dianne. "The Joy of Mid-Life Sex." *American Health,* January–February 1997, 78–81.

Hall, Stuart. "Culture, Community, Nation." *Cultural Studies* 7, 3 (October 1993): 349–63.

Hawksley, Emma. "Anniversary Waltz I." In Kensington Ladies, *Look Homeward Erotica,* 53–54.

Heeter, Carrie, and Bradley S. Greenberg. *Cableviewing.* Norwood, NJ: Ablex, 1988.

Hite, Shere. *The Hite Report: A Nationwide Study on Female Sexuality.* New York: Macmillan, 1976.

———. *The Hite Report on the Family: Growing Up under Patriarchy.* London: Bloomsbury, 1994.

Hobson, Dorothy. *Crossroads: Drama of a Soap Opera.* London: Methuen, 1982.

Hunter, Ian. *Culture and Government: The Emergence of Literary Education.* London: Macmillan, 1988.

Hunter, Ian, David Saunders, and Dugald Williamson. *On Pornography: Literature, Sexuality and Obscenity Law.* New York: St. Martin's, 1993.

Janus, Samuel, and Cynthia Janus. *The Janus Report on Sexual Behavior.* New York: John Wiley and Sons, 1993.

Jardine, Lisa, and Julia Swindells. "Homage to Orwell: The Dream of a Common Culture, and Other Minefields." In *Raymond Williams: Critical Perspectives,* edited by Terry Eagleton, 108–29. Cambridge: Polity Press, 1989.

Jauss, Hans Robert. *Toward an Aesthetic of Reception.* Translated by Timothy Bahti. Introduced by Paul de Man. Minneapolis: University of Minnesota Press, 1982.

Johnson, Eithne. "The Coloscopic Film and the 'Beaver' Film: Scientific and Pornographic Representations of Female Sexuality." Unpublished paper.

———. "Loving Yourself: The Spectacular Scene in Sexual Self-Help Advice for Women." Conference paper. Visible Evidence, Harvard University, 1995.

Johnson, Nora. "Return to the Land of the Loving: Journey of a Divorcee." *Cosmopolitan,* May 1975, 23–27.

Johnson, Virginia. "What's Good—and Bad—about the Vibrator." *Redbook,* March 1976, 85, 136.

Kaplan, Helen Singer. *The New Sex Therapy: Active Treatment of Sexual Dysfunctions.* New York: Brunner/Mazel, 1974.

Kappeler, Susan. *The Pornography of Representation.* Minneapolis: University of Minnesota Press, 1986.

Kazanjian, Dodie. "Victoria's Secret Is Out." *Vogue,* April 1992, 218, 220.

Kelly, Keith J. "Playboy's Fortunes Tied to the Bunny." *Advertising Age,* 24 October 1994, 6.

Kendrick, Walter. *The Secret Museum: Pornography in Modern Culture.* New York: Viking, 1987.

Kensington Ladies' Erotica Society. *Ladies' Own Erotica: Tales, Recipes, and Other Mischiefs by Older Women.* Berkeley: Ten Speed Press, 1984.

———. *Look Homeward Erotica: More Mischief by the Kensington Ladies' Erotica Society.* Berkeley: Ten Speed Press, 1986.

Kerr, Carmen. *Sex for Women Who Want to Have Fun and Loving Relationships with Equals.* New York: Grove, 1977.

Kipnis, Laura. *Bound and Gagged: Pornography and the Politics of Fantasy in America.* New York: Grove, 1996.

———. *Ecstasy Unlimited: On Sex, Capital, Gender, and Aesthetics.* Minneapolis: University of Minnesota Press, 1993.

Klein, Renate. "(Dead) Bodies Floating in Cyberspace: Post-Modernism and the Dismemberment of Women." In Bell and Klein, 346–58.

Koedt, Ann. "The Myth of the Vaginal Orgasm." In *Radical Feminism,* edited by Anne Koedt, Ellen Levine, Anita Rapone, 198–207. New York: Quadrangle Books, 1970.

Krantzler, Mel, and Barry Schwenkmcyer. "Trial Separation: Cop-Out or Marriage Saver? *Cosmopolitan,* February 1975, 180–82, 200–201.

Kronhausen, E., and Phyllis Kronhausen. *Pornography and the Law.* New York: Ballantine, 1959.

Kudaka, Geraldine, ed. *On a Bed of Rice: An Asian-American Erotic Feast.* Foreword by Russell Leong. New York: Doubleday, 1995.

Laclau, Ernesto, and Chantal Mouffe. *Hegemony and Socialist Strategy: Toward a Radical Democratic Politics.* London: Verso, 1985.

LaFay, Vivienne. *The Seductress.* London: Black Lace, 1995.

LaHaye, Tim, and Beverly LaHaye. *The Act of Marriage: The Beauty of Sexual Love.* Grand Rapids, MI: Zondervan, 1976.

Landis, Bill. "Sex Square." *Village Voice,* 18 July 1995, 27–32.

Levy, Steven. "No Place for Kids? A Parents' Guide to Sex on the Net." *Newsweek,* 3 July 1995, 46–50.

Lloyd, Frank W. "Access Indecency Rules Upheld: A Mixed Blessing for Cable?" *Cable TV and New Media,* June 1995, 6.

Lorde, Audre. "Uses of the Erotic: The Erotic as Power." In *Sister Outsider,* 53–55. Crossing Press Feminist Series. Freedom, CA: Crossing, 1984.

Love, Patricia, and Jo Robinson. *Hot Monogamy: Essential Steps to More Passionate, Intimate Lovemaking.* New York: Dutton, 1994.

Lowry, Thomas, ed. *The Classic Clitoris: Historic Contributions to Scientific Sexuality.* Chicago: Nelson Hall, 1978.

Lury, Celia. *Consumer Culture.* Cambridge: Polity Press, 1996.

Lydon, Susan. "The Politics of Orgasm." In *Sisterhood Is Powerful: An Anthology of Writings from the Woman's Liberation Movement,* edited by Robin Morgan. New York: Random House, 1970.

Machan, Dylan. "The Hef and Christie Saga." *Forbes,* 28 August 1995, 89.

———. "Sharing Victoria's Secrets." *Forbes,* 5 June 1995, 132–33.

MacKinnon, Catharine. "Vindication and Resistance: A Response to the Carnegie Mellon Study of Pornography in Cyberspace." *Georgetown Law Journal* 83 (1995): 1959–67.

Marcus, Steven. *The Other Victorians: A Study of Sexuality and Pornography in Mid-Nineteenth-Century England.* New York: Basic Books, 1966.

Mariposa, Eve. "Back to the Future with a Vibrator." In Sheiner, 121–28.

Massar, Shelley. "Nasty Business: The Inside Story of the Raid on Malibu Bay." *Octopus,* 20 June 1997, 6–10.

Massey, Doreen. *Space, Place, and Gender.* Minneapolis: University of Minnesota Press, 1994.

Masters, William H., and Virginia E. Johnson. *Human Sexual Response.* London: J. and A. Churchill, 1966.

May, Elaine Tyler. *Homeward Bound: American Families in the Cold War Era.* New York: HarperCollins, 1988.

McClintock, Anne. "Soft-Soaping Empire: Commodity Racism and Imperial Advertising." In *Travellers' Tales: Narratives of Home and Displacement,* edited by G. Robertson et al., 131–55. London: Routledge, 1994.

McManus, Michael. Introduction/reprinting. *Final Report of the Attorney General's Commission on Pornography.* Nashville: Rutledge Hill Press, 1986.

McRae, Shannon. "Coming Apart at the Seams: Sex, Text and the Virtual Body." In Cherny and Weise, 242–64.

McRobbie, Angela. *Postmodernism and Popular Culture.* London: Routledge, 1994.

Mead, Rebecca. "Is This Man from Mars?" *New York,* 18 September 1995, 67–69.

Mercer, Kobena. "Just Looking for Trouble: Robert Mapplethorpe and Fantasies of Race." In Segal and McIntosh, 92–110.

Meyer, Carlin. "Reclaiming Sex from the Pornographers: Cybersexual Possibilities." *Georgetown Law Journal* 83 (1995): 1969–2008.

Michael, Robert T., John H. Gagnon, Edward O. Laumann, and Gina Kolata. *Sex in America: A Definitive Survey.* Boston: Little, Brown, 1994.

Miller, Russell. *Bunny: The Real Story of Playboy.* New York: Holt, Rinehart and Winston, 1984.

Milliot, Jim. "Fewer Mall Stores, More Superstores in B&N's Future." *Publishers Weekly,* 20 May 1996, 15.

————. "Superstore Sales Up 45% to $2.4 Billion in '95." *Publishers Weekly,* 6 May 1996, 10.

Morley, David. *Television, Audiences, and Cultural Studies.* London: Routledge, 1992.

Morris, Kathleen, ed. *Speaking in Whispers: Lesbian African-American Erotica.* Chicago: Third Side Press, 1996.

Murray, Charles. "What to Do about Welfare." *Commentary,* December 1994, 26–34.

Mutter, John. "Barnes and Noble Pushes the Envelope." *Publishers Weekly,* 11 December 1995, 24.

Nagle, Jill. "First Ladies of Porn: A Conversation with Candida Royalle and Debi Sundahl." In *Whores and Other Feminists,* edited by Jill Nagle, 156–66. New York: Routledge, 1997.

Nin, Anaïs. *Delta of Venus.* New York: Harcourt, Brace, Jovanovich, 1977.

Nolan, Chris. "Watch Your Mouth." *Cablevision,* 25 March 1996, 46.

Norment, Lynn. "Sex and Sisters: What Turns Women On—and Off." *Ebony,* March 1997, 46, 48, 50.

Northcott, Allan. "Playboy Television: Notes towards a Cable Prehistory of Teledildonics." Unpublished paper.

O'Brien, Pat. *The Houseshare.* London: Black Lace, 1996.

O'Leary, Noreen. "The Old Bunny: Can Playboy Reinvent Itself?" *Brandweek,* 18 March 1996, 26–30.

Oliver, Suzanne. "The Porn Mandate." *Forbes,* 28 August 1995, 46–47.

Pally, Marcia. *Sex and Sensibility: Reflections on Forbidden Mirrors and the Will to Censor.* New York: Ecco, 1994.

Pear, Robert. "Senate Passes Welfare Measure, Sending It for Clinton's Signature." *New York Times,* 2 August 1996, A1, A10.

Pearce, Lynne, and Jackie Stacey, eds. *Romance Revisited.* New York: New York University Press, 1995.

Pearson, Elvira. "Ergasm." In Kensington Ladies, *Look Homeward Erotica,* 73.

————. "Marriage in the Morning." In Kensington Ladies, *Look Homeward Erotica,* 49–52.

Pomeroy, Wardell. "The Truth about Oral Sex." *Cosmopolitan,* March 1976, 158–61.

Port, Nell. "Nice Girls Don't." In Kensington Ladies, *Look Homeward Erotica,* 162–64.

Probyn, Elspeth. *Sexing the Self: Gendered Positions in Cultural Studies.* New York: Routledge, 1993.

Radner, Hillary. *Shopping Around: Feminine Culture and the Pursuit of Pleasure.* New York: Routledge, 1995.

Radway, Janice. *Reading the Romance: Women, Patriarchy, and Popular Literature*. Chapel Hill: University of North Carolina Press, 1984.

Reed, Stacy. "Night Talk." In Sheiner, 9–18.

Reinisch, June M., with Ruth Beasley. *The Kinsey Institute New Report on Sex: What You Must Know to Be Sexually Literate*. New York: St. Martin's, 1990.

Reynolds, Margaret, ed. *Erotica: Women's Writing from Sappho to Margaret Atwood*. Foreword by Jeanette Wintersen. New York: Fawcett Columbine, 1990.

Rice, Anne. *Exit to Eden*. New York: Dell, 1985.

Rice, Rebecca. "The Nine Secrets of Happy Couples." *Redbook,* February 1997, 92–96.

Rohan, Patrick J. *Zoning and Land Use Controls*. Vols. 2 and 6. New York: Matthew Bender, 1995.

Roiphe, Katie. *The Morning After: Sex, Fear, and Feminism on Campus*. Boston: Little, Brown, 1993.

"A Room of Our Own Seeks a Buyer/Investors of Its Own." *Publishers Weekly,* 11 December 1995, 26.

Rooney, Peter. "Panel Supports Obscenity Measure." *Champaign/ Urbana News-Gazette,* 10 March 1997, A1, A8.

Rose, Charlotte, ed. *The Fifty Best Playgirl Fantasies*. New York: Masquerade Books, 1997.

Rosenstock, Natasha. "Women Should Shun Pornography, Embrace Erotica." *Daily Illini,* 9 April 1997, 10.

Ross, Andrew. *No Respect: Intellectuals and Popular Culture*. New York: Routledge, 1989.

Rubin, Gayle. "Misguided, Dangerous, and Wrong: An Analysis of Anti-Pornography Politics." In *Bad Girls and Dirty Pictures: The Challenge to Reclaim Feminism*, edited by Alison Assiter and Avedon Carol, 18–40. London: Pluto Press, 1993.

Safran, Claire. "Plain Talk about the New Approach to Sexual Pleasure." *Redbook,* March 1976, 85–87, 136.

Schlosser, Eric. "The Business of Pornography." *Newsweek,* 10 February 1997, 42–50.

Schneller, Johanna. "Death of a Dream Merchant." *Gentlemen's Quarterly,* September 1994, 194, 196.

Segal, Lynn, and Mary McIntosh, eds. *Sex Exposed: Sexuality and the Pornography Debate*. New Brunswick: Rutgers University Press, 1993.

Selsdon, Esther, ed. *Love's Theater: Women's Erotic Writing*. New York: Carroll and Graf, 1995.

Sheba Collective, eds. *Serious Pleasure: Lesbian Erotic Stories and Poetry*. Pittsburgh: Cleis, 1991.

Sheiner, Marcy, ed. *Herotica 4: A New Collection of Erotic Writing by Women*. New York: Plume, 1996.

Silverstone, Roger. *Television and Everyday Life*. London: Routledge, 1994.

Sinclair, Carla. *Net Chick: A Smart-Girl Guide to the Wired World*. New York: Henry Holt, 1996.

Small, Michael. "His Favorite Martians." *People*, 30 May 1994, 20.

Smith, Michael David. "Fiction under Fire." *Daily Illini*, 2 May 1997, 1, 9.

Snitow, Ann. "Retrenchment vs. Transformation: Politics of the Anti-Pornography Movement." In Ellis et al., 10–17.

Solomon, Rose. "Constant Interruptus." In Kensington Ladies, *Look Homeward Erotica*, 41–43.

Sontag, Susan. "The Pornographic Imagination." In *Styles of Radical Will*. New York: Farrar, Straus and Giroux, 1967.

Soren, Tabitha. "What Femininity Means Now." *Elle*, May 1996, 142–49.

Spigel, Lynn. *Make Room for TV: Television and the Family Ideal in Postwar America*. Chicago: University of Chicago Press, 1992.

Stabile, Carol. *Feminism and the Technological Fix*. Manchester: Manchester University Press, 1994.

Stacey, Jackie. *Star Gazing: Hollywood Cinema and Female Spectatorship*. London: Routledge, 1994.

Steinem, Gloria. "Erotic and Pornographic: A Clear and Present Difference." In *Take Back the Night: Women on Pornography*, edited by Laura Lederer, 35–39. New York: Morrow, 1980.

"Stephanie's Secret." *Playboy*, February 1993, 71–75.

Stevens, Michelle. "Pornophobia." In Sheiner, 228–33.

Stewart, Garrett. "Films Victorian Retrofit." *Victorian Studies* 38 (winter 1995): 153–95.

Straayer, Chris. "The Seduction of Boundaries: Feminist Fluidity in Annie Sprinkle's Art/Education/Sex." In Gibson and Gibson, 156–75.

Strom, Stephanie. "When Victoria's Secret Faltered, She Was Quick to Fix It." *New York Times*, 21 November 1993, D1.

Swartz, Mimi. "For the Woman Who Has Almost Everything." *Esquire*, July 1980, 56–63.

Tan, Cecilia. "Porn Flicks." In Sheiner, 19–23.

Taormino, Tristan, ed. *The Best Lesbian Erotica, 1997*. Introduction by Jewelle Gomez. San Francisco: Cleis, 1997.

Thornton, Louise, Jan Sturtevant, and Amber Coverdale Sumrall, eds. *Touching Fire: Erotic Writings by Women*. New York: Carroll and Graf, 1989.

Toy, Vivian S. "Bill to Restrict Sex Businesses Is Approved by Council." *New York Times*, 25 October 1995, B9.

Trauth, Denise, and John L. Huffman. "Obscenity and Cable Television: A Regulatory Approach." *Journalism Monographs* 95 (March 1986): 1–34.

Tuttle, Lisa. "Story of No." In *Slow Hand: Women Writing Erotica*, edited by Michele Slung. New York: HarperCollins, 1992.

U.S. Commission on Obscenity and Pornography. *Report of the Commission on*

Obscenity and Pornography. Washington, DC: Government Printing Office, 1970.

U.S. Justice Department. *Attorney General's Commission on Pornography, Final Report*. 2 vols. Washington, DC: Government Printing Office, 1986.

Vaughan, Bernadette. "When the Bough Breaks." In Kensington Ladies, *Look Homeward Erotica*, 67–72.

Wajcman, Judy. *Feminism Confronts Technology*. University Park: Pennsylvania State University Press, 1991.

Wasko, Janet. *Hollywood in the Information Age: Beyond the Silver Screen*. Austin: University of Texas Press, 1994.

Watkins, Evan. *Work Time: English Departments and the Circulation of Cultural Value*. Stanford: Stanford University Press, 1989.

Weber, Thomas. "For Those Who Scoff at Internet Commerce, Here's a Hot Market." *Wall Street Journal*, 20 May 1997, A1, A8.

Webster, Paula. "Pornography and Pleasure." In Ellis et al., 30–35.

Weyr, Thomas. *Reaching for Paradise: The Playboy Vision of America*. New York: New York Times Books, 1978.

White, Mimi. *Teleadvising: Therapeutic Discourse in American Television*. Chapel Hill: University of North Carolina Press, 1992.

"Why Playboy Is Hot Again." *Business Week*, 24 February 1997, 122.

Wilke, John R. "A Publicly Held Firm Turns X-Rated Videos into a Hot Business." *Wall Street Journal*, 11 July 1994, A1, A8.

Williams, Linda. *Hard-Core: Power, Pleasure, and the "Frenzy of the Visible."* Berkeley: University of California Press, 1989.

———. "Pornographies On/Scene, or Diff'rent Strokes for Diff'rent Folks." In Segal and McIntosh, 233–65.

———. "Second Thoughts on Hard Core: American Obscenity Law and the Scapegoating of Deviance." In Gibson and Gibson, 46–61.

———. "A Provoking Agent: The Pornography and Performance Art of Annie Sprinkle." In Gibson and Gibson, 176–91.

Williams, Raymond. *Television: Technology and Cultural Form*. 1974. Reprint, London: Wesleyan University Press, 1992.

Yudice, George. "For a Practical Aesthetics." In *The Phantom Public Sphere*, edited by Bruce Robbins (for the Social Text Collective). Minneapolis: University of Minnesota Press, 1993.

Zimmer, Linda. "Cable TV Manager Gets Death Threat." *Champaign-Urbana News Gazette*, 25 January 1995, A2.

Index

Adult Video News, 46

Advocate, The, 239n. 2

Aesthetics, 105–8; and circulation, 123–30; and cultural studies, 108–15; as a means of distinguishing erotica from porn, 7, 113–14, 127, 154; relation between women as producers of erotica and women as consumers, 116–23; and relation to superstore book chains, 130–35; and publishing, 135–44

African American erotica, 24

Agency: and access, 8, 9–21, 31; and display of women's bodies, 219–20; as structured mobility, 23, 55–56, 112, 201, 229, 233; and transgression, 16, 233; and women's heightened consumerism, 160; and women's mobility as represented in adult cable programming, 220–32

Agosín, Marjorie, 119. See also Pleasure in the Word: Erotic Writing by Latin American Women

AIDS, 139–40, 184, 217, 223. See also Safe sex

Allison, Dorothy, 90, 92

Amateur porn, 185, 218, 252n. 12

American Health, 170

Antiporn feminists, 1, 4, 8, 9–12, 44, 62, 72, 100, 174, 239n. 1

Asian American erotica, 24. See also Identity

Attorney General's Commission on Pornography. See Meese Commission

Baker and Taylor, as distributors of erotica, 244n. 2

Balsamo, Anne, 230

Barbach, Lonnie, 78, 123; The Erotic Edge: Twenty-Two Erotic Stories for Couples, 140, 179; For Yourself: The

Fulfillment of Female Sexuality, 76–78, 82–84, 86–88, 91; Pleasures: Women Write Erotica, 244n. 2. See also Masturbation

Barnes and Noble, 6, 57, 130–35, 234, 246n. 10

Barr, Rep. Bob, 33. See also Family values

Bedroom, as space of privacy, 170–72, 185–87, 198

Behind the Bedroom Door (video series), 181, 183, 187, 189. See also Erotic education videos

Benjamin, Jessica, 227–28

Bennett, Tony, 136; Outside Literature, 21–23, 105–6, 108–15. See also Aesthetics

Bennett, William, 32, 145. See also Family values

Berlant, Lauren, 37, 44, 171–72

Bérubé, Michael, 116

Best American Erotica, 128–30. See also Bright, Susie; Simon and Schuster

Best Lesbian Erotica 1997, 121–22, 164–65

Better Sex (video series), 187–89. See also Erotic education videos

Black Lace, 29, 106–7, 122, 132–33, 136–39, 141–43, 157–58, 246n. 14. See also Literary erotica

Blank, Joani, 123–24, 243nn. 6, 8. See also Good Vibrations

Blockbuster, 242n. 15

Bloom, Alan, 71

Blue Moon Press, as publisher of Victorian erotica, 154

Borders bookstore chain, 6, 57, 107, 130–35, 246n. 10

Boston Women's Health Collective, 81

Bourdieu, Pierre, 26

Bowers v. Hardwick, 171